Information Literacy and the Digitalisation of the Workplace

Every purchase of a Facet book helps to fund CILIP's advocacy, awareness and accreditation programmes for information professionals.

Information Literacy and the Digitalisation of the Workplace

Edited by
Gunilla Widén and José Teixeira

© This compilation: Gunilla Widén and José Teixeira 2023
The chapters: the contributors 2023

Published by Facet Publishing
c/o British Library, 96 Euston Road, London NW1 2DB
www.facetpublishing.co.uk

Facet Publishing is wholly owned by CILIP: the Library and Information Association.

The editors and authors of the individual chapters assert their moral right to be identified as such in accordance with the terms of the Copyright, Designs and Patents Act 1988.

Except as otherwise permitted under the Copyright, Designs and Patents Act 1988 this publication may only be reproduced, stored or transmitted in any form or by any means, with the prior permission of the publisher, or, in the case of reprographic reproduction, in accordance with the terms of a licence issued by The Copyright Licensing Agency. Enquiries concerning reproduction outside those terms should be sent to Facet Publishing, c/o British Library, 96 Euston Road, London NW1 2DB.

Every effort has been made to contact the holders of copyright material reproduced in this text, and thanks are due to them for permission to reproduce the material indicated. If there are any queries please contact the publisher.

British Library Cataloguing in Publication Data
A catalogue record for this book is available from the British Library.

ISBN 978-1-78330-581-0 (paperback)
ISBN 978-1-78330-579-7 (hardback)
ISBN 978-1-78330-580-3 (PDF)
ISBN 978-1-78330-582-7 (EPUB)

First published 2023

Text printed on FSC® accredited material.

Typeset from editors' files in 10.5/13 pt Revival 565 and Frutiger by Flagholme Publishing Services.
Printed and made in Great Britain by CPI Group (UK) Ltd, Croydon, CR0 4YY.

Contents

Figures and Tables vii

Contributors ix

Introduction: Advancing Theory on Workplace Information Literacy xv
Farhan Ahmad and Gunilla Widén

1. **Literature Review: In Search of the Many Meanings of Information Literacy** 1
   José Teixeira and Muhaimin Karim

2. **Digital Literacy in a Post-Digital Era: Rethinking 'Literacy' as Sociomaterial Practice** 15
   Mika Mård and Anette Hallin

3. **Methodological Choices of Information Literacy in the Workplace: Qualitative, Quantitative or Mixed-Methods?** 29
   Shahrokh Nikou and Farhan Ahmad

4. **Investigating Information Seeking and Information Sharing Using Digital Trace Data** 45
   José Teixeira

5. **Making Do With Limited Transparency of Sensitive Information in Secretive Organisations: Collective Information Literacy Through Hinting** 59
   Inti José Lammi and Anette Hallin

6. **Information Literacy Competencies for Career Transitions in the Digital Age** 71
   Marina Milosheva, Hazel Hall, Peter Robertson and Peter Cruickshank

7. **The Importance of Information Literacy for Work Satisfaction in a World-Wide-Workplace Context** 101
   Angela Djupsjöbacka, Jannica Heinström and Eva Österbacka

8. **Entrepreneurs' Digital Information Sources Selection: A Perspective on the Impact of Information Literacy and Generational Differences** 121
Thao Orrensalo, Malin Brännback and Shahrokh Nikou

9. **Conclusion: Workplace Information Literacy as the Literacy of the Digital Workplace** 145
Isto Huvila, Gunilla Widén, Farhan Ahmad and José Teixeira

Index 153

Figures and Tables

Figures
1.1	Articles with 'information literacy' in the title according to Google Scholar	2
1.2	Articles with 'x literacy' in the title across each decade according to Google Scholar	6
4.1	Two-way communication as initially presented by Robson and Robinson (2015)	48
4.2	Examples for the operationalisation of the study of information cycles using digital trace data	50
6.1	Career information literacy and digital career literacy relative to career self-management skills	82
7.1	Shapley decomposition of R^2 based on specification (2)	114
8.1	Proposed conceptual model	130
8.2	Structural model results	134

Tables
1.1	Library databases and search engines used during the literature review efforts	4
1.2	Keywords used during the literature search	4
1.3	Top 20 journal publications interested in information literacy	9
4.1	Affordances by coupling of information sharing and information seeking with digital trace	53
6.1	Career self-management skills, digital literacy skills and career information literacy skills	81
7.1	Effects of self-determination factors, external and individual characteristics on work satisfaction, weighted adjusted-POLS	111
8.1	Construct reliability and validity	133
8.2	Discriminant validity	133

Contributors

The editors

José Teixeira is University Lecturer in Information Studies at Åbo Akademi University, Finland, and defended his dissertation entitled 'Coopetition in an Open Source Way' in 2018. With an educational background in both computer science and management, he worked in the industry developing and deploying information systems at Wipro, Tesco, Airbus and Nokia. During his professional ventures, José was an enthusiastic advocate of open source software. Before the strategic partnership between Nokia and Microsoft, he turned to academia where he approached the open source software phenomenon from a research and development strategy perspective. More recently, he developed a keen interest in theories of information and communications, which he uses to study the production of open source software ecosystems. José communicates his research results both to the Information Systems and the Library and Information Science research communities. In his spare time, José plays basketball.

Gunilla Widén is Professor of Information Studies and Vice-Rector for Education at Åbo Akademi University, Finland, and Docent in Information Management at University of Tampere, Finland. Her research interests have focused on the role of information as a resource in organisations as well as in everyday life. She has led several large projects financed by the Academy of Finland, including: individual and organisational key skills in an information intensive society (2006–10); Library 2.0 – a new participatory context (2008–13); and the impact of information literacy in the digital workplace (2016–20). Recently, she has been involved in European projects on youth information service development. She is currently leading research on trust in information, part of the *Diversity, Trust and Two-Way Integration (Mobile Futures)* project funded by the Strategic Research Council (SRC), Academy of Finland (2021–24), and on cultural policy decision-making, the case of Helsinki Central Library Oodi, in the PolyCul project funded by the Norwegian Research Council (2021–24). She has published widely in her areas of expertise, including in the *Journal of Information Science, International Journal of Information Management, Journal of Documentation, Journal of Information Literacy* and *Information Research*. She has edited several books and conference proceedings, including *Social Information*

Research with K. Holmberg (Emerald, 2012) and *Building Sustainable Health Ecosystems, 6th International Conference on Well-being in the Information Society* with H. Li, P. Nykänen, R. Suomi, N. Wickramasinghe and M. Zhan (Springer, 2016). Outside work, Gunilla spends time in the Turku archipelago and travelling with her relatives.

The contributors

Farhan Ahmad is a university teacher in Information Systems in Turku School of Economics, Finland. He is also doctoral supervisor at the Edinburgh Business School, Heriot-Watt University, Scotland. His research focuses on information and knowledge management, knowledge sharing, workplace information literacy and digitalisation. He is also interested in distinct research methods, such as fuzzy-set qualitative comparative analysis (fsQCA) and bibliometrics. Farhan's work has been published in international journals, including *Long Range Planning, International Journal of Information Management, Journal of International Management* and *Journal of Information Science*.

Malin Brännback is Professor of International Business at Åbo Akademi University, Finland. Currently, she is Dean of the faculty of Social Sciences, Business and Economics. She has published widely in entrepreneurship, entrepreneurial cognition, motivations, biotech, high-technology and high growth entrepreneurship, but also in information systems and knowledge management. She has published more than 50 peer review articles in journals such as *Entrepreneurship Theory & Practice, Journal of Small Business Management, Entrepreneurship & Regional Development, VINE* and *Knowledge Management Research & Practice*. She has co-authored 11 books with Dr Alan Carsrud. Malin is associate editor of the *Journal of Small Business & Entrepreneurship* and a member of the editorial board of the *Journal of Small Business Management* and the *Journal of Developmental Entrepreneurship* and was awarded a top reviewer award in 2020. She has been Vice-Rector of Åbo Akademi University and visiting professor at Stockholm University School of Business, Sweden.

Peter Cruickshank is Associate Professor at Edinburgh Napier University, Scotland. His main research area is information practices associated with engagement with digital systems. He also has an active interest in issues around identity and trust in using online systems. Peter has led a number of projects on the use of internet technologies by Community Councils in Scotland from a variety of information practice, knowledge management and learning perspectives. He has conducted other research in library and information science, as a member of the team that conducted market research on training provision for information professionals, and barriers to impact of research on library and information science practitioners. He is currently leader of the Social Informatics research group within the Applied Informatics subject group.

Angela Djupsjöbacka is an experienced university teacher of Economics at Åbo Akademi University, Finland. She holds a PhD in Economics. Her research interests are mainly centred around human capital formation and educational economics in general, but she has also ventured into the area of health economics. She primarily uses quantitative empirical methods in her research and also teaches courses in quantitative data analysis and econometrics, mainly at undergraduate level. In her role as a teacher, she focuses on guiding students on how to make sound empirical arguments in the social sciences where research is generally confined to the use of observational data.

Hazel Hall is Professor Emerita at Edinburgh Napier University, Scotland, and Docent in Information Studies at Åbo Akademi University, Finland. Between 2009 and 2022, she led the research of the Centre for Social Informatics at Edinburgh Napier University. Hazel's research expertise encompasses information behaviour and use (including information literacy), online communities and collaboration, library and information science research, and research impact. Her particular interest is information sharing in online environments. Most recently, she has explored audience engagement with archives across different digitised formats with reference to the writing of Lorna Beatrice Lloyd (1914–42), including Lloyd's World War 2 diary, which is available as a podcast at https://rss.com/podcasts/lornalloyd.

Over the course of her career, Hazel has won awards for her research and teaching, including the Jason Farradane Award (2016) and the Clarivate Analytics Outstanding Information Science Teacher Award (2019). Among Hazel's distinguished appointments are service for international peer-reviewed journals and conferences, such as editorial board membership of the *Journal of Information Science* and *Library and Information Science Research* and papers co-chair of the *78th Association for Information Science and Technology Annual Meeting* in 2015. She has served on several high profile committees, including the Communication, Cultural and Media Studies, Library and Information Management (Unit of Assessment 34) sub-panel of the UK Research Excellence Framework (REF) 2021 and as Chair of the UK Research and Innovations Digital Economy Programme Advisory Board. Hazel is a Fellow of the Royal Society of Edinburgh.

Anette Hallin is Professor in Organisation and Management at Åbo Akademi University, Finland, and Mälardalen University, Sweden. Anette has a long-established interest in how organisational practices change with the introduction and use of new technologies. In collaboration with colleagues and working with, for example, performativity and sociomaterial theory, she has explored this in different contexts, ranging from projects, high-tech companies, traditional industrial settings, public organisations and various types of management. She has published widely and is a sought-after speaker. In addition, she is Chair of the Swedish Academy of Management. In her spare time, Anette is renovating a little cabin in the woods in the Stockholm archipelago.

Jannica Heinström is Professor in Information Studies at the Department of Archivistics, Library and Information Science, Oslo Metropolitan University, Norway. She is also Docent in Information Studies at the University of Borås, Sweden. Her research focuses on psychological aspects of information interaction, particularly the role of personality and individual differences. Recent work includes studies on information avoidance, stigma, serendipity and everyday information mastering. In a workplace context, her work has focused on understanding emotional aspects of information processes, such as information sharing.

Isto Huvila is Professor in Information Studies at the Department of ALM (Archival Studies, Library and Information Studies and Museums and Cultural Heritage Studies) at Uppsala University, Sweden. His research focuses on information and knowledge management, information work, knowledge organisation, documentation, research data, and social and participatory information practices. The contexts of his research range from archaeology and cultural heritage, archives, libraries and museums to health information and e-health, social media, virtual worlds and corporate and public organisations.

Muhaimin Karim is a doctoral researcher in Information Studies at Åbo Akademi University, Finland. His research topics are centred around information and media literacy, information behaviour and practices, information service policy designing, and youth participation. As a doctoral student, he worked for several research projects centred around the concept of information literacy. Muhaimin currently conciliates his studies with his job as a business analyst for Kemppi, a Finnish manufacturing company developing equipment for the metal industry.

Inti José Lammi is Senior Lecturer in Organization and Management Studies at Mälardalen University, Sweden. He is a member of the New Organization and Management Practices (NOMP) research group at the university. In his research, Inti has studied private sector organisations, governmental agencies and municipal organisations with a specific interest in digital transformation. He is currently researching high security organising and inclusive leadership models. When Inti is not doing research, he prefers to spend his time reading books in the company of cats.

Mika Mård is University Lecturer in Organization and Management at Åbo Akademi University, Finland. He has comprehensive experience in teaching topics such as leadership, organisational behaviour and organisation theory. His main research interest concerns affects and emotions in organisations, but he also has a keen research interest in the intersection between sport (including play and games) and business. Mika's work has been published in international journals, including the *Nordic Journal of Working Life Studies*, *The International Journal of Sport and Society* and the *Scandinavian Journal of Public Administration*.

Marina Milosheva is a third-year PhD student in the School of Computing at Edinburgh Napier University, Scotland. She is an active member of the Social Informatics research group and holds both teaching assistant (TA) and research assistant (RA) responsibilities within the School of Computing. Her primary research interests lie in the areas of information behaviour, information and digital literacy, knowledge management, career development and lifelong learning. Her doctoral research is concerned with young people's career information literacy and with their career information behaviours for the purposes of career decision-making. This doctoral work is funded through an ESRC 1+3 collaborative PhD award and is conducted in partnership with the Scottish Graduate School of Social Sciences (SGSSS) and Skills Development Scotland (SDS).

Shahrokh Nikou is Senior Lecturer at the Faculty of Social Sciences, Business and Economics, Åbo Akademi University, Finland, and is also affiliated with the Department of Computer and Systems Sciences (DSV) at Stockholm University. His research interests relate to digitalisation in higher education, entrepreneurship and healthcare services, with a particular focus on digital transformation as an enabler for organisational change. He has been involved in national and international research projects and collaborates with international universities. Shahrokh has published on the impact of digitalisation on business models/business model innovation in healthcare services, entrepreneurship and higher education, using sophisticated and advanced research methods and data analysis techniques. He is an Associate Editor of the *Journal of Electronic Markets* and the *Digital Business Journal*, Academic Editor of PLOS ONE and Section Editor of the *Journal of Theoretical and Applied Electronic Commerce Research*.

Thao Orrensalo is a doctoral candidate at Åbo Akademi University, Finland. She has also co-founded an IT consulting services startup. Through the operation of her business and multiple first-hand experiences, Thao became interested in information access, especially administrative information, and the challenges faced by entrepreneurs. This experience inspires her study of entrepreneurs and their information behaviour in the digital age. Thao also examines how empowering critical literacies – information and digital literacy – support entrepreneurs to effectively and efficiently access information in the digital age. The context of her research is entrepreneurs in Finland. Her research is funded by Liikesivistysrahasto. Thao enjoys Finnish summer activities, such as mushroom picking, fishing and camping.

Eva Österbacka is Professor in Economics at Åbo Akademi University, Finland. Her research interests focus on the labour market, particularly on the importance of formal education, time use of individuals, economics of the family, and gender issues. How individuals manage on the labour market is crucial for their wellbeing. The path might not be straight, but once employed, a decent wage makes life easier. In addition, the work environment – including colleagues – contributes to work satisfaction and that eventually contributes to life satisfaction. She has been involved in several Nordic research projects, which have taken a comparative approach. She has served as an expert on national and international evaluation committees.

Peter Robertson is Professor at Edinburgh Napier University's School of Applied Sciences in Scotland. He trained in career guidance at Bristol Polytechnic, England, before working in Hertfordshire and North London specialising in supporting young people with disabilities. Peter became a training manager after studying occupational psychology at the University of East London, England. A chartered psychologist, he is currently lecturing on an initial professional training programme for career advisers at Edinburgh Napier University. He is a Fellow of the National Institute for Career Education and Counselling and edits the Institute's journal. He is also the lead editor of the *Oxford Handbook of Career Development*.

Introduction: Advancing Theory on Workplace Information Literacy

Farhan Ahmad and Gunilla Widén

In today's world, information plays an increasingly essential role in the smooth functioning of our society (Dufva and Wäyrynen, 2020). The last few decades have seen a considerable surge in the production and consumption of information at all levels and spheres of society across family, media, education, religion and the workplace. Even pre-industrial eras of humanity were dependent on information for societal advancement. Nevertheless, the phenomenal growth in the volume, velocity and variety of information alongside technological developments has resulted in the novel ways in which information contributes to social and economic development. At no point in history did human welfare and progress so much depend on efficient management of information as today (Floridi, 2009; Ziemba, 2019). Whether we can claim to have developed a perfect information society is subject to debate. But, without doubt, the world has experienced extensive 'informatisation' resulting in the information industry becoming a major part of modern economies while simultaneously changing the ways in which people interact with information in their day-to-day lives. All while technology is becoming embedded in everything and attention on equity aspects of digitalisation becomes increasingly important (Dufva, 2020).

The evolution of modern information societies has been possible largely because of technological developments and we have been living the digital transformation for quite a while now (Hilbert, 2022). Information and communication technology (ICT) has enabled us to connect in unprecedented ways. The information landscape of the world would not have been this dynamic if it was not for the affordances of information technology. Digital tools and technologies are increasingly part of our everyday life as well as our working life, affecting how we communicate, interact and perform different activities. Technology also comes with important challenges, such as risks with use of data, who decides how to develop technology and for what purposes (Dufva and Wäyrynen, 2020). Some technologies have been around for so long that they are already well integrated into our ways of acting. Still, we are in the midst of rapid technological development and new digital innovations are constantly knocking on the door, asking for an agile introduction to our everyday lives, to workplaces and to society at large.

Workplace digitalisation and informatisation

Work and workplaces constitute a substantial part of society and are defined as a place or activity to produce something, an intentional engagement that may or may not be compensated (Cairns and Malloch, 2011, 7). Workplaces are often described as complex, competing in markets and demanding innovation to survive (Lloyd, 2017). Digital innovations, particularly in information technologies, have greatly transformed the workplace domain of society. Organisations are investing in technologies and information infrastructure to enable employees to connect, collaborate and communicate seamlessly within and across organisational boundaries as well as time and space, leading towards the digitalisation of workplaces (Byström, Heinström and Ruthven, 2019; Holmström Olsson and Bosch, 2020). New forms of collaboration enabled by information technologies have connected different work processes, departments, geographic units and external stakeholders. Previous research has suggested that seamless information flow in digital workplaces has contributed greatly to improving work productivity as well as overall organisational performance (Eller et al., 2020). Moreover, an organisation's ability to have close customer and supplier relationships has been greatly enhanced by real-time information flow across organisational boundaries. In many organisations, emerging technologies such as big data, artificial intelligence and the internet of things have now integrated machine-driven information processing and knowledge creation into organisational decision-making, simultaneously building organisations' agility to respond to market changes (Van der Voort et al., 2021).

Digitalisation has made our work more associable, editable, interactive, programmable, traceable, communicable and distributable and is therefore shaping the workplace and its organising logic (Kallinikos, Aaltonen and Marton, 2013). But it also comes with substantial changes to ways of working. New technologies almost always translate into new work processes, work arrangements, collaborative engagements and hence disrupt the information environment and consolidate equilibria at work (Byström, Heinström and Ruthven, 2019). Although the pervasiveness of modern ICT benefits flexibility at work, it also exposes employees to new dynamics of information creation, sharing and management (Fuglseth and Sørebø, 2014). For example, as evidenced during the recent COVID-19 pandemic, the shifting of work-related employee interaction and task performance from a physical to a virtual environment reshapes the boundary of an organisation's information environment and consequently raises issues of privacy and data security (Teebken and Hess, 2021), work-life conflict (Adisa, Gbadamosi and Osabutey, 2017) and information overload (Bawden and Robinson, 2021). Digitalisation-driven alteration of work arrangements and communication also creates power asymmetry and digital inequality. There is evidence that the introduction of new ICTs disturbs the information ecosystem of an organisation (Palumbo, 2021). Technology savvy people are more proficient in dealing with information sharing, creating and access than technology neophytes whose information experiences are overshadowed by the complexity of new technologies and are hence put at a disadvantage. In the long term, this creates trust and fairness issues in organisations, which are known to affect knowledge sharing and an organisation's innovation potential (Palumbo, Manna and Cavallone, 2020).

Another major change experienced due to the intensive digitalisation of the workplace is loss of workflow control (White, 2012). Enhanced connection has been known to become a major source of distraction and work disruption in the workplace. The ability to send and receive e-mails at any time and at any place means there is less control on information inflow. According to Thomas (2019), it takes at least 20 minutes for an employee to get back to work after e-mail interruption. This often leaves people with exhaustion and the feeling that nothing has been accomplished during the day. Blurring of the boundary between work and home is further fuelling this problem as it is now difficult to completely disconnect or block information inflow while not at work. The concept of space in the workplace now encompasses virtual environments and extends far beyond the physical premises of the workplace. The COVID-19 pandemic further amplified these challenges (Vallo Hult, Islind and Norström, 2021).

There is also a paradigm shift so that many information activities once thought to be performed by specific professionals have now become part of the work of every employee. In addition to developing fluency in information tools, employees are now expected to understand and consume information in accordance with social, organisational and industry-specific ethical, legal and security standards. For example, even though information security professionals are responsible for protecting organisational information assets, other employees, such as marketing professionals, are expected to protect their work-specific information and be vigilant of threats such as hacking and phishing.

The rising complexity and amount of information, accompanied by developments in information technology, have transformed workplaces into complex systems of information flow making extremely efficient management of information a prerequisite for enhanced performance and innovation. To counteract the possible negative consequences, an explicit digitalisation strategy is needed, along with early communication and employee involvement and continuous training and lifelong learning (Eurofound, 2021). With rapid technological development, having modern information systems and devised information flow structures presents a risk for organisations. However, employees' capacity to effectively deal with information still needs to catch up, which brings up the importance of the continuous development of information literacy in the workplace.

It is crucial to continuously update information capabilities, both to navigate through the changing information landscape and to fully capitalise on new technologies and workplace digitalisation. Rather than focusing on how to master new information technology during digital transformation, there is a need to pay much more attention to how we master all the information that is produced as a result of new technologies. The need for digital skills is widely acknowledged, but the skills and competencies needed after first learning how to master the technology and tools is taken for granted. Clearly it is not only about technological skills. As the volume of information increases, so does the difficulty in differentiating between right and wrong, relevant and irrelevant, and real and fake information (Hemp, 2009). Also, there is a growing risk with the vast amount of data and information in relation to privacy, safety and security (Pal, Chua and Hoe-Lian Goh, 2019). To make the most out of digital transformation, it is critical that we also master the selection of relevant information sources in a complex information environment, that we foster our ability to think critically and make balanced judgements about any information we find and use, and that we better understand how to support and enhance new information and communication practices that emerge through digital innovation. This is possible only through continuous development of information literacy – all these capabilities are constituents of workplace information literacy.

Aim of the book

Information literacy is crucial in dealing with new forms of information experiences, realities and work organisations actualised by the permeation of ICT in organisations. There is a dearth of research on how workplace information literacy plays out in digital environments. This book aims to bring forward the role of workplace information literacy as a key condition for successful digitalisation or digital transformation in today's workplaces, as the compass through digital transformation, the conditions and the impact of information literacy in the digital workplace. Moreover, it aims to extend the critical debate on the impact of digitalisation on individuals and organisations. As technological innovations grow, so will their role in the workplace. In this regard, it is indeed timely to explore the multifaceted role of workplace information literacy in organisational operations. In doing so, we also contribute to the individual's perspective on the organisational digital transformation debate, which has often been overlooked and neglected. In the following section, we shed more light on information literacy in the workplace. After that, we provide an overview of the book and a short discussion of why it is important to advance workplace information literacy theory, research and practice together.

Defining workplace information literacy (WIL)

Information literacy (IL) has been addressed as an important capacity since the 1970s (e.g., Zurkowski, 1974). The need for information handling skills has been discussed in similar ways for nearly 50 years, referring to an overabundance of information exceeding our capacity to evaluate it. The IL concept has primarily been developed within educational contexts and is acknowledged as an important support for learning. However, it is also understood as a sociocultural construct, affected by situation and context (Lloyd, 2005; Tuominen, Savolainen and Talja, 2005). Since 2005, research on IL has increased, with strong technology-related motivations. The interest in IL has successively reached disciplines outside education and library and information science, such as health sciences and media, and the need for a number of new literacies, such as financial literacy, health literacy and internet literacy, has been introduced. With the growing interest in the concept of IL, a lack of good evaluation measures to study its impact has been identified (Li, Chen and Wang, 2021; Widén et al., 2021). In the workplace context, the interest in IL has grown in step with digital transformation. IL is often seen as a combination of formal information skills and the skills needed to master digital tools and technologies, but it is also constructed and affected by workplace information culture and information practices.

The number of IL definitions is almost endless and there are many systematic overviews of the different definitions, the development of the concept and its use in various contexts (e.g., Sample, 2020). The main challenge is that IL is highly context dependent and it is crucial that the concept is clearly defined every time it is studied or discussed. In this book, we are focusing on IL in the workplace context and follow to a large extent CILIP's definition:

> In the workplace, information literacy is knowing when and how to use information in order to help achieve organisational aims, and to add value to organisational activities. [...] The exact nature of information literacy is highly dependent on the context of the workplace, and it reflects workplace culture, practices and experiences.
>
> (CILIP, 2018)

In the workplace context, IL has increasingly been studied empirically, bringing an in-depth understanding of the information handling skills required in contemporary workplaces. IL has been identified as a key capability in workplace learning, helping organisations to effectively leverage information to create business value, such as innovation (Ahmad, Widén and Huvila, 2020; Forster, 2017; Middleton and Hall, 2021). As digital transformation is largely about change, that is, learning new information tools and technologies to master a complex information environment, the transition itself becomes a relevant context of study when developing WIL support (Hicks, 2020; Sharun, 2021).

In today's workplace, the digital aspect of IL is of course crucial and is often focused as digital literacy (DL). DL is defined as the awareness, attitudes and ability to appropriately use digital tools to manage information in the digital age. This includes the ability to identify, access, manage, integrate, evaluate, analyse, synthesise, construct, create and communicate information (Martin and Grudziecki, 2006; Bawden, 2008). IL is a broader concept than DL, including information in all forms and formats, while DL focuses on the ability to use digital tools to manage information. Different chapters in this book may have slightly different approaches to IL, as well as WIL and DL, and might focus on DL instead of the more general IL approach. However, the concept is clearly defined in relation to every chapter to make the conceptual understanding as clear as possible throughout the book. These definitions are further elaborated in Chapter 1.

The chapters

The chapters of this book are organised into four main perspectives: conceptual matters regarding WIL (Chapters 1–2); methodological aspects (Chapters 3–4); WIL from a process perspective (Chapters 5–6); and from an impact perspective (Chapters 7–8). The book is summarised in the final chapter, Chapter 9, where we also discuss future developments and the importance of research in this area.

Conceptual matters

In this section, the two chapters discuss the complexity of the IL concept and the importance of acknowledging the digital and technological infrastructure as an active part of forming WIL. Chapter 1 reports on a systematic literature review, pointing at the growing interest in the IL concept. The chapter also discusses the challenges in covering IL research due to the many related concepts and the many different disciplines in which IL is studied. With the growing interest in the concept as a result of the rapid development of digital transformation, there is clearly a challenge in effective knowledge exchange between disciplines, as well as between theory and practice.

Chapter 2 takes a post-digital approach to DL, shifting the focus from individual practice to a sociomaterial perspective looking at DL as a practice enacted by humans and technology combined. This is important in a workplace context where we need to have the consequences of practice in mind. The chapter builds on Lloyd's (2010) conceptualisation on IL as sociocultural practice, but adds the materiality aspect into the social setting, giving technology a more active role as an agent in producing practices. This means that we need to look at DL beyond the human-centric approach. It also gives a time factor to the process of developing DL practices. It is not only about DL giving humans the ability to use digital technology, but also how DL is enacted in practices performed by humans, materials, objects, technology and algorithms, all connected to each other.

Methodological aspects

As previously noted, the concept of WIL is complex and hard to study. Chapter 3 takes on the task of mapping out commonly used methods and practices for measuring IL. The chapter provides an overview of how qualitative, quantitative and mixed-methods have been used when studying IL, showing that the choice of methods depends not only on how IL is understood and defined, but also that there are different methodological practices in different disciplines. In the workplace context, qualitative methods have been applied more often, but to address the complexity of WIL, the chapter also puts forward the need for a mixed-method approach, such as fuzzy-set qualitative comparative analysis (fsQCA), to develop a multifaceted understanding of WIL.

Chapter 4 presents a methodological discussion and a novel approach to studying actual information seeking and sharing practices, following digital trace data. The growing amount of digital trace data provides a range of opportunities to observe and study information activities and how they have changed on a longitudinal scale. It also opens up possibilities for new insights regarding how to support employees' WIL. As organisations increasingly trace the information behaviour of their employees' overtime, and as digital records capture what information was shared and retrieved across the organisation, individuals should learn how to use these records from past operations to improve the current ones. As more and more information on individuals' behaviour is recorded in organisations, there is a need for skills and competencies to master those records to bring value to either the individual or the organisation. In other words, making sense of organisational digital trace data (that is often very context-specific) adds a dimension to WIL that is very dependent on context (e.g., organisational design, business processes, ICT systems in use). Independently of the workplace context, an information literate professional should be able to make sense of the digital trace data records from the past to bring value to the present.

Process and transition perspectives

In this section, the chapters focus on WIL in more specific contexts, with an emphasis on developing IL in a collective process and in a process of transition. Chapter 5 explores IL from a specific but very important and challenging perspective, namely in relation to sensitive information within high-security organisations, where information is not readily available to everyone. IL becomes a collective resource where the employees together achieve IL in terms of how to use, manage and benefit from the information to achieve common goals. When information cannot be openly available, hinting and the role of trust become important parts of building WIL in such high-security settings.

Chapter 6 looks at WIL in terms of how work-related IL can, and should be, transferred between jobs and during an individual's career. It is important to look at WIL beyond the single workplace and identify IL in terms of employability. In doing so, this chapter presents a roadmap of IL skills supporting employability, as well as how to manage these skills during career development and transitions between workplaces or professions.

Impact perspectives

Chapter 7 investigates the impact of WIL on work satisfaction, with special focus on one central component: information sharing. The insights in this chapter are based on an analysis of open access, large-scale quantitative data (Programme for the International Assessment of Adult Competencies (PIAAC)), contributing also to the methodological discussion. The study demonstrates that information sharing is associated with work satisfaction and it is put forward that management should encourage and facilitate information sharing in combination with supporting information sharing skills, willingness and motivation. A holistic understanding of WIL is emphasised, including not only skills but also mindset and motivation.

Chapter 8 discusses the importance of IL in the entrepreneurial work setting. The focus is on entrepreneurs' intentions to select and use digital information sources and shows that their IL influences their ability to find, select and access relevant information sources, contributing positively to the growth of their business. In light of the results, it is recommended that entrepreneurial programmes should focus on IL as a motivational factor independently of gender or age.

Importance of advancing WIL theory, research and practice

Digital transformation is primarily about change, which in turn requires a change in attitudes, skills and ways of working. It is obvious that we need more technical skills in the workplaces of the future, such as programming, digital production and data analytics. In addition to that, the future workplace needs people with more general technological competence who know how to use digital technologies and how to interact with computers taking over some of the work tasks previously managed by humans. These competencies must also be integrated with other workplace competencies to be efficient, such as leadership competencies, creativity, agile work practices, communication and negotiation (Ek and Ek, 2020). To drive digital transformation, we need good information and knowledge management to lead people and information processes, ensuring that information and knowledge are valued as important resources. Part of information and knowledge management is understanding and developing open information cultures in which it is easier to quickly adapt information and knowledge processes to continuous change. In this equation, WIL has a clear role, which is also shown in the chapters of this book in various ways.

The aim of the book is to bring forward the role of information literacy as a key condition for successful digitalisation in today's workplaces and extend the critical debate on the impact of digitalisation on individuals and organisations. The focus is on IL, which is a complex concept in terms of defining it clearly, finding suitable measures for studying it in the workplace context and in identifying its impact. In this book we have taken on all these challenges. The chapters contribute to mapping the development of the concept of WIL and bringing it into a post-digital era where employees, organisational culture and the digital infrastructure together shape the framework for WIL. The book clearly shows the need for methodological development in order to study WIL in various contexts. We need to go beyond traditional mono-method approaches to include mixed-methods and the use of digital data that is rapidly produced and can be traced to reflect our actual information activities and practices.

The book also discusses the need for understanding WIL as a collective process and that we cannot always focus on individual IL skills alone. For example, in settings where information is sensitive, the workplace might need other, collective actions to manage the information effectively. WIL should also be seen from a transition perspective, that is how employees' IL is transferred between workplaces or throughout their career so that it is utilised in the most effective way. Finally, the book gives examples of the actual impact of IL, both on a large scale that shows WIL across workplaces and countries and, more specifically, how IL significantly influences entrepreneurs' access to and selection of information sources for the benefit of their business success. Although the book advances a conceptual, methodological and practical understanding of WIL in today's digital workplaces, it is clear that we still need to develop all these areas – this is further discussed in the last chapter of the book, Chapter 9.

References

Adisa, T. A., Gbadamosi, G. and Osabutey, E. L. (2017) What Happened to the Border? The Role of Mobile Information Technology Devices on Employees' Work-life Balance, *Personnel Review*, **46** (8), 1651–71.

Ahmad, F., Widén, G. and Huvila, I. (2020) The Impact of Workplace Information Literacy on Organizational Innovation: An Empirical Study, *International Journal of Information Management*, **51**, 102041, www.sciencedirect.com/science/article/pii/S026840121930492X?via%3Dihub#bib0305.

Bawden, D. (2008) Origins and Concepts of Digital Literacy. In Lankshear, C. and Knobel, M. (eds), *Digital Literacies: Concepts, Policies, and Practices*, 17–32, Lang.

Bawden, D. and Robinson, L. (2021) Information Overload: An Overview. In *Oxford Encyclopedia of Political Decision Making*, Oxford University Press, https://doi.org/10.1093/acrefore/9780190228637.013.1360.

Berg, O. (2012) *Why the Digital Workplace is Both Relevant and Necessary*, www.infocentricresearch.com/Research/Publications/The-Digital-Workplace.aspx.

Byström, K., Heinström, J. and Ruthven, I. (2019) Work and Information in Modern Society: A Changing Workplace. In Byström, K. Heinström, J. and Ruthven, I. (eds), *Information at Work*, 1–32, Facet Publishing.

Cairns, L. and Malloch, M. (2011) Theories of Work, Place and Learning: New Directions. In Malloch, M. et al. (eds), *The Sage Handbook of Workplace Learning*, 3–16, Sage Publishing.

CILIP (2018) *CILIP Definition of Information Literacy 2018*, https://infolit.org.uk/ILdefinitionCILIP2018.pdf.

Dufva, M. (2020) *MEGATREND 4: Technology is Becoming Embedded in Everything*, SITRA, www.sitra.fi/en/articles/megatrend-4-technology-is-becoming-embedded-in-everything.

Dufva, M. and Wäyrynen, A. (2020) *Technology Provides A Lot of Opportunities for – and a Few Threats to – the Post-Coronavirus Times*, SITRA, www.sitra.fi/en/articles/technology-provides-a-lot-of-opportunities-for-and-a-few-threats-to-the-post-coronavirus-times.

Ek, I. and Ek, T. (2020) *Digitalisering i företag*, Studentlitteratur.

Eller, R., Alford, P., Kallmünzer, A. and Peters, M. (2020) Antecedents, Consequences, and Challenges of Small and Medium-sized Enterprise Digitalization, *Journal of Business Research*, **112**, 119–27.

Eurofound (2021) *Digitisation in the Workplace*, Publications Office of the European Union, www.eurofound.europa.eu/publications/report/2021/digitisation-in-the-workplace.

Floridi, L. (2009) The Information Society and its Philosophy: Introduction to the Special Issue on 'the Philosophy of Information, its Nature, and Future Developments', *The Information Society*, **25** (3), 153–8.

Forster, M. (2017) Information Literacy and the Personal Dimension: Team Players, Empowered Clients and Career Development. In Forster, M. (ed.), *Information Literacy in the Workplace*, 29–40, Facet Publishing.

Fuglseth, A. M. and Sørebø, Ø. (2014) The Effects of Technostress Within the Context of Employee Use of ICT, *Computers in Human Behavior*, **40**, 161–70.

Hemp, P. (2009) Death by Information Overload, *Harvard Business Review*, **87** (9), 82–9.

Hicks, A. (2020) Moving Beyond the Descriptive: The Grounded Theory of Mitigating Risk and the Theorisation of Information Literacy, *Journal of Documentation*, **76** (1), 126–44.

Hicks, A. (2022) Negotiating Change: Transition as a Central Concept for Information Literacy, *Journal of Information Science*, **48** (2), 210–22, https://doi.org/10.1177/0165551520949159.

Hilbert, M. (2022) Digital Technology and Social Change: The Digital Transformation of Society from a Historical Perspective, *Dialogues in Clinical Neuroscience*, **22** (2), 189–94.

Holmström Olsson, H. and Bosch, J. (2020) Going Digital: Disruption and Transformation in Software-intensive Embedded Systems Ecosystems, *Journal of Software, Evolution and Process*, **32** (6), e2249.

Kallinikos, J., Aaltonen, A. and Marton, A. (2013) The Ambivalent Ontology of Digital Artifacts, *MIS Quarterly*, **37** (2), 357–70.

Li, Y., Chen, Y. and Wang, Q. (2021) Evolution and Diffusion of Information Literacy Concepts, *Scientometrics*, **126**, 4195–224.

Lloyd A. (2005) Information Literacy: Different Contexts, Different Concepts, Different Truths?, *Journal of Librarianship and Information Science*, **37** (2), 82–8.

Lloyd, A. (2010) Framing Information Literacy as Information Practice: Site Ontology and Practice Theory, *Journal of Documentation*, **66** (2), 245–58.

Lloyd, A. (2017) Learning From Within for Beyond: Exploring a Workplace Information Literacy Design. In Forster, M. (ed.), *Information Literacy in the Workplace*, 97–112, Facet Publishing.

Lloyd, A. (2019) Foreword: Situating the Role of Information in the Messy and Complex Context of the Workplace. In Byström, K., Heinström, J. and Ruthven, I. (eds), *Information at Work*, 1–32, Facet Publishing.

Martin, A. and Grudziecki, J. (2006) DigEuLit: Concepts and Tools for Digital Literacy Development, *Innovation in Teaching and Learning in Information and Computer Sciences*, **5** (4), 249–67.

Middleton, L. and Hall, H. (2021) Workplace Information Literacy: A Bridge to the Development of Innovative Work Behavior, *Journal of Documentation*, **77** (6), 1343–63.

Pal, A., Chua, A. Y. K. and Hoe-Lian Goh, D. (2019) Debunking Rumors on Social Media: The Use of Denials, *Computers in Human Behavior*, **96**, 110–22.

Palumbo, R. (2021) Does Digitizing Involve Desensitizing? Strategic Insights into the Side Effects of Workplace Digitization, *Public Management Review*, **24** (7), 975–1000.

Palumbo, R., Manna, R. and Cavallone, M. (2020) Beware of Side Effects on Quality! Investigating the Implications of Home Working on Work-life Balance in Educational Services, *The TQM Journal*, **33** (4), 915–29.

Sample, A. (2020) Historical Development of Definitions of Information Literacy: A Literature Review of Selected Sources, *The Journal of Academic Librarianship*, **46** (2), 102116.

Sharun, S. (2021) Practicing Information Literacy: Practicum Students Negotiating Information Practice in Workplace Settings, *The Journal of Academic Librarianship*, **47** (1), 102267.

Tabrizi, B., Lam, E., Girard, K. and Irvin, V. (2019) Digital Transformation is Not About Technology, *Harvard Business Review*, **13**, 1–6.

Teebken, M. and Hess, T. (2021) Privacy in a Digitized Workplace: Towards an Understanding of Employee Privacy Concerns. In *Proceedings of the 54th Hawaii International Conference on System Sciences*.

Thomas, M. (2019) How to Overcome Your (Checks Email) Distraction Habit, *Harvard Business Review*, https://hbr.org/2019/12/how-to-overcome-your-checks-email-distraction-habit.

Tuominen K., Savolainen R. and Talja, S. (2005) Information Literacy as a Sociotechnical Practice, *Library Quarterly*, **75** (3), 329–45.

Vallo Hult, H., Islind, A. S. and Norström, L. (2021) Reconfiguring Professionalism in Digital Work, *Systems, Signs and Actions*, **12**, 1–17, www.sysiac.org/uploads/SySiAc2021-ValloHultEtal.pdf.

Van der Voort, H., van Bulderen, S., Cunningham, S. and Janssen, M. (2021) Data Science as Knowledge Creation: A Framework for Synergies Between Data Analysts and Domain Professionals, *Technological Forecasting and Social Change*, **173**, 121160.

White, M. (2012) Digital Workplaces: Vision and Reality, *Business Information Review*, **29** (4), 205–14.

Widén, G., Ahmad, F., Nikou, S., Ryan, B. and Cruickshank, P. (2021) Workplace Information Literacy: Measures and Methodological Challenges, *Journal of Information Literacy*, **15** (2), 26–44, https://doi.org/10.11645/15.2.2812.

Ziemba, E. (2019) The Contribution of ICT Adoption to the Sustainable Information Society, *Journal of Computer Information Systems*, **59** (2), 116–26.

Zurkowski, P. G. (1974) *The Information Service Environment Relationships and Priorities*, Related Paper No. 5, National Commission on Libraries and Information Science.

1

Literature Review: In Search of the Many Meanings of Information Literacy

José Teixeira and Muhaimin Karim

Introduction

The concept of information literacy is crucial for an educated and literate society (Weiner, 2011). According to Annemaree Lloyd (2010) and Weiner (2011), information literacy acts as a key catalyst for learning in everyday contexts (for example, school, university or working life). If the concept of information literacy was already relevant before the emergence of computers and the internet, it is even more relevant now as the knowledge economy undergoes digitalisation and globalisation (Shapiro and Varian, 1999; Nikou, Brännback and Widén, n.d.; Autio, Mudambi and Yoo, 2021).

The conceptual foundations of information literacy keep evolving with recurring discussions – and even disagreements – on what information literacy means (Behrens, 1994; Bawden, 2001; Tuominen, Savolainen and Talja, 2005; Stordy, 2015; Webber and Johnston, 2017; Secker, 2018). The starting point for our theoretical orientation is the definition originally proposed in 2000 by the Association of College & Research Libraries (ACRL):

> Information literacy is a set of abilities requiring individuals to recognize when information is needed and have the ability to locate, evaluate, and use effectively the needed information.
>
> (ACRL, 2000)

Complementing this definition, which takes a perspective centred on the individual and their skills and competencies, the ACRL (2000) also stated that an information literate individual is able to:

- determine the extent of information needed
- access the needed information effectively and efficiently
- evaluate the information and its sources critically
- incorporate selected information into one's knowledge base

2 INFORMATION LITERACY AND THE DIGITALISATION OF THE WORKPLACE

- use information effectively to accomplish a specific purpose
- understand the economic, legal, and social issues surrounding the use of information and access and use information ethically and legally.

Evidencing the growing attention devoted to the information literacy concept, Figure 1.1 shows a surge of research in information literacy that started in 1990 and continued until 2019. Here, we must remark that the decline of research in information literacy coincided with the emergence of the worldwide COVID-19 pandemic in 2019. Therefore, it can be speculated that the abrupt decline of research in information literacy is down to the pandemic. What stands out the most in Figure 1.1 is the steady increase in the attention devoted to information literacy since 1990.

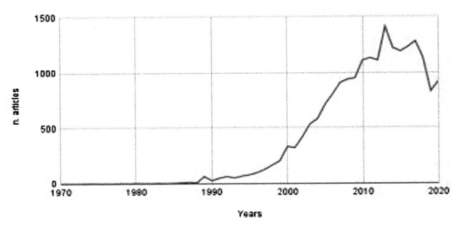

Figure 1.1 *Articles with 'information literacy' in the title according to Google Scholar*

Contributing to this line of research, which captured much attention in the last 30 years, we report on a systematic literature review on information literacy that was conducted at the initial stages of a large academic project that looked at the impact of information literacy in the digital workplace. Grounded in our literature review efforts, we discuss the meaning(s) of information literacy and point out promising avenues for future research on the topic. Furthermore, we also outline the methodological lessons that arose while conducting a comprehensive literature review at the beginning of a large collective research project on a topic that deals with vast amounts of literature.

Literature review

Sources, search and storage

The literature review was conducted semi-automatically to identify existing knowledge on information literacy in the workplace and it was carried out by two scholars working in parallel from the beginning of the project (see www.abo.fi/diwil for more detailed information on the project's context). As the literature review was conducted early, it contributed to the research team's collective understanding of the meanings of information literacy.

The literature review was conducted using both library databases and search engines (see Table 1.1 on the next page). Benefiting from licensing agreements with the EBSCO and ProQuest, we could access both the articles, metadata and full text within the Library, Information Science & Technology Abstracts (LISTA) and the Library and Information Science Abstracts (LISA) research databases. Furthermore, we also leveraged the Education Resources Information Center (ERIC) database provided by the US Department of Education and the Google Scholar search engine, which indexes literature more broadly across disciplines.

The literature review was based on a keywords search strategy and the results were made available to the overall team in a Google Drive folder. By storing the collected articles on a Google Drive, we considered several factors: (a) accessible storage (in terms of price); (b) automatic backups; (c) automatic synchronisation across project team members; (d) easy remote access from multiple devices; and (e) the indexing capabilities of Google allowed the team members to rapidly search for textual strings within the article collection content.

The article collection that grew with the literature review was organised within folders that reflect the adopted keywords search strategy. Duplicated files were identified and merged as the use of the different keywords (see Table 1.2) often led to the same articles. For example, the article entitled 'Information Literacy Assessment: Moving Beyond Computer Literacy' (Hignite, Margavio and Margavio, 2009) was retrieved both by using the 'information literacy' and the 'computer literacy' keyword. On the more operational side, we dealt with duplicate files by creating 'hard links' to the first retrieved article, which allowed us to save storage and optimise the indexing of the retrieved articles by the Google Drive.

We faced three main challenges during search and storing efforts. The first was the explosion of keywords. Even if we started by using only the 'information literacy' keyword, we soon realised that more keywords (see Table 1.2) were necessary to capture research dealing with the information literacy concept that does not necessarily employ the same term. The second was the vast amount of literature retrieved, especially when using the Google

4 INFORMATION LITERACY AND THE DIGITALISATION OF THE WORKPLACE

Table 1.1 *Library databases and search engines used during the literature review efforts*

Database	License	Provider	Scope	Type
LISTA with Full Text	Subscription	EBSCO	Information sciences	Bibliographic database
LISA	Subscription	ProQuest	Information sciences	Bibliographic database
ERIC	Free for public use	U.S. Depart. Edu.	Inf. and Edu. sciences	Bibliographic database
Scholar	Free for public use	Google	Broad	Web search engine

Scholar search engine. This forced us to dedicate much time to retrieving and filtering upon what we perceived sufficiently rigorous and relevant to our project. The third challenge was the actual file name of the retrieved full-text files. When downloading a full-text file from a publisher (usually a PDF), the file names varied a lot and often had no visible pattern (for example, 1524.pdf or AlberS16793254383.pdf). This forced us to develop a small software script that renamed PDF files according to the PDF content in the title page and the PDF metadata. This renamed all files in the more standard format of AUTHORS-YEAR-TITLE-JOURNAL-VOLUME-ISSUE.pdf. By having a standard file name for the full-text articles, we were able to locate them much faster (both on Google Drive and locally on our computer devices).

Table 1.2 *Keywords used during the literature search*

Keyword	n. articles with keyword in the title
Information literacy	25900
Data literacy	968
Digital literacy	6270
Computer literacy	3700
ICT literacy	738
IT literacy	129
Media literacy	8950
Health literacy	21600
Meta literacy	166

Analysis and communication

Regarding the retrieved literature, most of the literature was found within the fields of education, health and library and information science (LIS). A smaller number of articles was also found within the business, management, organisation, human resources and wellbeing fields of research.

Following months of searching, retrieving and storing full-text articles, the most relevant articles were added to a reference database using the RefWorks web-based reference management service. This would allow the remaining colleagues on the project (those not directly participating in the initial literature review process) to find and cite the literature on information literacy more easily.

After several months, the two scholars working in parallel from the beginning of the project concluded the more systematic literature review and retrieval process. This resulted in a collection of folders with articles on Google Drive that could be synchronised among the different team members and a RefWorks web-based reference database that could also be updated by the different team members. It was then time to leverage the literature review in a way that the overall research team could get an improved collective understanding of the meanings of information literacy and conduct further empirical research on the topic.

A seminar was organised to bring together the two scholars and the overall project teams. The scholars offered tips to their team on how to navigate the large collection of articles and the correspondent reference database. They also provided advice on how to search within the large collection of PDF files using the indexing capabilities of Google Drive and common operating systems (Mac and Linux). It was demonstrated how the articles could be cited from the RefWorks database. A list of seminal review articles (ranked by relevance to the overall project goals) and a list of articles discussing measures and metrics for the study of information literacy were also discussed. Finally, the journal publications most interested in information literacy were presented (see Table 1.3); this gave the overall research team an overview of what publication channels should be considered for future empirical research within the project scope. All the delivered information was then archived using the Moodle Learning environment and a dedicated web page (https://web.abo.fi/projekt/diwil/literature.html), which has been used by other scholars interested in information literacy.

Results and discussion

The many meanings of information literacy

When discussing the results, we must remark that while this research started as a literature review on 'information literacy', it evolved into a literature review on 'information literacies'. Early on, we realised that research dealing with the concept does not necessarily employ the same term. As we progressed, we expanded our search to capture research using other terms, such as computer literacy, digital literacy, meta literacy and health literacy among others (see Table 1.2 on page 4). To better understand the evolution of research on the many information literacies that conceptually approximate their meaning, we captured how each different 'x literacy' term was used over time (see Figure 1.2). From the results we can note that:

1 Research using all different terms increased over time (i.e., no research stream on the different types of literacy seems dead).
2 Research on digital literacy and health literacy surged over the last decade signalling them as promising avenues for future research.
3 Even if the ACRL endorsed the concept of meta literacy (Mackey and Jacobson, 2011; Mackey and Jacobson, 2014; ACRL, 2016), not many scholars employed the term in the title of their papers as compared with other terms such as information literacy, digital literacy or health literacy. According to our literature review records, meta literacy was used in the title of 324 publications from 1990 to 2020. This number is quite significant but is negligible when compared with hundreds of thousands of publications using 'information literacy' or 'health literacy' in their title.

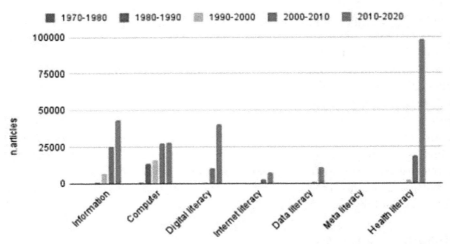

Figure 1.2 *Articles with 'x literacy' in the title across each decade according to Google Scholar*

It is worth reporting that we were able to identify other reviews of information literacy and related concepts (for example, Behrens, 1994; Saranto and Hovenga, 2004; Lloyd, 2005; Secker, 2014; Forster, 2015;

Stordy, 2015; Webber and Johnston, 2017; Secker, 2018). While on the one hand those reviews have merit by organising, reconceptualising and redefining information literacy and related concepts (for example, computer literacy or digital literacy); on the other hand, the successive reviews fragment even further the meaning of information literacy and the related concepts. Plenty of research on information literacy does not clearly define the concept (Saranto and Hovenga, 2004). Other research, trying to precisely define the concept, gets trapped in discussions and even disagreements (Lloyd, 2011) over the meaning.

While we agree with others (for example, Saranto and Hovenga, 2004; Bawden, 2001; Aharony, 2010) on information literacy as an ambiguous concept, we should not get trapped in recurring discussions over its meaning. Rather, we should empirically research its antecedents and its consequences across different contexts. After all, the concept can be linked and theorised both before or after other conceptual constructs (for example, information literacy as a antecedent or consequence). We also note that most literature commonly recognises the importance of information literacy, its connection and evolution from basic literacy, as well as its embodiment in the form of knowledge, skills and competences that can be learned. As put by Saranto and Hovenga (2004), information literacy is a foundational educational outcome.

Methodological lessons

This literature review on information literacy was conducted at the initial stages of a large academic project spanning across four years. It included members with backgrounds in library and information science, network science, economics, management and information systems. The review was carried out by the two authors working in parallel for nine months from the beginning of the overall project. As the literature review was conducted early, it contributed to the team's collective understanding of the meanings of information literacy. This was a setting in which part of the large project team (with more than ten participating researchers) did not have prior experience with the core concept of the project (that is, information literacy). The early literature review therefore informed not only the two scholars involved in the systematic literature review, but also the project team overall. Many challenges emerged and lessons were learned that are worth being reported to assist other large projects that kick off with systematic literature reviews.

Even if we started by using only the 'information literacy' keyword, we soon realised that more keywords (see Table 1.2) were necessary to capture research dealing with the concept that does not necessarily employ the same term (for example, digital literacy). Here, the prior existence of literature outlining different dimensions and types of information literacy and different perspectives on it (for example, Stordy, 2015) was helpful to guide the expansion of our search keywords. As a lesson learned, we would highlight the importance of using such literature to identify relevant search keywords. Topologies and taxonomies of different conceptualisations (such as Stordy, 2015) have proven invaluable.

As the literature search was executed, we started using several different software tools. For example, we used a bibliographic database (RefWorks), storage and indexing tools (Google Drive), a communication and education platform (Moodle) and a dedicated web page for the project. While we managed with a standard collection of widely available tools, we also ran into problems that could be eased by the use of specialised software tools that aid collaborative systematic literature reviews (for example, Synthesis, MAXQDA or Rayyan). However, the price, set-up time and expected learning curve prevented us from exploiting these specialised tools fully. We also learned that a project with a single person conducting a systematic literature review is very different from a two-person team conducting a systematic literature review in support of a larger team.

After identifying each relevant publication, we would download and import the reference into RefWorks. The use of the BibTex format allowed the use of the references across multiple bibliographic software tools and word processors and across all team members (for example, those using Windows, Mac and Linux operating systems). Whenever possible, and if the licensing agreements with the publishers allowed, we would save the file in a PDF format with a common file name format (AUTHORS-YEAR-TITLE-JOURNAL VOLUME-ISSUE). That way, it would be quick and easy for everybody to search on Google Drive for a given publication by doing a simple file search. Here, we found that different publishers and even different journals under the same publisher named their publication PDF files in a very distinct way. We found it too laborious to rename each downloaded PDF file by hand so we developed instead a small software tool that renamed PDF files based on their PDF metadata. It was a technical endeavour that took time, but it allowed project members to find and retrieve the full-text PDFs of each of the reviewed articles much more quickly.

As there were so many publications on information literacy and related literacies, it was impossible for two scholars to grasp it all. A set of secondary objectives therefore emerged that led to a set of deliverables that also proved useful for the overall project researchers. The first deliverable was the identification of seminal literature review articles, which we identified both for being the most cited and the most recent literature review articles on information literacy. Every project researcher was invited to read the five most cited review papers and the five most recent review papers. The second deliverable was the identification of articles with measuring instruments for information literacy. Both of these deliverables reduced duplication of effort across all project teams. Finally, we also identified which published journals were more interested in information literacy research, making it easier for research teams from different disciplines to find a suitable audience for their research (see Table 1.3 for journal publications that most match the 'information literacy' string on the abstract).

Table 1.3 Top 20 journal publications interested in information literacy

Journal	Publisher
Computers and Education	Elsevier
Journal of Information Literacy	CILIP
Communications in Information Literacy	Portland State University
Reference Services Review	Emerald
College & Research Libraries	Association of College and Research Libraries
College & Undergraduate Libraries	Taylor & Francis
Evidence Based Library and Information Practice	University of Alberta Library
Journal of Critical Library and Information Studies	Litwin Books
Library and Information Research	CILIP
Journal of Academic Librarianship	Elsevier
Journal of Library Administration	Taylor & Francis
Teacher Librarian	EL Kundyla
Journal of the Association for Information Science and Technology	Wiley-Blackwell
Information Research	University of Borås
Information Development	SAGE
Journal of Information Science	SAGE
Education for Information	IOS Press
Academic Exchange Quarterly	RIG
International Journal of Learning and Media	MIT Press
ITALICS Innovations in Teaching and Learning in Information and Computer Sciences	Taylor & Francis
New Directions for Teaching and Learning	Wiley

Agenda for future research

Research on information literacy is, so far, particularly bounded by the educational context – a context where libraries play a very important role (Secker, 2014; Lloyd, 2017). However, recent research has pointed out the importance of exploring the concept of information literacy in non-educational work contexts (see Lloyd, 2005; Lloyd and Williamson, 2008; Weiner, 2011; Mbatha, 2015; Secker, 2014; Forster, 2015; Secker, 2018, among others). Here, we take the position of information literacy as dependent and inseparable from the context in which it is investigated. This unexplored territory is also an opportunity for co-operating with the field of management and organisation studies. While those two fields have been intensively addressing the issue of knowledge management in organisations, they have devoted little attention to the issues of information literacy (Widén, Ahmad and Huvila, 2021). In our view, there is a limited understanding of how information literacy constrains knowledge management within the boundaries of the firm and the inter-organisational domain – a promising avenue for future research. Along those lines, we call for the further theorising of 'workplace information literacy' (see Lloyd, 2013; Crawford and Irving, 2009; Widén, Ahmad and Huvila, 2021). It is time to further theorise information literacy beyond its roots in the library and education contexts.

As organisations are embracing processes of digitalisation, the future theorising of information literacy should not ignore the role of digital technologies nor treat them as black boxes. Little is known about how the adoption of digital technologies influences information literacy at both the individual and organisational levels. So far, research on information literacy has taken very little account of the actual material nature of the digital technologies that enable information literacy to develop (see Tuominen, Savolainen and Talja, 2005; Lloyd, 2017). We recommend that future research on information literacy not only looks at it at an individual level but also explores it at the organisational level while considering the materiality (that is, the structural properties) of digital technologies (Tuominen, Savolainen and Talja, 2005; Lloyd, 2017; Orlikowski and Iacono, 2001). Competent organisations that link both individuals and technology are naturally interested in mastering information literacy in the workplace for better organisational outcomes.

Conclusion

In this chapter, we have reported our attempt to systematically review the literature on information literacy within the context of a multi-year, multi-team academic research project. Given the growing attention devoted to the topic by thousands of publications, the endeavour revealed itself to be too large to execute and did not meet the initial expectations. Rather than finding the meaning of information literacy, we needed to explore the many meanings of information literacy, all conceptualised in different ways. As other scholars have pointed out before, the meaning of information literacy is fragmented and evolving. Across decades of research, the concept of information literacy remains fuzzy and open to discussion. Nevertheless, the systematic literature review helped explore the multifaceted nature of information literacy and its contextuality. The literature review also revealed the lack of studies on information literacy in the emerging digital workplace context and pinpointed promising avenues for future research.

Besides all the challenges in developing a workable and agreed shared understanding of what information literacy means, it is worth reporting our efforts. Furthermore, our methodological lessons should also inform academic researchers who conduct literature reviews at the beginning of large collective research projects on topics that deal with vast amounts of literature.

References

ACRL (2000) *Information Literacy Competency Standards for Higher Education*, www.ala.org/acrl/standards/informationliteracycompetency.

ACRL (2016) *Framework for Information Literacy for Higher Education*, www.ala.org/acrl/standards/ilframework.

Aharony, N. (2010) Information Literacy in the Professional Literature: An Exploratory Analysis. In *Aslib Proceedings*, 261–82, Emerald Group Publishing Limited.

Autio, E., Ram M. and Youngjin, Y. (2021) Digitalization and Globalization in a Turbulent World: Centrifugal and Centripetal Forces, *Global Strategy Journal*, 11 (1), 3–16.

Bawden, D. (2001) Information and Digital Literacies: A Review of Concepts, *Journal of Documentation*, 57 (2), 218–59.

Behrens, S. J. (1994) A Conceptual Analysis and Historical Overview of Information Literacy, *College & Research Libraries*, 55 (4), 309–22.

Crawford, J. and Irving, C. (2009) Information Literacy in the Workplace: A Qualitative Exploratory Study, *Journal of Librarianship and Information Science*, 41 (1), 29–38.

Forster, M. (2015) Refining the Definition of Information Literacy: The Experience of Contextual Knowledge Creation, *Journal of Information Literacy*, 9 (1), 2–73.

Hignite, M., Margavio, T. M. and Margavio, G. W. (2009) Information Literacy Assessment: Moving Beyond Computer Literacy, *College Student Journal*, 43 (3), 812–22.

Lloyd, A. (2005) Information Literacy: Different Contexts, Different Concepts, Different Truths, *Journal of Librarianship and Information Science*, 37 (2), 82–8.

Lloyd, A. (2010) *Information Literacy Landscapes: Information Literacy in Education, Workplace and Everyday Contexts*, Chandos Information Professional Series, Elsevier Science.

Lloyd, A. (2011) Trapped Between a Rock and a Hard Place: What Counts as Information Literacy in the Workplace and How is it Conceptualized?, *Library Trends*, **60** (2), 277–96.

Lloyd, A. (2013) Building Information Resilient Workers: The Critical Ground of Workplace Information Literacy. What Have We Learnt?. In Kurbanoğlu, S. et al. (eds), *Worldwide Commonalities and Challenges in Information Literacy Research and Practice: European Conference on Information Literacy, ECIL 2013 Istanbul, Turkey, 22–25 October, Revised Selected Papers*, 219–28, Springer International Publishing.

Lloyd, A. (2017) Information Literacy and Literacies of Information: A Mid-Range Theory and Model, *Journal of Information Literacy*, **11** (1), 91–105.

Lloyd, A. and Williamson, K. (2008) Towards an Understanding of Information Literacy in Context: Implications for Research, *Journal of Librarianship and Information Science*, **40** (1), 3–12.

Mackey, T. P. and Jacobson, T. E. (2011) Reframing Information Literacy as a Metaliteracy, *College & Research Libraries*, **72** (1), 62–78.

Mackey, T. P. and Jacobson, T. E. (2014) *Metaliteracy: Reinventing Information Literacy to Empower Learners*, American Library Association.

Mbatha, B. T. (2015) Mapping and Auditing Digital Literacy of Civil Servants in Selected South African Government Departments, *Communicare: Journal for Communication Sciences in Southern Africa*, **34** (1), 49–64.

Nikou, S., Brännback, M. and Widén, G. (2019) The Impact of Digitalization on Literacy: Digital Immigrants vs Digital Natives. In *Proceedings of the 27th European Conference on Information Systems (ECIS)*, Stockholm & Uppsala, Sweden, 8–14 June, https://aisel.aisnet.org/ecis2019_rp/39.

Orlikowski, W. J. and Iacono, C. S. (2001) Research Commentary: Desperately Seeking the 'IT' in IT Research – A Call to Theorizing the IT Artifact, *Information Systems Research*, **12** (2), 121–34.

Saranto, K. and Hovenga, E. J. S. (2004) Information Literacy – What it is About?: Literature Review of the Concept and the Context, *International Journal of Medical Informatics*, **73** (6), 503–13.

Secker, J. (2014) Broadening the Scope of Information Literacy in 2015: Beyond Libraries, *Journal of Information Literacy*, **8** (2), 1–2.

Secker, J. (2018) The Revised CILIP Definition of Information Literacy, *Journal of Information Literacy*, **12** (1), 156–8.

Shapiro, C. and Varian, H. R. (1999) *Information Rules: A Strategic Guide to the Network Economy*, Harvard Business School Press.

Stordy, P. (2015) Taxonomy of Literacies, *Journal of Documentation*, **71** (3), 456–76.

Tuominen, K., Savolainen. R. and Talja, S. (2005) Information Literacy as a Sociotechnical Practice, *The Library Quarterly*, **75** (3), 329–45.

Webber, S. and Johnston, B. (2017) Information Literacy: Conceptions, Context and the Formation of a Discipline, *Journal of Information Literacy*, **11** (1), 156–83.

Weiner, S. (2011) Information Literacy and the Workforce: A Review, *Education Libraries*, **34** (2), 7–14.

Widén, G., Ahmad, F. and Huvila, I. (2021) Connecting Information Literacy and Social Capital to Better Utilise Knowledge Resources in the Workplace, *Journal of Information Science*, https://doi.org/10.1177/01655515211060531.

2

Digital Literacy in a Post-Digital Era: Rethinking 'Literacy' as Sociomaterial Practice

Mika Mård and Anette Hallin

Introduction: the need to rethink digital literacy in a post-digital era

The digital revolution has created a world where digital technologies are ubiquitous and operating as an integral part of everyday human life. Today, digital technologies are taken for granted to the extent that they are almost only noticed when they break down and no longer function as expected (Floridi, 2014). Since most contemporary practices 'entail the digital', it has been argued that the term 'digital' is no longer useful (Orlikowski and Scott, 2016, 88). Instead, it makes sense to say that we find ourselves in a 'post-digital era', where humans are *inextricably intertwined* with digital technologies (Cramer, 2015; Kalpokas, 2020; Pepperell and Punt, 2000; Reeves, 2019). This development has several consequences for the process of navigating the vast sea of information available in digital contexts, that is, for 'digital literacy' (see, for example, Bawden, 2001; Lankshear and Knobel, 2008). In the post-digital environment, it becomes important to rethink digital literacy, since the traditional way of understanding digital literacy as a competence of the individual risks hiding relational aspects that may explain the effects of its enactment.

In this chapter, we will argue that as we have entered the post-digital era, there is a need to rethink the concept of 'digital literacy' as a *sociomaterial practice* (Orlikowski, 2007). Rather than understanding digital literacy as a competence or skill possessed by individuals, we will, drawing upon sociomaterial and posthuman theories and empirical examples from existing literature, argue for a need to understand it as a sociomaterial practice enacted by humans and technologies in concert. This means shifting the focus from the ability of humans to use digital technologies, to acknowledging the role of material technologies in the enactment of practices whereby information is constructed and produced. Reframing digital literacy this way also allows for a deeper understanding of the way workplace information literacy is enacted sociomaterially. This increases the potential of understanding and explains not only how workplace information literacy is performed, but with what effects.

In order to do this, we will engage with Lloyd's (2010) conceptualisation of information literacy as sociocultural practice and her understanding of literacy as a product of the social, where 'meaning making is a negotiation between people in a particular setting' (Lloyd, 2010, 251). Although we will adopt Lloyd's concept of 'information literacy', which according to her refers to practices that build 'people's capacity to negotiate increasingly complex social and technological environments' and that facilitate ways of 'knowing about the modalities of information within an environment and how these modalities are constructed' (Lloyd, 2010, 245), we will throughout this chapter mostly use the term 'digital literacy'. We do so in order to accentuate our main argument: that the practice that Lloyd refers to needs to be understood as produced by humans and digital technologies *jointly*, especially in a post-digital environment where information is primarily digitalised and/or accessed through digital tools. In order to avoid the conceptual maze regarding information literacy versus digital literacy (see, for example, Bawden, 2001), we will here use the concept of digital literacy as a way of engaging with and extending Lloyd's proposition that information literacy is a practice, by emphasising that these practices are not merely socio*cultural*, but socio*material*.

Digital literacy as a competence in a particular site

Traditionally, definitions of digital literacy often either adopt a narrow, rational and positivist entity-based approach or a broader interpretative-relational approach, focusing on how literacy is constructed through sensemaking, understanding and critical thinking (Bawden, 2001; Martin, 2008). A typical definition may involve the various psychological traits of the person possessing digital literacy and the ability to use this. One example is:

> ... the awareness, attitude and ability of individuals to appropriately use digital tools and facilities to identify, access, manage, integrate, evaluate, analyze and synthesize digital resources, construct new knowledge, create media expressions, and communicate with others, in the context of specific life situations, in order to enable constructive social action; and to reflect upon this process.
>
> (Martin, 2008, 166–7)

It has however been argued that definitions such as the one above express opposing logics by, on the one hand, involving the measurable abilities/

skills/competences of the individual, while, on the other hand, also involving a particular activity on behalf of the individual (see, for example, Lloyd, 2010; Tuominen, Savolainen and Talja, 2005). This means that while being 'rooted in objectivism' and 'unanchored in relationship and context', through, for example, an emphasis on 'quantifiable and measurable' competencies, the definitions at the same time include dimensions of practice, which build on 'explicitly constructionist', 'inherently relational and collective' and 'situated and socially defined' ideas (Carroll, Levy and Richmond, 2008, 236). While the first logic focuses on the competency of the individual and privileges reason by assuming that an individual has an intellect, hence allowing for analysis on an individual level, the second focuses on the doings and actings of the individual, allowing for lived experiences that involve discursive, narrative and rhetoric as well as embodied and felt dimensions (Carroll, Levy and Richmond, 2008, 236).

Building on this, Lloyd points out that the doings and actings – that is, the practices – of information literacy need to be understood in the particular context in which they are performed:

> ... an analysis of practice cannot be reduced to its cognitive features, but needs to consider how the practice is constructed corporeally and socially and how these features are interwoven and mesh together within a social site.
> (Lloyd, 2010, 248)

Lloyd hence proposes conceptualising information literacy as a 'socio-cultural practice' and argues for a relational understanding where literacy is understood as a social product of sense-making in a particular setting (see also Tuominen, Savolainen and Talja, 2005). Inspired by Theodore Schatzki's idea of site ontology (Schatzki, 2002), Lloyd thus suggests a shift from understanding information literacy as a human competence to a social and cultural practice: 'the focus here is not on the skills of information literacy [...] but on the nexus of activities that form the practice' (Lloyd, 2010, 255). A similar argument is also made by Tuominen, Savolainen and Talja (2005), who propose a sociotechnical practice approach to information literacy in order to shift 'the focus away from the behavior, action, motives, and skills of monologic individuals' (2005, 339) and instead focus 'on the social, ideological, and physical contexts and environments in which information and technical artefacts are used' (340).

Even though we start from the same point and share the conviction that there is value in seeing practice 'as the central feature of social life' (Lloyd, 2010, 246) and the need for reframing literacy as something 'which is formed and understood through a social setting in which a person enters and operates' (Lloyd, 2010, 253), we argue that the notion of 'socio-cultural practices' still to a large extent assumes a human-centric understanding of practices (see Braidotti, 2019). While acknowledging that material aspects can play a role in sociocultural practices, materiality remains in Lloyd's (2010) account somewhat secondary to the doings of humans in a particular site and she does not give material objects the same agentic status as humans (see Orlikowski, 2007). Also, while we agree with Tuominen, Savolainen and Talja's argument that 'literacies cannot be separated from the domain-specific sociotechnical practices that give rise to them' (2005, 341), technology remains in their conceptualisation as something we humans interact with. In other words, while emphasising that information literacy is 'practiced by communities using appropriate technologies' (Tuominen, Savolainen and Talja, 2005, 341), technology still holds the status of a tool that we use and is hence never really explored as an agent in information literacy practices. But, in a post-digital context, where technologies are inextricably intertwined with humans in daily practices, material objects, technological tools and digital algorithms need to be considered as agents in producing practices and need to be acknowledged in depth to allow for a richer understanding of the enactment of literacy and its consequences (see Orlikowski, 2007; Barad, 2003; Latour, 1994).

Digital literacy as a sociomaterial practice

In the following, we draw on sociomaterial theory (Gherardi and Strati, 2017; Orlikowski, 2007) and posthumanism (Braidotti, 2019) in order to propose a sociomaterial conceptualisation of digital literacy. This approach means that we put emphasis on an understanding of social life as entangled with materiality; that is, a performing of life where every 'practice is *always* bound with materiality' (Orlikowski, 2007, 1436, emphasis in original). Such an understanding means that materiality is viewed as *integral* to social life, not an accidental by-product of it. However, it is important here to not ontologically privilege one over the other, that is, to neither focus on how humans interact with or use materiality (anthropocentrism) or how technology influences human action (materialism), but to view the social and material as *constitutively entangled*: 'the social and the material are considered to be inextricably related – there is no social that is not also material, and no material that is not also social' (Orlikowski, 2007, 1437). It is evident here that in her account of sociomaterial practices, Orlikowski draws inspiration from the work of other scholars interested in materiality and the social, mainly the work of Karen Barad (2003) and Bruno Latour (1994; 2005). Especially discernable are similarities to Latour's notion of technical mediation, by which he emphasises that 'action is simply not a property of humans, but of an association of actants' (Latour, 1994, 35). However, while aware of obvious connections to other scholars, we have in this chapter chosen to anchor our discussion in Orlikowski's notion of sociomaterial practices since her work is influenced by the same 'practice-turn' that Lloyd (2010) also draws upon.

In the case of digital literacy, this means that rather than focusing on the skills that are required of individuals, how these skills are made sense of or how humans use digital technologies, a sociomaterial understanding of digital literacy involves attention to *how humans and technologies are configured in practice*, that is, through the *enactment* of digital literacy (see Baptista et al., 2020; Grønsund and Aanestad, 2020; Suchman, 2012); to the *situated and embodied nature* of these practices; and how they *matter* (see Berkelaar, 2017; Clarke and Knights, 2018). In an attempt to give attention to such sociomaterial configurations, we will describe the four types of activities, or 'routine activities and arrangements', that, according to Lloyd (2010, 253), facilitate the enactment of information literacy as a sociocultural practice: *influence work*, *information work*, *information sharing* and *information coupling*. For each activity we will, drawing on existing literature, offer empirical illustrations from the post-digital context that demonstrate the sociomaterial nature of these activities. By doing so, we aim at outlining a new conceptualisation of digital literacy; one that does not only see it as a socio*cultural* practice, but also socio*materially* enacted.

Influence work

According to Lloyd, influence work is related to 'the mediating activities of members as they interact with newcomers and with each other' (Lloyd, 2010, 254). In this activity, Lloyd explains, 'experienced members of the community engage new members with explicit and implicit information' (Lloyd, 2010, 254) and hence:

> ... [this] interaction facilitates the negotiation and sharing of collective meaning, draws new members towards the community of practice and facilitates the mapping of the information landscape of the workplace, thus ensuring the continuity of the site and its unique characteristics.
>
> (Lloyd, 2010, 254)

Here, it is quite clear that Lloyd understands the members of this interaction to be human actors. However, influence work could also be seen to involve non-human actors. An example that is obvious to many people today is web portals, intranets or various Web 2.0 technologies that are mobilised in organisations in the 'mediating work' that Lloyd describes, whereby people interact with each other and hence become involved in various sense-making processes.

From a sociomaterial point of view, technology does not merely play the role of mediator in these processes. Instead, it may be understood as an actor that plays an important role in shaping influence work. An empirical illustration of this may be found in Orlikowski's (2007) account of a study of a company that equipped its staff with BlackBerry wireless e-mail devices; a change that in a fundamental way reconfigured the communication practices within the organisation. Even though the staff could choose when they opened and responded to certain e-mails, the implementation of the new digital device led to a change in practices, which meant that staff began to frequently check their devices and quickly respond to e-mails (sometimes even 24/7). Furthermore, they expected others to do the same, which further reinforced the emergence of the new practice:

> When such expectations are enacted in practice, they are reinforced over time, becoming intrinsically bound up with the device, and shifting how people think and act with it.
> (Orlikowski, 2007, 1442)

Orlikowski emphasises that this example should not only be interpreted as a matter of material technology having an impact on social life, but rather that:

> ... the performativity of the BlackBerry is sociomaterial, shaped by the particular contingent way in which the BlackBerry service is designed, configured, and engaged in practice.
> (Orlikowski, 2007, 1444)

In other words, when the device 'becomes entangled with people's choices and activities to keep devices turned on, to carry them at all times, to glance at them repeatedly, and to respond to email regularly' (Orlikowski, 2007, 1444) it is not only a 'matter of the technology interacting with the social, but of constitutive entanglement' (Orlikowski, 2007, 1444). What this example highlights is that material technology does not only play a mediating role in the influence work of humans when facilitating the enactment of digital literacy, but rather that 'the mediating activities of members as they interact with newcomers and with each other' (Lloyd, 2010, 254) are continuously formed, enacted and reconfigured *together with* technology (see Suchman, 2012).

Information work

According to Lloyd (2010), the second activity that facilitates information literacy practices is information work, that is, the work directed towards the developing or refining of practical information skills that are deemed effective and appropriate to collective practice and to the production and reproduction of collective knowledge about the ways things are done. Information work aims at changing the information practices of new members in order to direct them towards the modalities of information (social, corporeal or textual) that are constituted through collective and embodied knowledge (Lloyd, 2010). Central to this is the body and the 'corporeal, embodied and often contingent understandings it produces' (Lloyd, 2010, 54). Lloyd points out that 'the body plays a critical role in the shaping of workplace identity and in dissemination of information about the performance of workplace practices' (Lloyd, 2021, 254). In other words, the body becomes 'a source of information and central to information practice' (Lloyd, 2021, 254).

However, the body should not merely be seen as a sensory device, picking up information from its environment. Instead, the body, in the post-digital context, is entangled with digital technologies and cannot be considered as separate from these (van Doorn, 2011). An illustration of this could be the performing of online meetings via digital technologies such as Zoom, Teams or Skype. In these digital spaces, the virtual and the non-virtual (such as the body) converge and the 'immaterial potential of the virtual is materially actualized in the form of digital objects' (van Doorn, 2011, 534). More specifically, through these platforms, people come together in a virtual space, also with their bodies, enacting presence through video, audio and text. The bodies of the participants should not be viewed as mimetic mirrors of 'the real thing' or as representations, but as essential to the production of the encounter. In a post-digital setting then, the experiences of one's own body, as well as of others, change, for example, through the continuous looking at yourself in the moving image in a Zoom or Teams meeting. Our use of these virtual spaces should not be viewed only as disembodied presentations of ourselves, but rather spaces where the virtual and the body converge in a way that forms new experiences of our body – even our identity – and the bodies of others, or as van Doorn (2011, 535) puts it: 'the medium *is* the experience here'.

Not only does this mean that matter matters in online performances (van Doorn, 2011, 534), but that the bodywork performed in the virtual space is constitutively entangled with the digital technology that enables it. This is a fundamental aspect of information work. When Lloyd points out that 'through engagement with information work, the body becomes the source of information and the reflection of the site' (Lloyd, 2010, 255) we should not only think of the material body, but of the digital *actualisations* of our embodiments. In addition to the example of the convergence of the virtual and the body in Zoom meetings, another example here would be smartwatches. From a sociomaterial perspective, these devices are not merely understood as tools for collecting information *from* or *about* the body, but as fundamentally performative in nature by changing how the possessors' relate to their bodies (for example, counting steps and changing sleep patterns). In other words, these devices are constitutively entangled with people's bodily activities, and hence play an important role in contributing to the *shaping* of the practices of information work.

Information sharing

The third activity proposed by Lloyd in her description of information literacy as practice is information sharing. In her words, information sharing may be defined as 'a purposeful directed activity, which enables a member to give and receive information' (Lloyd, 2010, 255). Even though Lloyd discusses information sharing as a separate activity, she describes it 'as central to both information and influence work' (Lloyd, 2010, 255). This also highlights that even though Lloyd discusses each activity separately they are closely related – 'it is as an interwoven mesh of coterminous activities' (Lloyd, 2010, 253). However, with the notion of information sharing Lloyd attempts to highlight activities that purposefully enable members to share information and that are 'affected and influenced by the sayings and doings of the environment' (Lloyd, 2010, 255).

From a sociomaterial perspective, it could however be argued that this activity takes place in concert with digital technologies. When, for example, thinking of activities that enable members to share information it is easy to point to Wikipedia, which demonstrates the pivotal role that digital technology plays in information sharing. But technologies can also play a more crucial, agential role in the activity of information sharing. An example of this is when Facebook algorithmically decides which information we see in our news feeds (see, for example, Tufekci, 2015). As Tufekci (2015) suggests, Facebook's algorithms need to be conceptualised as having computational agency – they need to take the role of 'actants', as Latour would call them (Latour, 1991; 1994). In other words, by algorithmically curating what we see on our news feeds, the algorithms 'act with agency in the world' (Tufekci, 2015, 207).

Another example may be found in Orlikowski's article about Google searches, where she argues that Google searches are practices that are 'constitutively entangled through their everyday engagement with the materiality of the Google search engine' (Orlikowski, 2007, 1439). Orlikowski explains that a simple Google search involves 'multiple servers, directories, databases, indexes, and algorithms, and reflects considerable choices made about its design, construction, and operation' (Orlikowski, 2007, 1439). However, Orlikowski points out that the page rank of a Google search is not 'fixed or static, but dynamic and relative' (Orlikowski, 2007, 1439). Instead, the rankings of pages produced by certain Google searches are continually being updated due to new web pages being added and deleted, plus changes to existing web pages are continuously being made. It also needs to be noted here that this is not a neutral process, but rather heavily influenced by Google's commercial interests. Hence, 'these temporally emergent results are not dependent on either materiality or sociality [...] rather the performance and results of a Google-based search are sociomaterial' (Orlikowski, 2007, 1440). The practice and outcome of a Google search should be, according to Orlikowski, understood as a sociomaterial assemblage, constructed by a web of different agencies: human users and engineers, material computers and hardware, and digital algorithms and codes.

Understood this way, information sharing is an activity that involves social as well as material actants that are linked to each other in an intricate web, across space and time, and that support or hinder the sharing of information.

Information coupling

In the process of becoming a full member of a site, or an organisational context, a 'member engages not only with content but also acknowledges the effectiveness of their own information practice against the sanctioned ways of knowing within the site' (Lloyd, 2010, 255). This activity, that Lloyd calls information coupling, is the nexus of the above-mentioned activities. It is about the coupling together of explicit knowledge with 'experiential and relationally based knowledge to produce a way of knowing within the site that is intersubjectively understood' (Lloyd, 2010, 255). Information coupling, Lloyd explains, 'facilitates emergent awareness of where information is situated, and the strategies to access it within the various modalities' (Lloyd, 2010, 255).

Through the empirical illustrations above, relating to digital devices such as BlackBerry, Zoom/Teams/Skype and Google's search engine, it becomes clear that the activity of coupling together different forms of knowledge (explicit as well as implicit) is constitutively entangled with materiality and digital technology in today's post-digital world. In other words, coupling occurs not only through a sociocultural practice (as Lloyd points out), but also through a practice that is formed, enacted and reconfigured in a sociomaterial assemblage. It is important to not give ontological privilege to humans in understanding information coupling, but to instead acknowledge that 'in our information age the boundaries between anthropomorphic humans and quasi-human technological substitutes have been radically displaced' (Braidotti, 2019, 17).

Braidotti uses the example of reCAPTCHA to demonstrate this. ReCAPTCHA is the system used to identify you as a human when entering a website. Previously, this was done by ticking a box next to the following text 'I'm not a robot'. According to Braidotti:

> ... having to demonstrate one's humanity in order to access goods and services seems to be the imperative of a 'new' economy, centred on the algorithmic culture of computational networks, not good old Man/Homo/Anthropos – the human.
>
> (Braidotti, 2019, 17)

The main point here is not that reCAPTCHA restricts and affects the activity of information coupling for us humans. Instead, reCAPTCHA demonstrates that in this environment it is actually the 'algorithmic culture of computational networks' that is performing information coupling, gathering information about us humans, our clicks, preferences and desires, and coupling it together with other modalities and interests within this environment. Here, information coupling emerges as the result of the constitutive entanglement of the social and material and the only way for humans to participate in this process is to demonstrate that we are 'simple' humans.

The consequences of rethinking digital literacy as sociomaterial

By emphasising the role of material objects, technological tools and algorithms as agents in co-producing literacy practices, we have throughout this chapter had the conceptual aim to discuss digital literacy as a sociomaterial practice. We have done this by engaging with the four types of activities that, according to Lloyd (2010), facilitate the enactment of information literacy and offered empirical illustrations that show their sociomaterial nature. By doing that, we have aimed at extending Lloyd's work and suggested a conceptualisation of literacy that does not only see it as a socio*cultural* practice, but also socio*materially* enacted. What, then, does a rethinking of digital literacy as a sociomaterial practice mean for the understanding of literacy in a post-digital era? Below, we highlight three interrelated consequences of such a re-conceptualisation.

First, the relational ontology that is mobilised through the idea that digital literacy is enacted and practised by humans and technologies *together* enables us to question the assumed ontological dichotomy between human versus digital that comes with a human-centric understanding of digital literacy. Following this, rather than assuming that the full responsibility for acquiring or developing digital literacy lies with the working subject – the human – (see Bawden, 2008), a sociomaterial understanding of digital literacy allows for a more nuanced understanding whereby the complex web of material and discursive practices of organisational, business or societal structures are acknowledged (see Ebert, 2012).

Second, emphasising digital literacy as *emergent*, helps develop an understanding of how new subjectivities and their agency emerge, not only in relation to each other, but over time and in relation to other non-human agents (see Braidotti, 2019). This raises questions about change and allows for a clearer focus on how, and why, digital literacy improves, declines and generally changes.

Third, acknowledging the *subjectivities of materialities* allows for a better understanding of how these are different from other subjectivities. If the boundaries between humans and digital are fluid in a post-digital context, then different types of subjectivities will matter in the enactment of various practices. Previous research has, for example, pointed to the role of the algorithm when it comes to the enactment of practices, albeit not in the context of digital literacy (Andersson et al., 2021).

Conclusion

By bringing materiality into the understanding of digital literacy, it becomes clear that digital literacy not only concerns the ability of humans to *use* digital technologies or the sociocultural contexts or sites where humans engage in the practices of digital literacy, but that digital literacy is enacted in practices that are performed by humans, material objects, technological tools and algorithms *in concert*. As Lloyd (2010) points out, literacy is performed through a nexus of activities in practice – but here we want to add that these are not only sociocultural but also sociomaterial in that materialities also matter. By rethinking digital literacy in this way and illustrating how it is enacted sociomaterially, our hope is that this chapter contributes to the overall understanding of and discussion on digital literacy and especially to the practice perspective on workplace information literacy (Lloyd, 2010; Tuominen, Savolainen and Talja, 2005).

References

Andersson, C., Crevani, L., Hallin, A., Ivory, C., Lammi, I. J., Popova, I. and Uhlin, A. (2021) Hyper-Taylorism and Third-Order Technologies: Making Sense of the Transformation of Work and Management in a Post-Digital Era. In Ekman, P., Dahlin, P. and Keller, C. (eds) *Management and Information Technology after Digital Transformation*, 63–71, Routledge.

Baptista, J., Stein, M.-K., Klein, S., Watson-Manheim, M. B. and Lee, J. (2020) Digital Work and Organisational Transformation: Emergent Digital/Human Work Configurations in Modern Organisations, *The Journal of Strategic Information Systems*, **29** (2), https://doi.org/10.1016/j.jsis.2020.101618.

Barad, K. (2003) Posthumanist Performativity: Toward an Understanding of How Matter Comes to Matter, *Signs*, **28** (3), 801–31.

Bawden, D. (2001) Information and Digital Literacies: A Review of Concepts, *Journal of Documentation*, **57** (2), 218–59, https://doi.org/10.1108/EUM0000000007083.

Bawden, D. (2008) Origins and Concepts of Digital Literacy. In Lankshear, C. and Knobel, M. (eds), *Digital Literacies: Concepts, Policies and Practices*, 17–32, Peter Land.

Berkelaar, B. L. (2017) Different Ways New Information Technologies Influence Conventional Organizational Practices and Employment Relationships: The Case of Cybervetting for Personnel Selection, *Human Relations*, **70** (9), 1115–40, https://doi.org/10.1177/0018726716686400.

Braidotti, R. (2019) *Posthuman Knowledge*, Polity Press.

Carroll, B., Levy, L. and Richmond, D. (2008) Leadership as Practice: Challenging the Competency Paradigm, *Leadership*, **4** (4), 363–79, https://doi.org/10.1177/1742715008095186.

Clarke, C. A. and Knights, D. (2018) Practice Makes Perfect? Skillful Performances in Veterinary Work, *Human Relations*, **71** (10), 1395–421, https://doi.org/10.1177/0018726717745605.

Cramer, F. (2015) What is Post Digital? In Berry, D. M. and Dieter, M. (eds), *Postdigital Aesthetics: Art, Computation and Design*, 12–28, Palgrave Macmillan.

Ebert, N. (2012) *Individualisation at Work: The Self between Freedom and Social Pathologies*, Routledge.

Floridi, L. (2014) *The Fourth Revolution: How the Infosphere is Reshaping Human Reality*, Oxford University Press.

Gherardi, S. and Strati, A. (2017) Talking about Competence: That 'Something' Which Exceeds the Speaking Subject. In Sandberg, J., Rouleau, L., Langley, A. and Tsoukas, H. (eds), *Skillful Performance: Enacting Capabilities, Knowledge, Competence, and Expertise in Organizations*, 103–

24, Oxford University Press, https://doi.org/10.1093/oso/9780198806639.003.0005.

Grønsund, T. and Aanestad, M. (2020) Augmenting the Algorithm: Emerging Human-in-the-Loop Work Configurations, *The Journal of Strategic Information Systems*, **29** (2), https://doi.org/10.1016/j.jsis.2020.101614.

Kalpokas, I. (2020) Towards an Affective Philosophy of the Digital: Posthumanism, Hybrid Agglomerations and Spinoza, *Philosophy & Social Criticism*, **47** (6), https://doi.org/10.1177/0191453720916522.

Lankshear, C. and Knobel, M. (eds) (2008) *Digital Literacies: Concepts, Policies and Practices*, Peter Lang Publishing.

Latour, B. (1991) Technology is Society Made Durable. In Law, J. (ed.), *A Sociology of Monsters: Essays on Power, Technology and Domination*, 103–31, Routledge.

Latour, B. (1994) On Technical Mediation: Philosophy, Sociology, Genealogy, *Common Knowledge*, **3** (2), 29–64.

Latour, B. (2005) *Reassembling the Social: An Introduction to Actor Network Theory*, Oxford University Press.

Lloyd, A. (2010) Framing Information Literacy as Information Practice: Site Ontology and Practice Theory, *Journal of Documentation*, **66** (2), 245–58, https://doi.org/10.1108/00220411011023643.

Lloyd, A. (2021) *The Qualitative Landscape of Information Literacy Research: Perspectives, Methods and Techniques*, Facet Publishing.

Martin, A. (2008) Digital Literacy and the 'Digital Society'. In Lankshear, C. and Knobel, M. (eds), *Digital Literacies: Concepts, Policies and Practices*, 151–76, Peter Land.

Orlikowski, W. J. (2007) Sociomaterial Practices: Exploring Technology at Work, *Organization Studies*, **28** (9), 1435–48, https://doi.org/10.1177/0170840607081138.

Orlikowski, W. J. and Scott, S. V. (2016) Digital Work: A Research Agenda. In Czarniawska, B. (ed.), *Research Agenda for Management and Organization Studies*, 88–96, Edward Elgar Publishing.

Pepperell, R. and Punt, M. (2000) *The Postdigital Membrane: Imagination, Technology and Desire*, Intellect Books.

Reeves, T. (2019) A Postdigital Perspective on Organizations, *Postdigital Science and Education*, **1**, 146–62.

Schatzki, T. (2002) *The Site of the Social: A Philosophical Account of the Constitution of Social Life and Change*, Pennsylvania University Press.

Suchman, L. (2012) Configuration. In Lury, C. and Wakeford, N. (eds), *Inventive Methods: The Happening of the Social*, 48–60, Routledge.

Tufekci, Z. (2015) Algorithmic Harms Beyond Facebook and Google: Emergent Challenges of Computational Agency, *Journal on Telecommunications and High Technology Law*, **13**, 203–18.

Tuominen, K., Savolainen, R. and Talja, S. (2005) Information Literacy as a Sociotechnical Practice, *The Library Quarterly*, **75** (3), 329–45.

van Doorn, N. (2011) Digital Spaces, Material Traces: How Matter Comes to Matter in Online Performances of Gender, Sexuality and Embodiment, *Media, Culture & Society*, **33** (4), 531–47, https://doi.org/10.1177/0163443711398692.

3

Methodological Choices of Information Literacy in the Workplace: Qualitative, Quantitative or Mixed-Methods?

Shahrokh Nikou and Farhan Ahmad

Introduction

Digitalisation has not only impacted business and entrepreneurial activities (Urbach et al., 2019), but also workforce activities in workplaces (Farivar and Richardson, 2021). The digital revolution has created a new era of information-based society. Organisations need highly literate workforces to meet the challenges posed by digitalisation as well as the opportunities it presents (Iversen, Smith and Dindler, 2018). Literacy skills, and more fundamentally information literacy (hereinafter IL), have become an increasingly important prerequisite skill for lifelong learning in the 21st century (Lloyd, 2010). The traditional definition of IL refers to the ability to recognise information needs and to identify, assess and use the information (Bruce, 1999). In the workplace, IL includes the ability to use various information sources and tools, synthesise information, evaluate information, use information in practice and share information with colleagues (Gilbert, 2017). While IL has primarily been addressed, examined and measured in the educational context (for example, Jang et al., 2021; Johnston and Webber, 2003; O'Connor, Radcliff and Gedeon, 2002; Nikou and Aavakare, 2021), a few studies have investigated IL in the workplace, addressing the methodological choices and their consequences for workplace IL research (Gilbert, 2017; Widén et al., 2021a).

The aim of this chapter is to focus on the methodological choices (quantitative, qualitative or mixed-methods) that can be used in workplace IL research. This chapter also introduces a relatively new approach for analysing IL in the workplace called 'fuzzy-set Qualitative Comparative Analysis' (hereinafter fsQCA) (Ragin, 1987). The fsQCA is an analysis technique and enables researchers to better understand the complexity of workplace IL. It should be noted that we do not engage with philosophical traditions, such as positivism, interpretivism and pragmaticism – they are beyond the scope of this chapter. We recommend that interested readers check Lipu, Williamson and Lloyd (2007) for a better understanding of research philosophies in the context of IL.

This chapter is guided by the following research question: *What are the methodological choices for assessing IL in the workplace and what factors should be considered when selecting one?* Our method is to review the relevant literature to identify the most commonly used methodologies and procedures for measuring IL in the workplace. By doing so, we aim to highlight the underlying advantages and shortcomings of methodological choices, making recommendations and providing best practices for future research in this domain.

The next section in the chapter provides a brief summary of the literature on available methodologies for IL research and presents an overview of how each method has been used. We then introduce the concept of workplace IL, followed by a discussion of the challenges of the methodological choice and instruments for measuring IL. Finally, we conclude the chapter by discussing the contributions, limitations and suggestions for further research.

Research methodologies in information literacy research

During the last three decades, IL has mainly been discussed and assessed in the education area (Lloyd, 2010; Markless and Streatfield, 2007). In addition to providing rich insights on the theoretical intricacies of IL, education-specific research has also paid attention to IL assessment (Pinto, 2010; Walsh, 2009) and a number of IL measurement scales have been developed over the years (Kurbanoglu, Akkoyunlu and Uma, 2006; Larkin and Pines, 2005). For example, the Association of College and Research Libraries (ACRL, 2000) published *Information Literacy Competency Standards for Higher Education* containing five general IL standards, which has been widely used since its introduction (Jackman and Weiner, 2017; Iannuzzi, 2000). Some IL scales are very brief and consist of only a few measurement items, often as little as six (see, for example, Houlson, 2007), while others are comprehensive and built around IL standards, such as the Association of College and Research Libraries IL scale (see, for example, Cameron, Wise and Lottridge, 2007). Moreover, most, if not all, of the previous studies that attempted to measure IL conclude there is a lack of unified IL scales and instruments as well as a lack of agreement on which methodological approach – qualitative or quantitative – should be used in a given context (Baji et al., 2018; Davies-Hoffman et al., 2013). However, regardless of the context, it is critical to understand what IL constitutes, and hence what aspects of it should be measured, how we should conceptualise IL and which methodological choice is the most appropriate.

Qualitative, quantitative, and mixed-method research in information literacy

From a qualitative research methodology perspective, the IL research has gained momentum during the last decade (Forster, 2019; Gumulak and Webber, 2011). Prior studies aimed at exploring IL in the everyday life context, encompassing situations experienced over the course of life, such as critical life events (for example, Lloyd, 2010), participation in leisure activities (Demasson, 2014), citizenship activities (Correia, 2002) and immigration (Suárez-Orozco and Suárez-Orozco, 2009). The qualitative research trend is driven by the understanding that experiences of information are largely situated and sometimes even conflictual. Moreover, qualitative research deepens our understanding of multifaceted relationships with information in all its forms. To this end, qualitative research is mainly powered by interview data and encompasses different research designs, such as case study (Bryman, 2006), the Delphi method (Brady, 2015), discourse analysis (Wodak and Krzyżanowski, 2008) and ethnography (for example, Buchanan and Tuckerman, 2016; Comstock, 2012). In contrast to the educational domain, where students are the main subject, everyday life context covers much broader and diverse sets of the general population (Crawford and Irving, 2009). Therefore, depending upon the life situation, qualitative research-based investigations of IL in everyday life context explore day-to-day life information experiences of different groups of the population. Many authors, such as Oakleaf and Kaske (2009, 280), have argued that qualitative assessments should be used when the goals of the research can best be measured without having the need for numerical data, or when detailed descriptions provide the best information for modifying, judging or continuing research. What is not clear is whether qualitative research and its results would provide sufficient insights on the relationships between the antecedent factors and their impact on the outcome variable. Therefore, many researchers have recommended a quantitative approach to address such conditions in studying workplace IL.

In the education setting, quantitative research is clearly the dominant research methodology. Kurbanoglu, Akkoyunlu and Umay (2006) have developed an IL self-efficacy scale, which is one of the most widely used instruments in the educational context. Based on the self-efficacy concept of Bandura (Bandura, Freeman and Lightsey, 1999), a 17-item IL scale was proposed to measure perceived capabilities regarding study-related information seeking and evaluation skills, such as use of electronic and print bibliographic records, construction of bibliographies and capability to find information relevant to essays. Another IL scale, with multiple applications, was developed by Pinto (2010) to measure four aspects of the students' IL abilities (information search; information assessment; information processing; and information communication/dissemination) and three self-reporting dimensions (motivation; self-efficacy; and favourite source of learning). Moreover, in the educational context, a widespread practice of measuring IL through surveys has contributed significantly to extensive use of quantitative methods (Nikou and Aavakare, 2021; Nikou, De Reuver and Mahboob Kanafi, 2022). Studies using a quantitative approach often use survey-based IL measurement scales to gain descriptive and inferential statistical insights using different techniques to analyse the data collected through surveys. In addition to survey-based research, some studies have assessed IL using student essays, bibliographies and portfolios as a source of data (Lockhart, 2015). Others have collected data from alternative sources, for example, by using a marking rubric mapped on some kind of IL standard (Walsh, 2009). However, some authors, such as Machin-Mastromatteo, Lau and Virkus (2013, 51), argued that there are several critical issues, such as validity, trustworthiness and sample size, that need to be carefully considered when conducting quantitative research.

To address some of the flaws in qualitative and quantitative approaches, Williamson (2007) recommended exploiting mixed-method research in library and information research. This approach has recently made its way into IL research. In one piece of recent mixed-method research, Wakimoto (2010) employed pre- and post-tests, as well as focus group sessions, aiming at a better understanding of students' IL and satisfaction after finishing an IL course. The results showed that students' awareness about IL increased in the post-test compared to the pre-test survey responses. Furthermore, the results of the focus group revealed that those students who had participated in the discussion felt that their perception of IL and what it comprises had improved (Wakimoto, 2010, 87). In addition, Middleton and Hall (2021) also adopted a mixed-method approach and collected quantitative and qualitative data through questionnaire, interview and focus groups. The authors have found that information sharing and workplace IL are information-related determinants for the development of the employees' innovative work behaviour. Such understanding could, perhaps, not be gained if a single research method was applied. However, as Williamson (2007, 5) argued, regardless of whether researchers use a quantitative, qualitative or mixed-method approach, there is a wide variety of views on how the research landscape should be configured, which limits researchers' attempts to choose the most appropriate methodology to understand, assess or measure IL.

Workplace information literacy

People spend a significant amount of their lifetime at work. In a way, the workplace is an extension of everyday life context, albeit with different dynamics. Based on the notion that workers' information-related interaction capabilities and experiences can shape their performance at work, researchers are particularly interested in assessing the role of IL in the workplace (for example, Partridge, Edwards and Thorpe, 2010). Workplace IL is an emerging field of research, although some earlier works on workplace IL date back to the late 1990s (for example, Bruce 1999; Cheuk Wai-yi, 1998). As is the case with everyday life IL research, this emerging area of research is also dominated by qualitative research (Bruce, 1999). The complexity of the workplace information environment is usually presented as a main reason for the adoption of a qualitative research approach. As such, since the seminal work of Bruce (1999), several qualitative studies have been conducted on workplace IL specifically on the information experiences of professionals, such as auditors, lawyers (Golenko and Siber, 2017), firefighters (Lloyd, 2005) and ambulance workers (Lloyd, 2007). In addition, through qualitative research, Crawford and Irving (2009, 28) found that IL in the workplace is mainly seen as a pedagogical concept and information in the workplace is often used for social interaction with people, both within and outside the organisation.

From the methodological standpoint, qualitative methods can be used when the aim is to understand experiences of a specific group of individuals operating in a system. In addition, the conceptualisation of a phenomenon as a subjective experience can also influence the selection of the research method as well as the research target group. A tendency to study IL in specific professions has indeed contributed to the dominance of qualitative research in workplace IL studies. However, the quantitative approach has also been used to assess workplace IL, particularly in recent studies. In one of the first attempts to develop a scale for the measurement of workplace IL, Ahmad, Widén and Huvila (2020), investigated the impact of the IL capability of the senior management on the innovation performance of SME organisations in Finland. Using the same scale, Widén, Ahmad and Huvila (2021) explored the impact of employees' IL on the development of social capital. Recently, Middleton and Hall (2021) quantitatively measured IL in the workplace and discovered that it serves as a link between innovative work behaviour development and workplace learning.

In summary, even though the quantitative approach has gained some attention in workplace IL research, the qualitative approach is clearly dominating the literature, which potentially imposes challenges.

Methodological challenges of workplace information literacy assessment

The determination of the most appropriate method for assessing IL, as well as where to start, what to measure and how to analyse the instruments' reliability and validity, are all potential issues inherent in the IL research methodology choices. Although traditional classroom assessments based on multiple choice or fill-in-the-blank questions are commonly used to assess students' information competence, such assessments are unable to correctly evaluate an individual's ability at a higher level, such as their search abilities in real-world situations (Walsh, 2009, 19). Furthermore, there is a vast body of literature, notably in the US, that includes study findings from case studies and IL evaluations. In many such studies, the ACRL's IL competency standards were used (Emmett and Emde, 2007).

Some authors, such as Walsh (2009, 25), have noted the importance of balancing the need for an easy-to-administer test and one that accurately assesses the various transferable information abilities that IL entails. In other words, this implies that researchers must carefully evaluate which tool to use to assess IL and if such an instrument will be able to analyse various underlying components of literacy skills properly and efficiently. In this regard, Forster (2017) argues that while there is growing interest in assessing IL in different environments, we cannot be sure if the existing instruments, methodological choices and definitions would also work in another situation, such as the workplace. For example, as the younger workforce moves from school to work, they are confronted with new ways of using, comprehending and applying information in contexts other than the classroom. In the workplace, employees must adjust to a new attitude, new viewpoints and new ways of thinking in their working environments as to what information means and what values it entails. There is therefore a need for an analytical method that can overcome the shortcomings of the conventional methods, such as scale validation, reliability of measurement items, convergent and discriminant validity. In this regard, fuzzy-set Qualitative Comparative Analysis (fsQCA) is deemed to be an appropriate analytical approach to study IL in the workplace (Ragin, 1987). This method allows for combining both qualitative and quantitative approaches, making the best of both methods and complementing the results.

Fuzzy-set Qualitative Comparative Analysis (fsQCA): an alternative approach

Ragin (1987) introduced fsQCA and since then it has been widely used in a variety of fields to overcome the pitfalls of conventional regression analysis and suchlike (for example, Chen et al., 2022). Although, the fsQCA was originally developed to analyse a small number of cases in qualitative studies (Fiss, 2011), Woodside (2013) has demonstrated how it can be applied in quantitative studies with a large dataset and sample size.

Prior research on IL has frequently employed traditional statistical methods, yielding empirical and practical discoveries that are generally noteworthy and, in some circumstances, compelling (Pinto and Fernández-Pascual, 2014). However, the validity and reliability of the measurement items, as well as the causal links, are critical when conventional regression analysis is used. In addition, such approaches may fail to assess the intricate interdependencies, conjunctive paths and the causal asymmetrical relationships between variables (Çoklar, Yaman and Yurdakul, 2017). When adopting fsQCA analysis, these issues could be alleviated.

In terms of fsQCA, necessity analysis and sufficiency analysis are two critical factors for understanding data validity and causality, which are both regarded as limitations of the traditional regression-based approaches. In addition, traditional statistical analyses focus on the symmetric relationships between a set of antecedent variables. For example, if IL has a positive relationship to job performance, then an increase in IL should lead to high job performance and vice versa. Moreover, the R-square (the explained variation denoted as a percentage) is used to denote the model fit, but researchers cannot know how variables interact together to lead to a certain outcome, or, more importantly, how to account for the causal (asymmetrical) relationships between independent variables and the dependent variable (outcome) (Liu et al., 2015). In this regard, Woodside (2013) introduced the conjunctional causation concept in which the combinations of several causal variables must be accounted for in determining the outcome and not merely one variable. While both regression analysis (quantitative) and semi-structured interviews (qualitative) may help to account for symmetric relationship, fsQCA enables researchers to account for asymmetric relationships and gain in-depth analysis on how various causal variables contribute to the presence or absence of an outcome of interest (El Sawy et al., 2010; Fiss, 2007).

While regression-based analysis focuses on the influence of the individual variable on a particular outcome (the net effect), fsQCA focuses on the asymmetric relations between the outcome of interest and the antecedent (the conditions in terms of fsQCA) (Pappas and Woodside, 2021). In other words, how the combined conditions cause the outcome. Thus, there may be more than one combination of configuration that leads to a given outcome. Such flexibility helps researchers to understand the impact of IL in the workplace and gain an in-depth knowledge on how multiple configurations of conditions simultaneously lead to such an impact (El Sawy et al., 2010).

Furthermore, the fsQCA technique is distinct from traditional regression-based methods like structural equation modelling (SEM) and how the relationships between variables are handled. SEM only allows for the analysis of latent variables and the assessment of their linear associations using observable indicators, whereas fsQCA allows for asymmetric relationships and equifinality. The concept of equifinality refers to the existence of multiple distinct configurations of conditions leading to the outcome of interest, where, instead of one solution, there might be multiple pathways to a given outcome (Fiss, 2011). It should also be mentioned that fsQCA analysis depends on the researchers' knowledge of examined variables (conditions), the theory being used and the context in which the method is applied (Pappas and Woodside, 2021).

FsQCA procedures

The implementation of fsQCA requires certain procedures to be carefully followed. The first step is to transform the variables under investigation into fuzzy sets, which is known as calibration (Ragin, 2008). There are two methods for data calibration: direct and indirect (Ragin, 2008). Indirect calibration rescales the original measurement scales in line with qualitative assessments, whereas direct calibration determines three qualitative breakpoints of the fuzzy sets. It should be highlighted that the researchers' domain knowledge is critical to the calibrating procedure.

Direct calibration can take several forms when transforming variables, depending on the types of variables and scales used. For example, if one of the variables is gender, we can express it with crisp (0–1) sets. When a variable is converted into a set in this situation, it becomes crisp and can only take two values: 0 for male and 1 for female, or vice versa. If variables are measured by Likert-scales, we can calibrate the data using three values from the range of the variable. These three values further correspond to: (i) a full-membership; (ii) the most ambiguous membership; and (iii) a full non-membership. The most popular method involves using three values: 1, 0.5 and 0. To fit into these three values, the other values of the original scale (for example, 5-point scales or 7-point scales) are calibrated using a linear function. The next step after calibration and converting all the variables into a condition set is to assess all the possible variable combinations. This means that with k condition sets, there will be 2^k possible combinations to be assessed. For example, if we have five variables, in addition to our outcome variable, we will have 2^5 or 32 possible combinations to be assessed – this practice is called constructing a truth table.

The final step in fsQCA analysis is the sufficiency analysis, which produces the solutions. The output produces three types of solution sets: complex, parsimonious and intermediate solutions (Ragin, 2008). The solution (which also refers to causal conditions) generated by fsQCA analysis can be divided into core and peripheral conditions. Core conditions indicate the presence of a condition (variable) in both the parsimonious and intermediate solutions; peripheral conditions indicate the presence of a condition only in the intermediate solutions.

In summary, fsQCA provides several advantages compared to conventional regression analysis or semi-structured interview data. For example, with fsQCA analysis, the researchers gain knowledge on what variables are necessary or what variables are sufficient for the outcome to occur. In addition, fsQCA provides different combinations of causal conditions capable of producing the same outcome, whereas in regression analysis, researchers only obtain the R-square values and the net effects between variables.

Discussion

As digitalisation is changing the information landscape of organisations, workplace IL is seen as a critical resource for individual performance as well as organisational innovativeness. Workplace IL is an important part of employees' knowledge schema that needs to be constantly updated and developed in order to effectively deal with a rapidly changing organisational environment. We've reviewed the current literature on workplace IL research and identified methodological choices commonly used in such studies. The literature review findings show that the qualitative method (interview, case study) has been a dominant paradigm in workplace IL research. We also found that qualitative exploratory research on workplace IL has enhanced our understanding of information practices of employees in different work contexts. Although there has been some interest in applying quantitative approaches (survey-based research) to study workplace IL, such studies are quite limited in number (Ahmad, Widén and Huvila, 2020).

In addition, we found that both approaches have their pros and cons. For example, the results of the qualitative studies have contributed to enriching workplace IL theory and provided us with new insights into the information experiences of individuals in different contexts other than the traditional educational context. Moreover, this stream of research has also addressed the conceptualisation of IL, explaining its constituents and different facets. But due to the inherently context-specific nature of qualitative research, along with the tendency of previous workplace IL research to focus on specific professions, applicability of such insights to other workplaces is limited. Moreover, for practitioners, it is difficult to transform such insights into practical actions and policies.

Similarly, using a quantitative approach in research is beneficial in terms of generating measurement scales to assess the impact of workplace IL (for example, Ahmad, Widén and Huvila, 2020). But this approach also suffers from the same reductionism as it limits workplace IL to measurable information activities, which makes it difficult to capture the complexity of the IL phenomenon.

To address the methodological issues discussed in this chapter, we suggested using a relatively new methodological approach that has not been extensively applied in workplace IL research, namely: fuzzy-set Qualitative Comparative Analysis (fsQCA). This method combines and complements the advantages of both qualitative and quantitative methods as a way forward to advance workplace IL research in the future. As there is a history of both quantitative and qualitative research on IL, albeit in different domains, it is possible to draw insights from these previous streams of research to develop comprehensive investigations providing deeper insights into the role of IL in today's workplace. In addition, fsQCA can be considered as both an analytical approach and a data analysis technique that can resolve many of the issues associated with the traditional quantitative and qualitative research approaches and statistical data analysis methods. For example, assessing how a combination of different variables impacts the outcome and that there is always more than one solution for the outcome to occur. This method is versatile in terms of sample size and does not necessitate a huge dataset for analysis, but it does reveal more detailed insights to help better comprehend the phenomenon being studied. It also accounts for asymmetric relationships between the variables and the outcome of interest.

The findings of this chapter have practical implications for IL researchers, instructors, educators and others interested in learning more about the influence of IL in the workplace. They can apply fsQCA in their activities to gain a deeper understanding of how variables interact to produce the desired outcome. This method enables IL practitioners to gain knowledge on how individuals comprehend and perceive the importance of IL in the workplace and, if needed, design and create training to improve the IL level of employees. In addition, the fsQCA approach enables workplace IL researchers and practitioners to understand the statistical associations and the set relations of the conjunctions and conditions combined leading to the occurrence of the outcome.

Conclusion

This chapter contributes to workplace IL research by providing a brief overview of methodological alternatives and suggesting a relatively new methodological approach (fsQCA) to be used in this stream of research. This latter method has the potential to solve some of the methodological issues that have plagued traditional approaches, such as measurement validity and sample size issues. Future workplace IL research can utilise this new technique to get a more fine-grained understanding of the role of IL in the workplace. As IL is known as a multifaceted concept, it would be beneficial to understand which combinations of workplace IL capabilities and skills are helpful in different organisational contexts and situations. For example, in highly uncertain and unknown environments, employees' information access and evaluation capabilities might be much more important than other workplace IL capabilities such as information environmental awareness. Such understanding might be difficult to gain if conventional statistical methods, such as regression analysis or content analysis, are used to analyse the data. Instead, through the use of the fsQCA approach, researchers can obtain multiple configurations of conditions that together lead to the occurrence of the outcome. In other words, fsQCA enables workplace IL researchers to understand what combination of factors leads to employees' information access and evaluation capabilities.

Moreover, as fsQCA can be applied on both quantitative and qualitative data, it does not have any data type restriction and allows the application of similar analytical procedures and parameters on both types of data. Using fsQCA, future workplace IL research can utilise the complementary strengths of each data type and develop convergent mixed-method study designs, which help in the concurrent evaluation of quantitative and qualitative data and hence help in developing a multifaceted understanding of complex phenomena (Kahwati and Kane, 2018, 86).

Limitations and future work

While we sought to conduct a thorough literature review to identify the most generally used methodological technique in workplace IL research, our findings may not be as comprehensive as we had expected. However, we are convinced that the search results lead us to the conclusion that qualitative research is the most often employed method in workplace IL research, although quantitative studies are also gaining ground. Furthermore, while we find that fsQCA analysis can solve most of the methodological issues underpinning workplace IL research, we strongly encourage future studies to use this method in their research and experimentally test whether our judgements and results are valid. As fsQCA is very different from traditional quantitative and qualitative research approaches, the researcher's domain knowledge plays an important role. Nevertheless, a considerable advancement has been made on the standardisation of fsQCA. Future research on workplace IL can consult previous research, particularly in the business and management field where most of the work on fsQCA has been done (see Greckhamer et al., 2018; Pappas and Woodside, 2021), to gain a better understanding of its theoretical applications and methodological assumptions as well as good practices.

References

Ahmad, F., Widén, G. and Huvila, I. (2020) The Impact of Workplace Information Literacy on Organizational Innovation: An Empirical Study, *International Journal of Information Management*, **51**, 102041.

Association for College and Research Libraries (ACRL), American Library Association (2000) *Information Literacy Competency Standards for Higher Education*, ACRL, https://repository.arizona.edu/handle/10150/105645.

Baji, F., Bigdeli, Z., Parsa, A. and Haeusler, C. (2018) Developing Information Literacy Skills of the 6th Grade Students Using the Big 6 Model, *Malaysian Journal of Library & Information Science*, **23** (1), 1–15.

Bandura, A., Freeman, W. H. and Lightsey, R. (1999) *Self-Efficacy: The Exercise of Control*, W. H. Freeman/Times Books/Henry Holt & Co.

Brady, S. R. (2015) Utilizing and Adapting the Delphi Method for Use in Qualitative Research, *International Journal of Qualitative Methods*, **14** (5), https://doi.org/10.1177/1609406915621381.

Bruce, C. S. (1999) Workplace Experiences of Information Literacy, *International Journal of Information Management*, **19** (1), 33–47.

Bryman, A. (2006) Integrating Quantitative and Qualitative Research: How is it Done?, *Qualitative Research*, **6** (1), 97–113.

Buchanan, S. and Tuckerman, L. (2016) The Information Behaviours of Disadvantaged and Disengaged Adolescents, *Journal of Documentation*, **72** (3), 527–48.

Cameron, L., Wise, S. and Lottridge, S. (2007) The Development and Validation of the Information Literacy Test, *College and Research Libraries*, **68** (3), 229–36.

Chen, M., Zhou, C., Wang, Y. and Li, Y. (2022) The Role of School ICT Construction and Teacher Information Literacy in Reducing Teacher Burnout: Based on SEM and fsQCA, *Education and Information Technologies*. https://doi.org/10.1007/s10639-022-10989-7.

Cheuk Wai-yi, B. (1998) An Information Seeking and Using Process Model in the Workplace: A Constructivist Approach, *Asian Libraries*, **7** (12), 375–90.

Çoklar, A. N., Yaman, N. D. and Yurdakul, I. K. (2017) Information Literacy and Digital Nativity as Determinants of Online Information Search Strategies, *Computers in Human Behaviour*, **70**, 1–9.

Comstock, S. (2012) A Case Study of Legitimate Literacies: Teens' 'Small World' and the School Library, PhD thesis, University of Illinois, IL, www.ideals.illinois.edu/handle/2142/34419.

Correia, A. M. R. (2002) *Information Literacy for an Active and Effective Citizenship*, White Paper prepared for UNESCO, the US National Commission on Libraries and Information Science and the National Forum on Information Literacy, for use at the Information Literacy Meeting of Experts, Prague, The Czech Republic.

Crawford, J. and Irving, C. (2009) Information Literacy in the Workplace: A Qualitative Exploratory Study, *Journal of Librarianship and Information Science*, **41** (1), 29–38.

Davies-Hoffman, K., Alvarez, B., Costello, M. and Emerson, D. (2013) Keeping Pace with Information Literacy Instruction for the Real World: When Will MLS Programs Wake Up and Smell the LILACs?, *Communications in Information Literacy*, **7** (1), 9–23.

Demasson, A. E. (2014) Information Literacy and the Serious Leisure Participant: Variation in the Experience of Using Information to Learn, PhD thesis, Queensland University of Technology, http://eprints.qut.edu.au/78615/1/Andrew_Demasson_Thesis.pdf.

El Sawy, O. A., Malhotra, A., Park, Y. and Pavlou, P. A. (2010) Research Commentary – Seeking the Configurations of Digital Ecodynamics: It Takes Three to Tango, *Information Systems Research*, **21** (4), 835–48.

Emmett, A. and Emde, J. (2007) Assessing Information Literacy Skills Using the ACRL Standards as a Guide, *Reference Services Review*, **35** (2), 210–29.

Farivar, F. and Richardson, J. (2021) Workplace Digitalisation and Work-Nonwork Satisfaction: The Role of Spillover Social Media, *Behaviour & Information Technology*, **40** (8), 747–58.

Fiss, P. C. (2007) A Set-Theoretic Approach to Organizational Configurations, *Academy of Management Review*, **32** (4), 1180–98.

Fiss, P. C. (2011) Building Better Causal Theories: A Fuzzy Set Approach to Typologies in Organization Research, *Academy of Management Journal*, **54** (2), 393–420.

Forster, M. (2017) Information Literacy and the Workplace: New Concepts, New Perspectives? In Forster, M. (ed.), *Information Literacy in the Workplace*, 1–9, Facet Publishing.

Forster, M. (2019) 'Ethnographic' Thematic Phenomenography: A Methodological Adaptation for the Study of Information Literacy in an Ontologically Complex Workplace, *Journal of Documentation*, **75** (2), 349–65.

Gilbert, S. (2017) Information Literacy Skills in the Workplace: Examining Early Career Advertising Professionals, *Journal of Business & Finance Librarianship*, **22** (2), 111–34.

Golenko, D. and Siber, L. (2017) Information Literacy of Lawyers in Their Working Environment. In *European Conference on Information Literacy*, 78–86, Springer.

Greckhamer, T., Furnari, S., Fiss, P. C. and Aguilera, R. V. (2018) Studying Configurations with Qualitative Comparative Analysis: Best Practices in Strategy and Organization Research, *Strategic Organization*, **16** (4), 482–95.

Gumulak, S. and Webber, S. (2011) Playing Video Games: Learning and Information Literacy, Aslib Proceedings, **63** (2/3), 241–55, https://doi.org/10.1108/00012531111135682.

Houlson, V. (2007) Getting Results from One-Shot Instruction: A Workshop for First Year Students, *College and Undergraduate Libraries*, **14** (1), 89–108.

Iannuzzi, P. (2000) Information Literacy Competency Standards for Higher Education, *Community & Junior College Libraries*, **9** (4), 63–7.

Iversen, O. S., Smith, R. C. and Dindler, C. (2018) From Computational Thinking to Computational Empowerment: A 21st Century PD Agenda. In *Proceedings of the 15th Participatory Design Conference: Full Papers, Volume 1*, 1–11, Association for Computing Machinery (ACM).

Jackman, L. W. and Weiner, S. A. (2017) The Rescinding of the ACRL 2000 Information Literacy Competency Standards for Higher Education – Really?, *College & Undergraduate Libraries*, **24** (1), 117–19.

Jang, M., Aavakare, M., Nikou, S. and Kim, S. (2021) The Impact of Literacy on Intention to Use Digital Technology for Learning: A Comparative Study of Korea and Finland, *Telecommunications Policy*, **45** (7), 102154.

Johnston, B. and Webber, S. (2003) Information Literacy in Higher Education: A Review and Case Study, *Studies in Higher Education*, **28** (3), 335–52.

Kahwati, L. C. and Kane, H. L. (2018) *Qualitative Comparative Analysis in Mixed Methods Research and Evaluation*, SAGE Publishing.

Kurbanoglu, S. S., Akkoyunlu, B. and Umay, A. (2006) Developing the Information Literacy Self-Efficacy Scale, *Journal of Documentation*, **62** (6), 730–43.

Larkin, J. E. and Pines, H. A. (2005) Developing Information Literacy and Research Skills in Introductory Psychology: A Case Study, *The Journal of Academic Librarianship*, **31** (1), 40–5.

Lipu, S., Williamson, K. and Lloyd, A. (2007) *Exploring Methods in Information Literacy Research*, Centre for Information Studies, Charles Sturt University.

Liu, Y., Mezei, J., Kostakos, V. and Li, H. (2015) Applying Configurational Analysis to IS Behavioural Research: A Methodological Alternative for Modelling Combinatorial Complexities, *Information Systems Research*, **27** (1), 59–89.

Lloyd, A. (2005) Information Literacy: Different Contexts, Different Concepts, Different Truths?, *Journal of Librarianship and Information Science*, **37** (2), 82–8.

Lloyd, A. (2007) Learning to Put Out the Red Stuff: Becoming Information Literate Through Discursive Practice, *The Library Quarterly*, **77** (2), 181–98.

Lloyd, A. (2010) *Information Literacy Landscapes: Information Literacy in Education, Workplace and Everyday Contexts*, Chandos Publishing.

Lockhart, J. (2015) Measuring the Application of Information Literacy Skills After Completion of a Certificate in Information Literacy, *South African Journal of Libraries and Information Science*, **81** (2), 19–25.

Machin-Mastromatteo, J. D., Lau, J. and Virkus, S. (2013) Participatory Action Research and Information Literacy: Revising an Old New Hope for Research and Practice. In *European Conference on Information Literacy*, 48–53, Springer.

Markless, S. and Streatfield, D. R. (2007) Three Decades of Information Literacy: Redefining the Parameters. In Andretta, S. (ed.), *Change and Challenge: Information Literacy for the 21st Century*, 15–36, Auslib Press.

Middleton, L. and Hall, H. (2021) Workplace Information Literacy: A Bridge to the Development of Innovative Work Behaviour, *Journal of Documentation*, **77** (6), 1343–63.

Nikou, S. and Aavakare, M. (2021) An Assessment of the Interplay Between Literacy and Digital Technology in Higher Education, *Education and Information Technologies*, **26**, 1–23.

Nikou, S., De Reuver, M. and Mahboob Kanafi, M. (2022) Workplace Literacy Skills – How Information and Digital Literacy Affect Adoption of Digital Technology, *Journal of Documentation*, **78** (7), 371–91.

O'Connor, L. G., Radcliff, C. J. and Gedeon, J. A. (2002) Applying Systems Design and Item Response Theory to the Problem of Measuring Information Literacy Skills, *College & Research Libraries*, **63** (6), 528–43.

Oakleaf, M. and Kaske, N. (2009) Guiding Questions for Assessing Information Literacy in Higher Education, *Portal: Libraries and the Academy*, **9** (2), 273–86.

Pappas, I. O. and Woodside, A. G. (2021) Fuzzy-Set Qualitative Comparative Analysis (fsQCA): Guidelines for Research Practice in Information Systems and Marketing, *International Journal of Information Management*, **58**, 102310.

Partridge, H., Edwards, S. L. and Thorpe, C. (2010) Evidence-Based Practice: Information Professionals' Experience of Information Literacy in the Workplace. In Lloyd, A. and Talja, S. (eds), *Practising Information Literacy: Bringing Theories of Learning, Practice and Information Literacy Together*, 273–98, Centre for Information Studies, Charles Sturt University.

Pinto, M. (2010) Design of the IL-HUMASS Survey on Information Literacy in Higher Education: A Self-Assessment Approach, *Journal of Information Science*, **36** (1), 86–103.

Pinto, M. and Fernández-Pascual, R. (2014) Information Literacy Competencies Among Social Sciences Undergraduates: A Case Study Using Structural Equation Model. In *European Conference on Information Literacy*, 370–8, Springer.

Ragin, C. C. (1987) *The Comparative Method: Moving Beyond Qualitative and Quantitative Strategies*, University of California Press.

Ragin, C. C. (2008) *Redesigning Social Inquiry: Fuzzy Sets and Beyond*, 86–91, University of Chicago Press.

Suárez-Orozco, M. M. and Suárez-Orozco, C. (2009) *Globalization, Immigration, and Schooling*, 82–96, Routledge.

Urbach, N., Ahlemann, F., Böhmann, T., Drews, P., Brenner, W., Schaudel, F. and Schütte, R. (2019) The Impact of Digitalization on the IT Department, *Business & Information Systems Engineering*, **61** (1), 123–31.

Wakimoto, D. K. (2010) Information Literacy Instruction Assessment and Improvement Through Evidence-Based Practice: A Mixed Method Study, *Evidence Based Library and Information Practice*, **5** (1), 82–92.

Walsh, A. (2009) Information Literacy Assessment: Where Do We Start?, *Journal of Librarianship and Information Science*, **41** (1), 19–28.

Widén, G., Ahmad, F., Nikou, S., Ryan, B. and Cruickshank, P. (2021) Workplace Information Literacy: Measures and Methodological Challenges, *Journal of Information Literacy*, **15** (2), 26–44.

Widén, G., Ahmad, F. and Huvila, I. (2021) Connecting Information Literacy and Social Capital to Better Utilise Knowledge Resources in the Workplace, *Journal of Information Science*, https://doi.org/10.1177/01655515211060531.

Williamson, K. (2007) The Broad Methodological Contexts of Information Literacy Research. In Lipu, S., Williamson, K. and Lloyd, A. (eds), *Exploring Methods in Information Literacy Research*, 1–12, Centre for Information Studies, Charles Sturt University.

Wodak, R. and Krzyżanowski, M. (eds) (2008) *Qualitative Discourse Analysis in the Social Sciences*, Palgrave Macmillan.

Woodside, A. G. (2013) Moving Beyond Multiple Regression Analysis to Algorithms: Calling for Adoption of a Paradigm Shift from Symmetric to Asymmetric Thinking in Data Analysis and Crafting Theory, *Journal of Business Research*, **66** (4), 463–72.

4
Investigating Information Seeking and Information Sharing Using Digital Trace Data

José Teixeira

Introduction

We live in an 'information age' and an 'information economy' (see Sampler, 1998; Boisot, 1998). As argued before by Shapiro and Varian (1999), 'information rules' in the age of the internet. Information is available so quickly, ubiquitously and inexpensively that markets, organisations and individuals are now facing the problem of information overload (Shapiro and Varian, 1999). While 'information' is a very broad term, information theorists pointed out that information is better understood by conceptually dissecting it as an interaction between information seeking and information sharing (Robson and Robinson, 2015). Either by taking a perspective of information as a medium (for example, storage) or information as a process (for example, communication) the concepts of information seeking and information sharing come into play (Robson and Robinson, 2015).

Much of this information 'revolution' has been driven by advancements in technology. Particularly, the adoption of computers and the internet have shaped to a large extent how we seek and share information (Boisot, 1998; Shapiro and Varian, 1999). Information seeking and sharing moved away from paper and happens now online using computers in a transformation process known as digitalisation (Nikou, Brännback and Widén, n.d.; Meyer, Schaupp and Seibt, 2019; Olson and Pollard, 2004). With digitalisation also came a growing availability of digital data in a phenomenon known as 'big data'.

Evidencing the academic relevance of digitalisation and big data, many journals across disciplines issued special issues on the concepts (for example, *Journal of Communication* and *Social Science Computer Review* among others). Furthermore, some renowned academic publishers have also launched new journals devoted to the topic, such as *Big Data & Society* (SAGE), *Big Data Research* (Elsevier) and *Journal of Big Data* (Springer). Digitalisation is now mentioned in the 'official aims and scope information' of journals across many disciplines, including sociology, marketing, organisation studies, innovation studies, information science and software engineering. This all points to the need for multidisciplinary research efforts to fix problems that emerge with the digitalisation of information.

Literature review
Digital trace data
Before defining the concept of 'digital trace data', it is good to revisit the three characteristics of all trace data as proposed by Howison, Wiggins and Crowston (2011). Those are not just characteristics of digital trace data, but instead of all trace data:

- It is found data (rather than produced for research).
- It is event-based data (rather than summary data).
- It is longitudinal data (as events occur over a period of time).

Therefore, trace data contrasts with data traditionally collected through surveys and interviews in social sciences. As an illustrative example, we can think about how banks and accounting firms used to collect trace data of the financial transactions of their customers (for example, deposits, withdrawals, tax payments) way before computers entered the industry.

In line with Howison, Wiggins and Crowston (2011, 769) we conceptualise *trace* as 'a mark left as a sign of passage; it is recorded evidence that something has occurred in the past'. We take then the definition of 'digital trace data' as records of activity (trace data) undertaken through an online computer-based information system (thus, digital). In digital trace data, the information system acts as a data collection tool and data is then stored in a digital format that allows future retrieval using computer-based technologies. As an illustrative example, we can think again about how banks and accounting firms keep track of the financial transactions of their customers in the digital era. Such data is very important for those organisations as they need to be knowledgeable about their customers' behaviour. While digital trace data is mostly collected for operational purposes, it can also be used for research purposes – after all, digital trace data captures human behaviour over time in a very tangible way.

Even if a lot of digital trace data exists, it can be challenging to use it for research purposes as they are a by-product of operational activities rather than produced by a designed research instrument. For example, Wikipedia was not designed to test theories about knowledge production, nor are corporate e-mail systems designed to collect research data. As pointed out before, trace data, as found data, must be 'adapted' for research purposes (Howison, Wiggins and Crowston, 2011; Ekström, 2021; Jungherr and

Theocharis, 2017, among others). This chapter offers guidance on how to adapt digital trace data to research on information seeking and information sharing. As pointed out by Ekström (2021), trace data extends current methods for investigating information behaviour as it enables researchers to focus on practices as recorded through interactions with digital computer-based information systems.

Due to digitalisation and the widespread usage of digital devices, massive volumes of digital trail data are generated. Individuals and organisations utilise these in their own pursuits, but researchers studying human behaviour should also be interested in them. Because most of this data is owned by private individuals or organisations, digital trace data study frequently necessitates some type of public-private partnership involving licensing or other contractual arrangements. Private businesses and university researchers each have their own set of goals, some of which are aligned, while others may be at odds. As gathering digital trace data from private organisations can be challenging (Breuer, Bishop and Kinder-Kurlanda, 2020), many researchers turned to explore digital trace data in the context of large-scale open source software projects, the Wikipedia, epidemic data, blogs and social media platforms (for example, Howison, Wiggins and Crowston, 2011; Teixeira, Robles and González-Barahona, 2015; Adar and Adamic, 2005; Bakshy, Messing and Adamic, 2015) that provide vast amounts of naturally occurring digital trace data under public domain (that is, with no need to negotiate or license it).

Even if a lot of digital trace data is available, such data is not readily made to test or build theory – researchers need to map it to theory. For anyone interested in information and knowledge management in organisations, we offer here insights to theoretically and methodologically couple information seeking and information sharing with digital trace data. As previously noted by Choi (2020), traditional social science research implements sampling and conjectures regarding a population by drawing statistical inferences from samples, whereas digital trace data allows researchers to gather information about the population of a certain digital platform rather than sampling a few users. There are issues on how researchers set the boundary regarding the digital trace data collection and on their generalisation aims. What would be more valuable? A study of a social mechanism using the same survey instrument across hundreds of individuals within a few organisations or a study of the same social mechanism across millions of users of large-scale social networks (for example, Facebook and LinkedIn among others)?

Information seeking and information sharing

Information has always been a key concept theorised across many disciplines (see Belkin, 1978; Brillouin, 2013). On the more technical side, information was theorised in the fields of telecommunications, computing, physics and biology among others (Brillouin, 2013; Gappmair, 1999). In social sciences, the information concept has also been extensively theorised for the study of information behaviour, information literacy, information systems and knowledge management in organisations (Alavi and Leidner, 1999; Robson and Robinson, 2015; Glazer, 1991).

As information became increasingly available and digitised, many disciplines also integrated the concept of information into their core theories. The discipline of information science – historically concerned with the analysis, collection, classification, manipulation, storage, retrieval, movement, dissemination and protection of information – developed several theoretical models conceptualising information and communication. Those that captured a lot of attention include: Wilson's (2000) theory of information behaviour, which centres around the concept of information need; McKenzie (2003) and Lloyd (2006) on context-specific practice-based theories based on the observation of professionals dealing with information (for example, librarians, lawyers and firefighters); and models such as Robson and Robinson (2015) that centre around the concept of communication and the interaction between information seeking and information sharing. Among those, we find the work of Robson and Robinson (2015), based upon the observation of medical professionals within a hospital with supporting information systems, to be well suited to study information and communication in a digital world.

Besides being more elaborated, the model from Robson and Robinson (2015) can be broken down into simpler components (see Figure 4.1). The model depicts a two-way flow of information between provider and user. The model emphasises the fact that information behaviour is highly

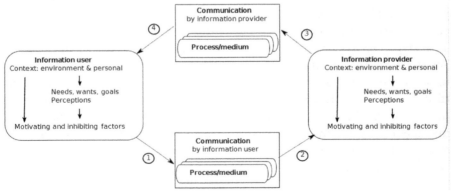

Figure 4.1 *Two-way communication as initially presented by Robson and Robinson (2015)*

interactive, with users communicating with other users (in their role as providers) and sharing information. An important insight from the model is that the 'information user' depicted in many information science models does not play a fixed role but a dual one. One can act both as a seeker of information and a provider of information. As in a two-way conversation, one person can ask (that is, the 'user' role in information seeking), as well as answer (that is, the 'provider' role in information sharing). This alternation between the user and provider roles is of course commonplace in information behaviour – people are both consumers and producers of information. In our view, the Robson and Robinson (2015) model has merit by conciliating scholars that tend to view information as a medium (for example, a database) with the ones that tend to view information more as a process (for example, knowledge transfer).

An operationalisation for the study of information behaviour

After introducing the concept of digital trace data and highlighting its importance for researching information behaviour in a world undergoing digitalisation, we illustrate how to use digital trace data to study both 'information as a process' as well as 'information as a medium'. We take the Robson and Robinson (2015) two-way communication model as the underlining conceptual framework. In addition, we support our arguments with examples of digital trace data created by open source software developers, as well as examples from Wikipedia and corporate knowledge management systems (for example, Confluence, Microsoft Teams, Salesforce). We hopefully generate a research agenda for researching information seeking and information sharing using the largely untapped potential of using digital trace data.

As previously discussed (Robson and Robinson, 2015), we should think about information behaviour as something very interactive where users can take the dual role of information users and information providers. In addition, there are also two ways of thinking about information: 'information as a process' and 'information as a medium'. While the latter invites us to theorise information around the concepts of media, channel, storage and encoding, 'information as a process' invites us to theorise information around the concepts of communication, information processing, information cycles and information flows. Therefore, it makes sense to consider four different facets for operationalising the study of information behaviour from digital trace data (see Figure 4.2 on the next page). First, we can capture the behaviour of information providers that share information as a process (for example, communication via e-mail); second, we can also capture the behaviour of the information providers that share information as a medium (for example, save a document in a PDF format). Furthermore, the same applies to information seekers, both when seeking the information as a process (for example, asking in an online forum) and information as a medium (for example, downloading an official document or buying an e-book). By conveying those four facets of information behaviour, we will be more encompassing than if we focused on only one of those aspects. However, time and resource constraints might force researchers to focus solely on one of the four aspects.

Our proposed operationalisation invites researchers to consider four different aspects (see Figure 4.2) when studying information behaviour using digital trace data. The four aspects are outlined by juxtaposing 'information seeking' versus 'information sharing' and juxtaposing 'information as medium' versus 'information as a process'. Starting with the first aspect of **information sharing as a process**, plenty of data is available from computational information systems. For example, many knowledge management systems (for example, Confluence, Microsoft Teams and Salesforce) allow researchers to investigate when and how users access documents over time. With recent advancements, the geolocation of users is also often available. Digital trace data can be used to associate information sharing behaviour with geographical locations and geographical proximity. Other avenues of research can explore

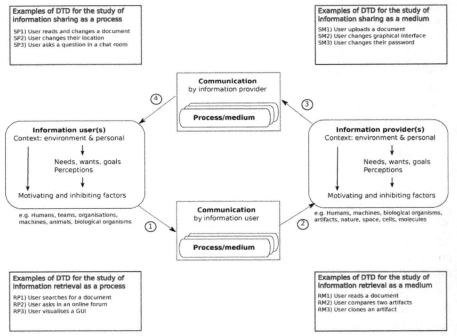

Figure 4.2 *Examples for the operationalisation of the study of information cycles using digital trace data*

how users question and answer each other on online platforms within or outside their organisations. The study of question and answer platforms, such as Quora and StackExchange, has been capturing scholarly attention (see Patil and Lee, 2016; Fu, Yu and Benson, 2020) from a social network perspective; however, to the best of our knowledge, the potential of those platforms for the study of the information sharing processual mechanisms remains untapped.

A thorough investigation of information behaviour will not only view **information sharing as a process** but should also view **information sharing as a medium**. The digital revolution brought us massive amounts of naturally occurring digital trace data. Modern knowledge management systems deployed in organisations store many documents and other artefacts that can be used for the study of information behaviour. With many text, document, audio, video and software formats available, researchers interested in studying information behaviour using such massive data need to be creative with the problem of the variety of formats that they could need to deal with. Researchers interested in information sharing by looking at the medium available at organisations will also most likely face issues of volume (large amounts of data), velocity (the speed with which data emerges), veracity (the trustworthiness of the data), ethics, privacy and security (see Ekbia et al., 2015; Jungherr and Theocharis, 2017).

As depicted by Robson and Robinson (2015), communication goes in two ways (see Figure 4.1). While on the one hand, we care about information sharing, we also care about information retrieval. Therefore, a thorough investigation of information behaviour in the digital age must also consider **information retrieval as a process** and **information retrieval as a medium**. When thinking about information retrieval as a process (for example, searching on Google, querying a database or exploring a visual map), many cognitive and computational micro-processes are enacted. Much remains unknown about how users search, ask and explore information (Qiu, Gadiraju and Bozzon, 2020) and there is a lack of knowledge on how the different information retrieval mechanisms differ in the physical and digital worlds (Qiu, Gadiraju and Bozzon, 2020; Tyner, 2014; Huvila, 2012).

For the study of information retrieval from the perspective of the medium, research should explore the nature of digital artefacts (see Kallinikos, Aaltonen and Marton, 2013), its affordances (Leonardi, Bailey and Pierce, 2019) and the implications for information retrieval. As pointed out by Orlikowski (2010), the actual digital artefacts should take part in the theorising of social theory. In other words, we need more research linking the characteristics and affordances of digital artefacts while theorising about information retrieval. Research along these lines would combine well with the theories on sociomateriality (see Leonardi, Bailey and Pierce, 2019; Orlikowski, 2010) and digital information infrastructuring (see Bygstad, 2010) that gained momentum in the last decade in the social sciences.

While much of the related research addresses communication and knowledge management, our proposed operationalisation of the Robson and Robinson (2015) model is organised around the concept of information. To our view, even if the concepts of data, knowledge and communication approximate to the concept of information, they are not the same thing. Nevertheless, research using similar concepts with approximate meanings remains useful for the study of information behaviour from digital trace data. Research on information seeking and information sharing in the digital era should take into consideration that existing theory might be organised around the concepts of data, knowledge and communication.

Discussion

This chapter raises our attention to the emergence of digital trace data and its untapped potential for advancing social sciences. Rather than using traditional methods established in information science (sampling, interviewing, questionnaires), we invite information scientists to shift the study from perceived behaviour to actual behaviour by using digital traces. As the world adopts digital technologies, we can find more and more digital trace data capturing the behaviours of information sharing and information seeking. Computer systems store more and more data that can be used for research purposes. Digitalisation opens up opportunities for information scientists to analyse data that is naturally produced by information providers and information users. Rather than provoking research data on information sharing and information seeking, information scientists now have plenty of records that capture information behaviour. It is therefore important for information scientists to be able to collect, analyse and make sense of large datasets, which can take the form of databases, repositories and computer-generated logs among other ways of storing digital traces. Social scientists need to grasp digital trace data datasets that are longitudinal in nature and contrast from the traditional social science datasets (for example, interviews and questionnaires). Here, cross-disciplinary co-operation with scholars with experience in the analysis of large datasets (for example, computer science, network science sociophysics) should be encouraged.

Besides shifting from the study of perceived behaviour to the study of actual behaviour by using digital trace, the digitalisation of work practices and the growing amount of digital trace data also enables new theoretical enquiries by re-configuring the granular level of interactivity, observing the longitudinal change of interactions and discovering the neglected presence of outliers and the invisibles (for example, observations that are not noticed by the researchers but are recorded in trace data). Furthermore, we also suggest a possible direction for the theoretical and methodological coupling of information sharing and information seeking with digital trace data by operationalising the Robson and Robinson (2015) two-way communication model in the study of information behaviour. Also, importantly, we derived five affordances with implications for research on information seeking and information sharing (see Table 4.1).

First, we can note the co-existence of multiple layers and multiple levels of analysis that will methodologically challenge the research enquiry. For example, when studying information behaviour in open source software ecosystems (that is, networks of individuals and organisations jointly producing software) we can conceptualise multiple layers of collaboration among individuals and firms (for example, sales, marketing, product development and product testing). Different information systems providing support to different operations can also be modelled as different layers of information. Prior research on open source software ecosystems also points out that research with digital trace data is often multi-level. Information can be aggregated at the individual, team, organisation and inter-organisational level (see Teixeira, Robles and González-Barahona, 2015). To sum up, researching information seeking and information sharing from digital trace data often requires researchers to leverage methodological advances in multi-level and multi-layer research. Observations cannot be assumed to be independent but are influenced by the layer and level in which they are recorded.

Table 4.1 *Affordances by coupling of information sharing and information seeking with digital trace data*

Affordance	Description
Multiple layers of analysis	Studies that look at information behaviour captured by different digital systems
Multiple levels of analysis	Studies that look at the individual, group or organisational levels in unison
Longitudinal orientation	As most digital trace data is time stamped
Sampling and outliers	Less of a need for sampling decision or the disregard of outliers
Sociomaterial integration	Information behaviour can be theorised with the materiality of systems and artefacts

As most digital trace data is time-stamped, it naturally allows information scientists to focus on the evolution of information behaviour over time. While questionnaires and interviews are recorded in a particular timeframe, research using digital trace data is recorded continuously. In many cases, such data is naturally occurring as a necessary output of production activities. For example, in open source software ecosystems, every time a user updates software, every time a developer improves software, every time a developer tests and reviews the work done by a peer, every time a developer asks for guidance online and every time a developer fixes a bug or vulnerability, digital trace data will be captured in some kind of website, database, repository or other digital infrastructure. Note, for example, that many open source software projects and Wikipedia can be studied from their beginning as digital trace data is recorded and stored in the public domain. Within the corporate domain, many firms also have capabilities to analyse the past information behaviour of their employees using digital traces.

In addition, as digital trace data is often recorded continuously and stored in digital means using computers, there is less of a need for the sampling decisions or the disregard of outliers often required in statistical research. Traditionally, sampling is done because it is hard to collect data on the overall population and the overall timeframe. For example, when studying the popular Linux open source software project or Wikipedia it can be hard to argue for sampling when data for the overall timeframe of the project might be available. As the digital information behaviour of all users across all the system existence time can be captured, information scientists can explore users and behaviours that are deviant, invisible or unknown. To sum up, sampling decisions and identification outliers are different when working with digital trace data as compared with the more traditional social science methods based upon interviews and questionnaires.

Finally, it is important to note that digital trace data is often orchestrated by computer-based information systems. Similar operations can be supported by many different information systems (for example, hospital health records) and the actual material characteristics of each different information system can influence their behaviour. As previously mentioned, research should take into account the characteristics and affordances of digital artefacts while theorising about information seeking and information sharing. Using the sociomateriality jargon (see Leonardi, Bailey and Pierce, 2019; Orlikowski, 2010), information sharing and information seeking with digital trace data should take into consideration the material part of the information systems that support their users. After all, the same accounting practice might be executed very differently depending on what accounting software is used. In the case of open source software development, much of the software developers' behaviour is heavily influenced by the different sets of software tools and infrastructures that were chosen to support the project.

From a practical perspective, and as information literacy plays an important role in information sharing and information seeking, the growing amount of digital trace data brings forward an avenue of possibilities not only for researchers but also for individual practitioners (for example, employees in an organisation, firefighters and nurses among others). As organisations increasingly trace the information behaviour of their employees over time, and as many digital records capture information digitally shared and retrieved across the organisation, individuals should learn how to use records from past operations to improve current ones. As digitalisation has allowed organisations to keep more and more records, there is a need for skills and competencies to master those records to bring value to either the individual or the organisation. In other words, making sense of organisational digital trace data (that is often very context-specific) adds a dimension to workplace information literacy that is very dependent on context (for example, organisational design, business processes, ICT systems in use). Independently of the workplace context, an information literate professional should be able to make sense of digital trace data records from the past to bring value to the present.

Conclusion

This chapter discusses the emergence of digital trace data and its importance for research. In addition, the chapter suggests directions for the theoretical and methodological coupling of research on information seeking and information sharing with digital trace data. By using the Robson and Robinson (2015) two-way communication model as the underlining conceptual framework, we illustrated how to use digital trace data both by taking the perspective of 'information as a process' as well as 'information as a medium'. We proposed an operationalisation that invites researchers to consider four different aspects of studying information behaviour that were derived by juxtaposing both 'information-seeking' versus 'information-sharing' and 'information as medium' versus 'information as a process' (see Figure 4.2). Furthermore, we enumerated and discussed with examples five different affordances (see Table 4.1) of the coupling of information sharing and information seeking with digital trace data.

Our main contribution illustrates the power of digital trace data for the study of information sharing and information seeking. We outlined a possible theoretical background, five affordances of research investigating information behaviour with digital trace data (multi-level, multi-layer, longitudinal, sampling/outliers and sociomateriality) and the related challenges, which were discussed with examples from the open source software community and general corporate information systems.

While we highlighted the power of digital trace data, we also pinpointed many of the methodological challenges of research exploiting it (for example, large longitudinal datasets, multi-layer and multi-level orientation). Besides expertise in computational tools, storage and processing power capable of handling large datasets of digital trace data, social scientists interested in leveraging digital trace data should benefit from collaboration with other disciplines with more experience in dealing with large longitudinal datasets (for example, computer science and information systems) and with emergent fields (such as data science, network science, sociophysics and computational social science).

References

Adar, E. and Adamic, L. A. (2005) Tracking Information Epidemics in Blogspace. In *The 2005 IEEE/WIC/ACM International Conference on Web Intelligence (WI'05)*, 207–14, IEEE.

Alavi, M. and Leidner, D. E. (1999) Knowledge Management Systems: Issues, Challenges, and Benefits, *Communications of the Association for Information Systems*, **1** (7), 1–28.

Bakshy, E., Messing, S. and Adamic, L. A. (2015) Exposure to Ideologically Diverse News and Opinion on Facebook, *Science*, **348** (6239), 1130–2.

Belkin, N. J. (1978) Information Concepts for Information Science, *Journal of Documentation*, **34** (1), 55–85.

Boisot, M. H. (1998) *Knowledge Assets: Securing Competitive Advantage in the Information Economy*, Oxford University Press.

Breuer, J., Bishop, L. and Kinder-Kurlanda, K. (2020) The Practical and Ethical Challenges in Acquiring and Sharing Digital Trace Data: Negotiating Public-Private Partnerships, *New Media & Society*, **22** (11), 2058–80.

Brillouin, L. (2013) *Science and Information Theory*, 2nd edn, Dover Publications.

Bygstad, B. (2010) Generative Mechanisms for Innovation in Information Infrastructures, *Information and Organization*, **20** (3–4), 156–68.

Choi, S. (2020) When Digital Trace Data Meet Traditional Communication Theory: Theoretical/Methodological Directions, *Social Science Computer Review*, **38** (1), 91–107.

Ekbia, H. et al. (2015) Big Data, Bigger Dilemmas: A Critical Review, *Journal of the Association for Information Science and Technology*, **66** (8), 1523–45.

Ekström, B. (2021) Trace Data Visualisation Enquiry: A Methodological Coupling for Studying Information Practices in Relation to Information Systems, *Journal of Documentation*, **78** (7), 141–59.

Fu, X., Yu, S. and Benson, A. R. (2020) Modelling and Analysis of Tagging Networks in Stack Exchange Communities, *Journal of Complex Networks*, **8** (5), cnz045.

Gappmair, W. (1999) Claude E. Shannon: The 50th Anniversary of Information Theory, *IEEE Communications Magazine*, **37** (4), 102–5.

Glazer, R. (1991) Marketing in an Information-Intensive Environment: Strategic Implications of Knowledge as an Asset, *Journal of Marketing*, **55** (4), 1–19.

Howison, J., Wiggins, A. and Crowston, K. (2011) Validity Issues in the Use of Social Network Analysis with Digital Trace Data, *Journal of the Association for Information Systems*, **12** (12), 2.

Huvila, I. (2012) *Information Services and Digital Literacy: In Search of the Boundaries of Knowing*, Elsevier Science.

Jungherr, A. and Theocharis, Y. (2017) The Empiricist's Challenge: Asking Meaningful Questions in Political Science in the Age of Big Data, *Journal of Information Technology & Politics*, **14** (2), 97–109.

Kallinikos, J., Aaltonen, A. and Marton, A. (2013) The Ambivalent Ontology of Digital Artifacts, *MIS Quarterly*, **37** (2), 357–70.

Leonardi, P. M., Bailey, D. E. and Pierce, C. S. (2019) The Coevolution of Objects and Boundaries Over Time: Materiality, Affordances, and Boundary Salience, *Information Systems Research*, **30** (2), 665–86.

Lloyd, A. (2006) Information Literacy Landscapes: An Emerging Picture, *Journal of Documentation*, **62** (5), 570–83.

McKenzie, P. J. (2003) A Model of Information Practices in Accounts of Everyday-Life Information Seeking, *Journal of Documentation*, **59** (1), 19–40.

Meyer, U., Schaupp, S. and Seibt, D. (2019) *Digitalization in Industry: Between Domination and Emancipation*, Springer International Publishing.

Nikou, S., Brännback, M. and Widén, G. (2019) The Impact of Digitalization on Literacy: Digital Immigrants vs Digital Natives. In *Proceedings of the 27th European Conference on Information Systems (ECIS)*, Stockholm & Uppsala, Sweden, 8–14 June, https://aisel.aisnet.org/ecis2019_rp/39.

Olson, S. R. and Pollard, T. (2004) The Muse Pixeliope: Digitalization and Media Literacy Education, *American Behavioral Scientist*, **48** (2), 248–55.

Orlikowski, W. J. (2010) The Sociomateriality of Organisational Life: Considering Technology in Management Research, *Cambridge Journal of Economics*, **34** (1), 125–41.

Patil, S. and Lee, K. (2016) Detecting Experts on Quora: By Their Activity, Quality of Answers, Linguistic Characteristics and Temporal Behaviors, *Social Network Analysis and Mining*, **6** (1), 1–11.

Qiu, S., Gadiraju., U. and Bozzon, A. (2020) Towards Memorable Information Retrieval. In *Proceedings of the 2020 ACM SIGIR on International Conference on Theory of Information Retrieval*, ICTIR '20, 69–76, Association for Computing Machinery.

Robson, A. and Robinson, L. (2015) The Information Seeking and Communication Model: A Study of its Practical Application in Healthcare, *Journal of Documentation*, **71** (5), 1043–69.

Sampler, J. L. (1998) Redefining Industry Structure for the Information Age, *Strategic Management Journal*, **19** (4), 343–55.

Shapiro, C. and Varian, H. R. (1999) *Information Rules: A Strategic Guide to the Network Economy*, Harvard Business School Press.

Teixeira, J., Robles, G. and González-Barahona, J. M. (2015) Lessons Learned from Applying Social Network Analysis on an Industrial Free/Libre/Open Source Software Ecosystem, *Journal of Internet Services and Applications*, **6** (1), 14.

Tyner, K. (2014) *Literacy in a Digital World: Teaching and Learning in the Age of Information*, Taylor & Francis.

Wilson, T. D. (2000) Human Information Behavior, *Informing Science*, **3** (2), 49–56.

5
Making Do With Limited Transparency of Sensitive Information in Secretive Organisations: Collective Information Literacy Through Hinting

Inti José Lammi and Anette Hallin

Introduction

A key feature of digitalisation is making information available through digital technologies (McAfee and Brynjolfsson, 2014). Through the exponential increase in the capacity of digital infrastructures, a fact of contemporary digitalisation is the increased amount of digital information available and the new platforms available to work together digitally (Yoo et al., 2012). With these aspects comes the increased challenge of understanding, using and managing information – the challenge of information literacy (Bawden, 2001).

The concept of information literacy entails all sorts of skills and abilities related to the managing of information, such as identifying, accessing or constructing it; evaluating and managing it; and analysing and synthesising it (Martin and Grudziecki, 2006). These skills and abilities have been argued to be collectively anchored (Martin and Steinkuehler, 2010) and are fundamental for modern workplaces (Ahmad, Widén and Isto, 2020), more so due to digitalisation. Indeed, organisations today critically depend on their ability to use and manage information in an era of information overload.

However, not all organisations are necessarily overwhelmed with information. Some information may, for example, deliberately be kept amongst those at the executive level of the organisation or within specific groups or departments through deliberate information management processes (Whyte and Levitt, 2010). Often, organisations also work hard on managing which information is made available to people outside of the organisation (Costas and Grey, 2014). In some organisations, this deliberate limiting of information is a way to prevent third parties accessing critical information, since information that falls 'into the wrong hands' may disrupt organisational activities in different ways (Cram, Proudfoot and D'Arcy, 2017). In these situations, information is considered 'sensitive'. Studies of sensitive information have in the past engaged with the problems of how sensitive information is still drawn upon, despite being subjected to a sharing-protecting tension, particularly in contexts of inter-organisational co-operation where distrust and disparate motives reign among involved parties (Bouty, 2000; Das and Teng, 2000; Jarvenpaa and Majchrzak, 2008). These studies indicate the need to not only use and manage information, but also point to the importance of organisational members 'sensing' how to navigate information without risking detrimental 'oversharing' across organisational boundaries (Jarvenpaa and Majchrzak, 2016).

In this chapter, we build on the concept of information literacy when exploring sensitive information within workplaces. Drawing on an empirical study of project work in a high-security organisation, we find that when information is sensitive and not readily available to everyone, information literacy is only made possible because of how organisational members work collectively to make do with the signs and cues they are able and allowed to disclose to each other. In these cases, only the group together can achieve information literacy whereby information may be used, managed and drawn upon to overcome the challenges of *fragmented knowing*. Information literacy is in such workplaces anchored in interconnected social practices (Lloyd, 2010), for example, security practices, through which the ability and competence is highly contextualised and collective (Cetindamar Kozanoglu and Abedin, 2021). We present one particular activity that most notably makes information literacy possible in these settings: *hinting*.

Understanding how information literacy is possible in settings where the availability of information is limited has important implications for a richer understanding of the organisational challenges of managing information. It also allows for the application of the concept of information literacy to a range of organisational settings often excluded in the hyperbolic discussions of digitalisation that emphasise the abundance and availability of information (see Christensen and Cornelissen, 2015) and which assume open co-operative processes (Yoo et al., 2012).

The structure of the chapter is as follows. First, we give an account of the research setting to introduce its particularities. Then, we give a brief account of the research design and our chosen analytical approach. Following this, we account for the main findings concerning the challenges of information literacy in high-security settings, highlighting fragmented knowing, hinting and the role of trust. Finally, we discuss our contribution to studies of information literacy.

Research setting: the high-security organisation

The empirical study is a case study of a high-security organisation in the nuclear energy sector. The organisation is divided into different legally and geographically separated sub-entities that operate on their own, legally as well as in daily practice. Due to safety and security regulations, each entity organises its affairs relatively autonomously from another, which means that they have their own security procedures, their own IT systems and their own security clearances.

However, most major initiatives pursued in the organisation take place across sub-entities, often in the form of joint projects that range from technological development and implementation to the construction of new work sites or storage for nuclear waste. The importance of keeping each sub-entity separate and ensuring that projects are managed as securely as possible means that project members rarely have the same access to the information that is relevant to the project. This also means that project managers are tasked with learning how to navigate the legal boundaries of each sub-entity of the organisation. Often, the project managers carry multiple security passes, multiple computers with access to distinctly different and separate IT environments and so on. One project manager illustrated this in the following way:

> When I travel between sites for my projects, I often carry 3 different computers in 3 different bags. I can never leave any of these out-of-sight when I travel between sites. You can imagine the hassle when I go into a shop and have to carry all my bags!

Data collection

The study was performed as part of a larger research programme, *The Digitized Management – What Can We Learn from England and Sweden?*, financed by FORTE, the Swedish Research Council for Health, Working Life and Welfare (grant no: 2016-07210). It was initiated with the explorative aim of understanding the use of digital technologies in project organising in a high-security context.

Given the high-security nature of the organisation, the first author of this paper had to undergo (just like all potential organisational members) a two-step security clearance, involving a health check-up and a security interview. After having been given clearance to access the organisation, he performed interviews with project managers and workers from four different sub-entities (two support offices and two nuclear reactor sites). A total of 30 interviews, each of 1–1½ hours, were performed between 2019 and 2021. In addition, the researcher was given access to participate in project meetings from 2020 to 2021. A total of 50 hours of structured observations were done. Notes were taken during meetings, which were held in person as well as virtually. Due to how research access was negotiated, the authors of this chapter also participated in workshops with upper management and project managers from the organisation to discuss the findings of the research. This gave an opportunity to assess the validity of the findings.

Analysis

For the purpose of this chapter, the empirical material was re-read with a focus on how information was managed in and across projects. In particular, we paid attention to the way the team members handled the fact that they did not have access to all information that was relevant to the projects in which they were involved.

Based on this reading, we will first describe the work of the team members when pursuing joint projects in a context where information is not accessible to everyone in the team as *fragmented knowing*. Then, we will describe the activity of *hinting*, which was the way the team members shared information in a way that makes the management of fragmented knowing possible. Third, we will discuss *the importance of organisational trust* as a way of making do with the scarce information provided through hinting.

Fragmented knowing

As described above, the team members in each project in the organisation have different security clearance and hence access to information. This means that contrary to projects in most other settings where team members share all information that is relevant to the project with each other, for example, through project management information systems (for example, Caniëls and Bakens, 2012; Raymond and Bergeron, 2008) and Web 2.0 technologies (for example, Jackson, 2010; Kanagarajoo, Fulford and Standing, 2019), the team members here only share information on a need-to-know basis. This does not mean that the organisation lacks digital systems for storing and sharing information – these systems do indeed exist – but due to differences in security clearance, not all team members can access the same information. Not even project managers have free access to all information related to a project they are managing. Team members are also fully aware of this and there is a strong culture of not sharing information with colleagues that are not entitled to it.

As a consequence of this, projects have to be achieved through work that is marked by what we describe as *fragmented knowing*. By this, we refer to the practices that the team members need to engage in, despite having little information. Fragmented knowing is thus a way of describing the team members' (fragmented)-knowledge-in-work (Rennstam and Ashcraft, 2013; Thompson, Warhurst and Callaghan, 2001).

In a project that is, for example, aimed at constructing a building, all team members had general information about the overall design of the building but they didn't have the detailed information about the technical specificities of the door (for example, measures, weight, material, etc.) nor about the exact position of the door in the building. While specific teams could share specific information among themselves, this specific information pertaining to the construction was not available to all. Construction workers and in-house programmers thus lacked full knowledge about what was being built.

This fragmented knowing was a continuous challenge for project managers, not least when working with external sub-contractors. While it might be relatively easy to know how to build a door, to ensure that the door works in the specific milieu it is intended for requires more than simply knowledge about how a door is constructed.

Hinting

An important activity through which fragmented knowing was made manageable was *hinting*. By hinting, we refer to the ways by which the team members gave each other limited signs and cues to avoid the unnecessary sharing of sensitive information. Hinting can be compared to other more transparent activities that enable information literacy (see Martin and Steinkuehler, 2010), but in this setting, hinting emerged as a means of navigating the tension of sharing and protecting information (Jarvenpaa and Majchrzak, 2016). This activity was demonstrated through social practices (Lloyd, 2010), such as virtual project meetings.

One example of this was observed during a project meeting where the team members discussed the construction of a pipe in a building. During the meeting, the team members responsible for the construction of the pipe realised they needed to know the approximate conditions of the part of the building where the pipe was to be installed. While everyone in the team knew approximately where the pipe would go, no detailed information regarding the pipe had been provided. To ascertain that the construction of the pipe would fit the rest of the building, the team members responsible for the pipe thus asked questions related to the temperature of the environment where the pipe was to be installed and the approximate distance of where the pipe would go in relation to other aspects of the building (for example, other rooms, the bedrock, etc.). Rather than providing the exact details, the answer involved approximations that were deemed sufficient for the construction.

Depending on the security level of a project, there would be individuals participating in the meetings who, because of having the right security clearance, actually had access to the specifics of the project. They would, for example, have access to most plans and models related to the project (documents that were stored locally physically, not digitally, in a non-disclosed location). These people – *the ones who knew* – were not always active in discussions during the project meeting, though. Instead, they were occasionally asked to address specific points at certain points in time during the meeting. Their answers were often brief and vague, such as: 'What you suggest is OK'. Furthermore, even if these team members had access to the complete information about the project, they were not necessarily familiar with the specifics of particular, often technical, aspects of the project. Their role was rather to act as gatekeepers to the information that was deemed high-security while ensuring that no major misunderstandings took place that would endanger the successful completion of the project.

This means that project meetings were rather silent and structured encounters, where only those called forth made themselves heard. Occasionally, discussions would intensify as relevant parties tried to ascertain that whatever activity they were pursuing was in line with other pursued or planned project activities. But also on these occasions, most participants were not active in the discussions. Given that each team member had their specific specialisation and piece of information, discussions about other information and aspects of the projects only made sense to them if this had any bearing on whatever they knew and were responsible for achieving in the project.

Hinting also occurred during limited visibility. Cameras were seldom turned on and documents or slides rarely shared, unless containing only vague information. If data was discussed, team members were assumed to have accessed this from the systems they had access to prior to the meeting. Occasionally, a team member would share his or her screen, as this was seen as less risky from a security point of view than sending a file or storing it virtually. Virtual work thus made the sharing of information an even more limited affair.

The importance of trust for making do with limited information

Despite the lack of shared information and, in fact, with very little information, project teams still had to make do and perform their tasks. Surprisingly, when asked, respondents rarely complained about this arrangement. Even the virtual meetings were, despite their relative silence and darkness, appreciated by project team members. For many, this was all they knew, as a sizeable part of the workforce had worked for the organisation for most of their careers. They trusted the organisation and they trusted each other, dimensions that we know from previous literature are key for knowledge sharing in organisations (for example, Searle, Weibel and Hartog, 2011).

The trust in the organisational processes at hand, that is, the *organisational trust*, in fact went beyond the specific sub-organisational entities and stretched to the wider umbrella of the high-security organisation and its procedures. The role and responses of *the one-who-knows* in projects were for example never questioned. The organisational members trusted the routines through which projects were initiated and performed. The team members also trusted that the projects that were initiated were up to par, as all projects had to undergo extensive and routine-based assessments for safety and security before being initiated, as well as during execution. Another consequence of this high level of organisational trust was also the willingness to accept that things could take time. This was, for example, obvious in one meeting when the project team realised that many team members lacked access to a specific file that was crucial for the development of the project. This was, however, not seen as problematic. The discussion simply moved on to focus on a future meeting, with somebody saying: 'We'll let them [those responsible for giving access to files] know, and we can come back to this later.'

People would also often express *interpersonal trust* in colleagues and in the project team. Even when working in arrangements with limited visibility and access, project organising was not a major concern due to a strong interpersonal trust. As one project manager remarked: 'We have worked together as a group for a long time. We know each other and we know how to get things done.'

During the pandemic, the intensification of virtual meetings was not seen as a major security concern as most assumed that their colleagues would follow the security protocol as usual. This may, partly, be explained by the fact that employees engaged in 'insecure' behaviour and who break protocol could be charged individually for committing a crime against national security. It may also be explained that the team members trust each other's expertise, which meant that drawing on the *hinting* of others during meetings was something all found to be common and relatively unproblematic. Team members trusted each other to manage their information – their own slice of the whole – and that they were sufficiently competent to share the particular piece of information that was needed in a timely but still secure way. Knowing that others knew was sufficient.

The role of trust in this setting can be compared with studies that show how organisational secrecy can foster a political attitude towards 'who gets to know what' (Fan, Grey and Kärreman, 2021). Unlike studies of high-security information among different organisations inclined to distrust one another due to different aims and motives (Jarvenpaa and Majchrzak, 2008), the setting displayed a cohesive and strong culture of control (Perin, 2006) among actors, in a way that fostered both interpersonal and organisational trust.

Conclusion

As seen in the empirical narrative above, project work may be pursued jointly despite the fact that not all project members have the relevant information. The case thus reveals an alternative picture of the often-espoused notion that information is ever-present in organisations and projects – and increasingly more so (Whyte, Stasis and Lindkvist, 2016). The spread of digitalisation as a means of ensuring openness in work and organising (see Glister, 1997) does not reach everywhere nor does it have to.

By describing how the work of the team members in this context is performed as *fragmented knowing*, through the activity of *hinting*, our findings support the calls to problematise individualistic and non-situated accounts of literacy (Cetindamar Kozanoglu and Abedin, 2021; Lloyd, 2010). Unlike previous theories that have aimed at explaining how collective systems composed of what individual people know and their knowing of who knows, such as transactive memory systems (Lewis and Herndon, 2011; Wegner, 1987) or the relational co-ordination of work (Gittell, 2006), we would like to argue for a different type of collective capability when it comes to information literacy; one anchored in trust. It was not enough to know who knew what, but also to trust one another under conditions of limited visibility. In the case discussed in this chapter, trust was present, but without the often assumed openness of collective systems of knowledge collaborations (see McEvily, Perrone and Zaheer, 2003). Instead, trust was expressed both in relation to organisational processes as well as to other individuals in the organisation, allowing for the possibility of engaging in joint projects *despite* limited openness and availability of information. This was possibly due to a culture of control (Perin, 2006) manifested across practices, painting a different picture than studies that highlight social capital accumulation among actors in social information exchange and literacy processes (Bouty, 2000; Martin and Steinkuehler, 2010).

Our chapter contributes to the practice of theoretical understandings of information literacy (Lloyd, 2010). We would particularly like to point out the role of *hinting* as an alternative mode of collectively managing sensitive information (Martin and Steinkuehler, 2010). Hinting serves as a mode of dialogic co-ordination activity (Faraj and Xiao, 2006) that enables a collective capacity to engage with information collectively on a case-by-case basis without full visibility and access. Even though our study reflects a particular case, we argue that its findings are illustrative of a wider concern of how we contend with information collectively. Managing information collectively is a common mode of work and one bound by ambiguity and tensions in interpreting information (Carlile and Rebentisch, 2003; Te'eni, 2001). The practical implications of our findings point to the general importance of appropriate practices, interpersonal skills and trust to balance information protection and information sharing while pursuing organisational aims. However, how exactly these practices, skills and trust manifest might vary across organisational settings. We suggest further studies to explore how organisations make do with fragmented knowing to better understand how hinting can take shape and under what conditions it proves effective to manage sensitive information.

References

Ahmad, F., Widén, G. and Isto, H. (2020) The Impact of Workplace Information Literacy on Organizational Innovation: An Empirical Study, *International Journal of Information Management*, **51**, 102041, https://doi.org/10.1016/j.ijinfomgt.2019.102041.

Bawden, D. (2001) Information and Digital Literacies: A Review of Concepts, *Journal of Documentation*, **57** (2), 218–59, https://doi.org/10.1108/EUM0000000007083.

Bouty, I. (2000) Interpersonal and Interaction Influences on Informal Resource Exchanges Between R&D Researchers Across Organizational Boundaries, *Academy of Management Journal*, **43** (1), 50–6.

Caniëls, M. C. J. and Bakens, R. J. J. M. (2012) The Effects of Project Management Information Systems on Decision Making in a Multi Project Environment, *International Journal of Project Management*, **30** (2), 162–75, https://doi.org/10.1016/j.ijproman.2011.05.005.

Carlile, P. and Rebentisch, E. (2003) Into the Black Box: The Knowledge Transformation Cycle, *Management Science*, **49** (9), 1180–95.

Cetindamar Kozanoglu, D. and Abedin, B. (2021) Understanding the Role of Employees in Digital Transformation: Conceptualization of Digital Literacy of Employees as a Multi-Dimensional Organizational Affordance, *Journal of Enterprise Information Management*, **34** (6), 1649–72, https://doi.org/10.1108/JEIM-01-2020-0010.

Christensen, L. T. and Cornelissen, J. (2015) Organizational Transparency as Myth and Metaphor, *European Journal of Social Theory*, **18** (2), 132–49.

Costas, J. and Grey, C. (2014) Bringing Secrecy into the Open: Towards a Theorization of the Social Processes of Organizational Secrecy, *Organization Studies*, **35** (10), 1423–47.

Cram, A. W., Proudfoot, J. G. and D'Arcy, J. (2017) Organizational Information Security Policies: A Review and Research Framework,

European Journal of Information Systems, **26** (6), 605–41, https://doi.org/10.1057/s41303-017-0059-9.

Das, T. K. and Teng, B.-S. (2000) Instabilities of Strategic Alliances: An Internal Tensions Perspective, *Organization Science*, **11** (1), 77–103.

Fan, Z., Grey, C. and Kärreman, D. (2021) Confidential Gossip and Organization Studies, *Organization Studies*, **42** (10), 1651–64, https://doi.org/10.1177/0170840620954016.

Faraj, S. and Xiao, Y. (2006) Coordination in Fast-Response Organizations, *Management Science*, **52** (8), 1155–69.

Gittell, J. (2006) Relational Coordination: Coordinating Work Through Relationships of Shared Goals, Shared Knowledge and Mutual Respect. In Kyriakidou, O. and Özbilgin, M. F. (eds), *Relational Perspectives in Organizational Studies: A Research Companion*, 74–94, Edward Elgar.

Glister, P. (1997) *Digital Literacy*, Wiley.

Jackson, P. (2010) *Web 2.0 Knowledge Technologies and the Enterprise: Smarter, Lighter and Cheaper*, Chandos Publishing.

Jarvenpaa, S. L. and Majchrzak, A. (2008) Knowledge Collaboration Among Professionals Protecting National Security: Role of Transactive Memories in Ego-Centered Knowledge Networks, *Organization Science*, **19** (2), 260–76.

Jarvenpaa, S. L. and Majchrzak, A. (2016) Interactive Self-Regulatory Theory for Sharing and Protecting in Interorganizational Collaborations, *Academy of Management Review*, **41** (1), 9–27, https://doi.org.10.5465/amr.2012.0005.

Kanagarajoo, M. V., Fulford, R. and Standing, C. (2019) The Contribution of Social Media to Project Management, *International Journal of Productivity and Performance Management*, **69** (4), 834–72, https://doi.org.10.1108/IJPPM-09-2018-0316.

Lewis, K. and Herndon, B. (2011) Transactive Memory Systems: Current Issues and Future Research Directions, *Organization Science*, **22** (5), 1254–65.

Lloyd, A. (2010) Framing Information Literacy as Information Practice: Site Ontology and Practice Theory, *Journal of Documentation*, **66** (2), 245–58, https://doi.org/10.1108/00220411011023643.

Martin, A. and Grudziecki, J. (2006) DigEuLit: Concepts and Tools for Digital Literacy Development, *Innovation in Teaching and Learning in Information and Computer Sciences*, **5** (4), 249–67, https://doi.org/10.11120/ital.2006.05040249.

Martin, C. and Steinkuehler, C. (2010) Collective Information Literacy in Massively Multiplayer Online Games, *E-Learning and Digital Media*, **7** (4), 355–65, https://doi.org/10.2304/elea.2010.7.4.355.

McAfee, A. and Brynjolfsson, E. (2014) *The Second Machine Age: Work, Progress and Prosperity in a Time of Brilliant Technologies*, Norton and Company.

McEvily, B., Perrone, V. and Zaheer, A. (2003) Trust as an Organizing Principle, *Organization Science*, **14** (1), 91–103.

Perin, C. (2006) *Shouldering Risks: The Culture of Control in the Nuclear Power Industry*, Princeton University Press.

Raymond, L. and Bergeron, F. (2008) Project Management Information Systems: An Empirical Study of Their Impact on Project Managers and Project Success, *International Journal of Project Management*, **26** (2), 213–20, https://doi.org/10.1016/j.ijproman.2007.06.002.

Rennstam, J. and Ashcraft, K. L. (2013) Knowing Work: Cultivating a Practice-Based Epistemology of Knowledge in Organization Studies, *Human Relations*, **67** (1), 3–25, https://doi.org/10.1177/0018726713484182.

Searle, R., Weibel, A. and Hartog, D. (2011) Employee Trust in Organizational Contexts. In Hodgkinson, G. P. and Ford, J. K. (eds), *International Review of Industrial and Organizational Psychology*, 143–91, Wiley Blackwell.

Te'eni, D. (2001) A Cognitive-Affective Model of Organizational Communication for Designing IT, *MIS Quarterly*, **25** (2), 251–312.

Thompson, P., Warhurst, C. and Callaghan, G. (2001) Ignorant Theory and Knowledgeable Workers: Interrogating the Connections Between Knowledge, Skills and Services, *Journal of Management Studies in Continuing Education*, **38** (7), 923–42.

Wegner, D. (1987) Transactive Memory: A Contemporary Analysis of the Group Mind. In Mullen, B. and Goethals, G. R. (eds), *Theories of Group Behavior*, 185–208, Springer.

Whyte, J. and Levitt, R. E. (2010) Information Management and the Management of Projects. In Morris, P., Pinto, J. K. and Söderlund, J. (eds), *Oxford Handbook of Project Management*, 365–88, Oxford University Press.

Whyte, J., Stasis, A. and Lindkvist, C. (2016) Managing Change in the Delivery of Complex Projects: Configuration Management, Asset Information and 'Big Data', *International Journal of Project Management*, **34** (2), 339–51, https://doi.org/10.1016/j.ijproman.2015.02.006.

Yoo, Y., Boland, R. J., Lyytinen, K. and Majchrzak, A. (2012) Organizing for Innovation in the Digitized World, *Organization Science*, **23** (5), 1398–408.

6

Information Literacy Competencies for Career Transitions in the Digital Age

Marina Milosheva, Hazel Hall, Peter Robertson and Peter Cruickshank

Introduction

The digitalisation of society is an issue subject to scholarly attention (for example, Tsekeris, 2018; Valenduc and Vendramin, 2017, 2–4), particularly in respect of its reshaping of economic, political and cultural landscapes, including the transformation of work (for example, Toven-Lindsey, 2017). It is now possible to delegate decision-making for workplace practices such as hiring, training and on-boarding to non-human entities and 'algorithmic bosses' and work placements can be reconfigured into an online format (Beer, 2017; Duffy, 2020, 103; de Haas et al., 2020). While workplaces are subject to continuous change and pressure to innovate (Oeij et al., 2019), automation and alterations to the spatiotemporal organisation of labour also impact individual work experiences (Hoskyn et al., 2020; Kingma, 2019; Gill, 2020, 146).

In addition to the challenges associated with working within such an environment, many workers face considerable job precarity: an increased experience of inequality and insecurity accompanied by the destabilisation of institutions (Kwon and Lane, 2016, 10). Job precarity has grown steadily since the 2008 financial crisis and has led to the development of multiple anti-precarity agendas that call for an improvement of working conditions through trade union and government engagement (Paret, 2016, 111). When employers no longer offer job stability and/or vertical progression opportunities to their employees, working trajectories can become disassociated from the identification of a single career for life (Rodrigues and Guest, 2010). Thus, individuals need to be prepared to navigate a number of career transitions across their working lifespan (Bezanson, Hopkins and Neault, 2016; Lyons, Schweitzer and Ng, 2015; Todolí-Signes, 2017).

Attitudes to work are also changing in ways that may prompt voluntary career mobility and necessitate an increased preparedness for managing changeable career pathways. In pursuit of a better work-life balance, greater job satisfaction and career advancement opportunities, many workers seek more fulfilling work (for example, Chan et al., 2020; Kidd, 2008). This trend has been especially pronounced in recent years. For example, the COVID-19 pandemic has prompted a global phenomenon known as 'the great resignation', whereby large numbers of workers resign from their jobs in protest at poor working conditions (Sheather and Slattery, 2021, 1). In addition, those born after 1995 (also known as 'Gen Z') have specific expectations of organisational culture, work-life balance and job stability. Of note, they ascribe meanings to the term 'stability' that are different from that of earlier generations: to them, stability is not concerned with job tenure within a specific organisation or profession, but with financial rewards such as competitive salaries and job benefits (for example, Barhate and Dirani, 2021). At the same time, this generation is strongly motivated by learning and skills development and may pursue lateral career moves over hierarchical career moves, especially if these provide ample learning and mentoring opportunities (for example, Barhate and Dirani, 2021; McCrindle and Fell, 2019, 23).

As a consequence of these developments, employability is no longer a matter of securing employment following formal education. Rather, it is a matter of managing transitions and of remaining agile in response to industrial and occupational demands over time (Meijers, Kuijpers and Gundy, 2013). It has been suggested that this can be addressed when individuals proactively navigate the world of work, self-managing the process of building their careers by applying problem-solving and entrepreneurial skills (Bridgstock, 2019, 34; Buheji and Buheji, 2020; Bufquin et al., 2021). Others have argued for notions of lifelong and sustainable employability to be incorporated into the employability discourse (Goldstein, 2016, 92; van der Klink et al., 2016).

More specifically, various skills and competencies have been proposed as means to address the challenges of working in information-intensive, digitised and dynamic work environments. These include: digital working competencies (Meske and Junglas, 2020, 5); digital literacy (Bejaković and Mrnjavac, 2020; Vrana, 2016); and workplace information literacy (Hepworth and Walton, 2013; Williams, Cooper and Wavell, 2014, 1; Zhang, Majid and Foo, 2010, 721). However, while the development of skills such as workplace information literacy can be associated with processes that facilitate organisational productivity (for example, Wu, 2019), it is important to make the distinction between skills for work and skills for employability. This is because the vitality of developed economies is dependent on the flexibility and productivity of the labour market, as well as on the extent to which labour and human capital is utilised within them. Inequality, unemployment, skills mismatch and skills under-utilisation all affect the ability of individuals to obtain and maintain work and have direct implications for the availability and uptake of labour in global economies (for example, Helpman, Itskhoki and Redding, 2010; McGuinness, Pouliakas and Redmond, 2017). For this reason, the conceptual framing of information literacy as related to work should extend beyond the physical boundaries of a single workplace.

This principle has been acknowledged in the use of the term 'professional information literacy' in prior work to represent the collective information skills of groups of employees who work in different organisations, yet al.l share the same goal for enhancing their professional development (for example, Abdi and Bruce, 2015). Similarly, the need for individuals to be equipped with information literacy to navigate fragmented and precarious post-industrial labour markets from workplace to workplace has previously been identified (Crawford and Irving, 2014). However, it is only recently that employability literacy and career information literacy have been distinguished in the literature and labelled as such (for example, Milosheva et al., 2022).

As an extension to workplace information literacy, employability information literacy takes into account the wider labour market in which workplaces operate (for example, Bušelić and Banek Zorica, 2018). It is most readily associated with the graduate employability agenda: the focus of much of the literature on employability information literacy relates to the preparation of university students for employment following graduation. In contrast, career information literacy is concerned with career decision-making and lifelong career development (Milosheva et al., 2022). This is because 'career', in general, is a much broader concept than 'employability'. Employability should not be conflated with notions of inclusion, social justice or career, nor should labour market power be equated to the obtainment of formal qualifications (for example, Atkins, 2013). To be strong contenders on the labour market, workers need to be able to manage their career pathways effectively. Such management entails nuanced understandings of career pathways, achieved through career identity formation and knowledge of opportunity infrastructures (Higgins, Nairn and Sligo, 2010, 23).

In this chapter, manifestations of work-related information literacy beyond the single workplace are provided, with a focus on the importance of employability information literacy and career information literacy to sustainable employment in largely digitised work environments. Here the two key terms are deployed as noted below:

1 *Employability information literacy* is an employability competency that enables people to seek jobs and to communicate their information literacy skills to future employers. To date, this type of information literacy has been articulated as a graduate attribute that facilitates university-to-work transitions.

2 *Career information literacy* is a competency for career transitions in the digital age that facilitates career decision-making at multiple transition points throughout the life span. Career decision-making is achieved through the development of knowledge of the self and the world of work.

First in this chapter, two main forms of employability information literacy – generic and subject-specific – are reviewed, with attention drawn to the narrow graduate employability focus of the concept of employability information literacy. Next, the concept of sustainable employability is discussed and perspectives on lifelong career development and self-management are reviewed. The notion of sustainable employability is used to illustrate global trends within the changing employability landscape and to elucidate the important role of career information literacy skills within this. The main focus of the remainder of the chapter falls on career information literacy. This incorporates competencies from three skills clusters: (1) career management skills; (2) digital career literacy skills; and (3) career information literacy skills. The convergence and divergence of emphasis across these skill clusters is considered and suggestions for refining the conceptualisation of career information literacy are presented.

The chapter concludes with an overview of best practices and potential innovations in the development of employability information literacy and career information literacy. The themes of skill transferability and transition are regarded as central themes to discussions of employability information literacy and career information literacy. It is proposed that greater advocacy for information literacy training is needed in the workplace as a way of scaffolding continued competence and operational efficiency in workers and in graduates who are commencing employment for the first time. Suggestions for supporting career information literacy in practice are also provided, with an emphasis on hybrid career education and multi-institutional support. It is concluded that career information literacy has the potential to enable career transitions across precarious and digitised career environments.

Employability information literacy

Discussions of employability information literacy in the published literature generally link the themes of information literacy and the employability of new graduates, showing strong interest from universities (Barkas and Armstrong, 2021; Christie, 2017). Research on this theme typically reports the embedding of transferable information literacy skills into the curriculum (alongside other employability skills) to demonstrate the contribution of libraries to the development of graduate attributes (for example, Johnston,

2010; Smith and Edwards, 2012). Significant amongst these initiatives in higher education is the graduate employability lens added to the Society of College, National and University Libraries (SCONUL) 'Seven Pillars of IL' model, reflecting the importance of information literacy for graduate employability purposes (Goldstein, 2015).

Such initiatives are often led by academic librarians. For instance, Towlson and Rush (2013) endeavoured to develop a graduate licence of employability information literacy skills by mapping common information literacy and employability skills against the skills developed by librarians and learning developers at De Montfort University in the UK. They found that self-management skills, digital skills, metacognition skills, academic study skills and information literacy skills were already being developed in students and that further instruction in teamworking, business awareness, media literacy, problem-solving and communication was necessary.

The reason for the strong participation of librarians in this work on employability information literacy is their historical ownership of information literacy instruction (and its predecessor 'user education'). The inclusion of librarians here also accounts for the first of the two types of employability information literacy skills found in the literature: generic employability literacy skills. These are skills that can be aligned to conventional bibliographic training for effective library use, such as organisation of information, resource discovery, searching strategies and critical evaluation strategies (Fiegen, 2011). In information literacy instruction tasks set by librarians, students complete assignments that will: prepare them to seek information on jobs and employers; help them complete job applications; and teach them about social media use for professional purposes, with an emphasis on reputation management (Oakley, 2013; Woods and Murphy, 2013, 156).

Other partnerships for this kind of work are struck between librarians and academic staff (for example, Farrar et al., 2007; Monge and Frisicaro-Pawlowski, 2014), academic librarians and librarians within business organisations (for example, Waters, Kasuto and McNaughton, 2012) and academic librarians and university careers advisers (Hollister, 2005). Thus, employability information literacy is a shared objective across numerous institutions with an interest in graduate employability. This interest is expressed through quantitative skills measurement, formal instruction and the development of specialised courses and qualifications, with the goal of developing tangible graduate attributes in university students (for example, Boden and Nedeva, 2010, 50).

The second type of employment information literacy – subject-specific employability literacy – comprises the teaching of subject-specific skills as preparation for work in a specific industry or occupation (Klusek and Bornstein, 2006). In designing instruction of this nature, the importance of information literacy skills to the domain is established through analyses of its presence in job information (for example, in advertisements) or directly from employers through interview (Gilbert, 2017; Head et al., 2013). The results of these analyses are matched against existing employability information literacy provision on degree programmes and then subject-specific employability information literacy curricula are developed/enhanced for embedding into modules/courses. Degrees that lead to employment in information-intensive business occupations benefit most from this approach. This is because they fit most readily with the skills articulated in competency standards developed for higher education, such as the US Information Literacy Competency Standards (Conley and Gil, 2010).

The generic employability information literacy skills as described above readily facilitate study-to-work transitions, whereas subject-specific employability information literacy skills are more focused on the skills required for a particular workplace setting. However, there is one key issue in the conceptualisation of both types of employability literacy skills: they are concerned exclusively with graduate employability and therefore the importance of attending to work-to-work transitions and adult literacies is overlooked. Matters such as adult employability literacies and skills continuity across different contexts do not receive the same amount of funding, institutional support and attention as graduate employability literacies. To date, only one exception to this can be found in the literature: Crawford and Irving's (2012) report of the provision of information literacy instruction in public libraries. Targeted specifically at citizens who are at risk of long-term unemployment or digital exclusion, this type of instruction includes training in computing skills and job-seeking skills (Crawford and Irving, 2012, 80).

Crawford and Irving's work in this area is significant because they address the challenge of managing one's career within digitised and precarious working environments. Yet their reported intervention represents a single, short-burst initiative with localised impact, in which only basic information literacy skills were taught. More can be done to support career management in the digital age through information literacy.

Sustainable employability

It has been noted that the shift to precarious labour markets, underpinned by principles such as volatility, uncertainty, complexity and ambiguity, has been accompanied by an increase in social instability and injustice (for example, Bone, 2021). As a result, social justice narratives feature in the literatures of career development, and of librarianship, in respect of sustainable employability and emancipatory modes of career guidance have emerged as antitheses to neo-liberal and normative regimes of injustice (Hooley and Sultana, 2016; Saunders, 2017; Sultana, 2017). Career development scholars have critiqued the state of the labour market, contending that workers are faced with precarity to the point of absurdity and that the free market offers a false vision of choice, freedom and flexibility (Southwood, 2017). They have also reflected upon the erosion of working practices and emphasised as an aspirational goal and basic human right the importance of 'decent work' (Blustein et al., 2016), that is, work that is stable and secure and associated with appropriate renumeration, community cohesion and strong trade unions (Blustein, 2019).

Within these social justice narratives, it is argued that there is a need to promote *sustainable employability* throughout working lives and to ensure a sense of continuity, contentment and progress in workers' experiences of career transitions and work (for example, Fleuren et al., 2016). Vocal proponents of fair work and sustainable employability, such as Sen (1987) and those inspired by his work (for example, van der Klink et al., 2016) contend that work should create value for the worker and not just the organisation. Related to this discourse are critiques of the de-politicisation of higher education, which inhibits the democratic potential of education and models future employees after employer standards, leaving little room for employers to consider employees' expectations of their place of work in return (for example, Clarke, 2012, 289). As a consequence of neo-liberal education policy, employability training becomes a commodity that does not live up to the promise of sustainable employability.

Work creates value for the workers when it is personally meaningful, congruent with their values and allows them to achieve their personal goals (van der Klink et al., 2016). This suggests that societal and organisational structures should allow for the exercise of personal agency and choice in respect of employment. Indeed, while external structural influences exert influence on individual outcomes and advocacy for fair and secure work is crucial, modern employability discourses tend to emphasise the importance of entrepreneurialism and individual responsibility over structural thinking and systemic change (Sofritti et al., 2020). Complex negotiations between global issues and local identities are to be conducted through reinvention of the self, termed as 'se faire soi', that is, 'make yourself' (Guichard, 2009) and 'career construction' (Savickas, 2013). By this logic, the responsibility for career progression resides, ultimately, with the individual. Sustainable employability is achieved not through institutional policy, but through self-constructed meanings of career.

While the development of societal structures to support decent work and the reduction of work precarity is a main priority for reducing injustices in society, self-management serves an important function. At a time of job precarity, career self-management allows individuals to carve dignified and empowered lives for themselves during career transitions (for example, Sultana, 2014). Such self-management is dependent on an individual's ability to articulate their career intentions and to position them within available opportunity structures and occurs in a continuous manner throughout the lifespan (for example, Savickas et al., 2009).

The importance of attending to lifelong career development and facilitating individual empowerment during career transitions has been recognised in other research areas beyond career development, including information literacy. Information literacy is relevant here as a key competency for personal effectiveness across many aspects of life, not limited to work, for example, education and leisure. Indeed, 'information literacy is for life, not just for a good degree' (Inskip, 2014, 1; Webber and Johnston, 2014, 15) and employability is an important part of the information literate life course. However, graduate employability (as described earlier in this chapter) represents only one form of career preparedness. Digital working competencies, career decision-making, adult literacies and skills to support the information literate life course could be further integrated into employability literacy discourses.

Within increasingly dynamic, fragmented and digitally mediated career trajectories, *learning about career options* is of paramount importance (for example, Smith et al., 2018). The possession of adequate knowledge of available career options is one of the pillars of self-directed career development, hence individuals are advised to carry out career research and planning rather than to leave their career choice to serendipity (Pennington, Mosley and Sinclair, 2013, 9). The provision of career information to individuals is one of the key means by which such knowledge can be developed (for example, Sampson et al., 2018).

There is therefore a natural fit between information literacy skills and career development processes, as exhibited in initial research on career information literacy and digital career literacy conducted in response to the challenges of job precarity and digitalisation (for example, Zalaquett and Osborn, 2007; Hooley, 2017). In order to unify disparate ideas pertaining to digital career literacy and career information literacy, the remainder of this chapter explores prospects for further development of the concept of career information literacy.

Career information literacy

Considerable skills are required to manage career information as part of career development processes. When attempting to make informed occupational, educational and training decisions, individuals need to be able to interpret the career information available and interrogate it in an effective way (for example, Hooley, 2017; Longridge, Hooley and Staunton, 2013, 6). Furthermore, since career information is commonly disseminated through information and communication technology (ICT), skills in accessing digital career services and managing digital career information are also required (Bimrose, Kettunen and Goddard, 2015). Taking into account the destabilisation and digitalisation of working lives, three clusters of career competencies are posited as central to the development of career resilience:

1 Career self-management skills (or simply, career management skills), which relate to the development of lifelong career development skills in citizens (for example, Akkermans et al., 2013). These skills incorporate a wide range of competencies not limited to the ability to handle digital or career information.
2 Digital career literacy skills (or 'digital career management'), which are/is concerned with the skills and knowledge needed to use online sources for career purposes, following Hooley (2012, 3). Digital literacy differs from information literacy as its primary focus is on digitally mediated career information, rather than on other types of engagement with career information.
3 Career information literacy skills, which can be framed as career information competencies that support career decision-making and career development learning by drawing on prior work by Lin-Stephens et al. (2019), Milosheva et al. (2022), and Zalaquett and Osborn (2007). Career information literacy is a holistic concept that encompasses all forms of engagement with career information, including social modes of career learning (for example, Arur and Sharma, 2022).

While prominence of different capabilities is given within these three clusters, there are still multiple points of convergence between them. This is evident in Table 6.1 on page 81 where conceptual overlap between the skills profiles for each cluster is presented. These overlaps have implications for the means by which these skills could be represented in academic narratives and developed in practice. By analysing the extant literature thematically, the following patterns can be recorded:

1 Information skills, social skills and self-regulated learning competencies are present in all three clusters. Skills that refer to learning about the self and learning about the world of work can be found in both the

career self-management and the career information literacy clusters. Information literacy is not listed as a career management skill, yet the information skills found within the career management skill cluster resemble those articulated as part of the digital career literacy skillset.
2 In addition to the production of information and the use of information systems, digital career literacy skills also include the management of one's online presence. Hooley's seven Cs of digital career literacy – changing, collecting, critiquing, connecting, communicating, creating, curating – appear to be a blend of traditional information literacy skills for information seeking, as well as career management skills and digital literacy skills (Hooley, 2012).
3 Career information literacy incorporates the informational aspects of several of the self-management tasks that are articulated as part of career management skills. For instance, Valentine and Kosloski (2021) developed a classification of 50 career literacy skills using the Delphi method. This skills classification incorporates some career self-management skills and represents the most comprehensive assemblage of career information literacy skills to date. Nevertheless, digital career literacy skills were not included in Valentine and Kosloski's (2021) skills classification and are not currently incorporated within the career information literacy literature more broadly.

Overall, on the basis of the available evidence, it can be inferred that information skills (in general) are an essential part of career self-management. However, only information skills relating to the production of information and the use of information systems have been considered as part of the career self-management discourse. There are multiple opportunities for further conceptual specialisation in this regard. One opportunity is to expand the description of information skills within the career management skills matrix. Here, information literacy skills relating to the access, use and evaluation (that is, beyond the production of information outputs) can be added to the 'information' cluster. In addition, digital career literacy and career information literacy may be merged in a new meta-concept retaining either the designation of 'digital career literacy' or 'career information literacy'.

Whether information literacy and digital literacy are competing or complementary concepts, two separate entities or constituent parts of the same concept of meta literacy is subject to debate (Cordell, 2013; Jacobson and Mackey, 2013). In a digitised world, however, it is difficult to imagine a clear segregation between the two concepts. With more career services delivered online, the digitisation and automation of work are pervasive phenomena that are not happening 'out there' but 'here and now' (Hirschi,

Table 6.1 *Career self-management skills, digital literacy skills and career information literacy skills*

Career self-management skills	Sources
• <u>General</u>: life skills, meta-competencies, work readiness skills, personal management, skilful practices relating to academic endeavour, employment, and life, transversal competencies • <u>Information</u>: developing and presenting information, understanding information systems • <u>Planning</u>: career planning, problem-solving, personal management, organisational skills, goal-setting • <u>Learning about the world of work</u>: self-regulated learning, horizons (exploring the world of work, training, and learning career exploration, person–environment fit); work exploration (exploring behaviour), career action (proactive behaviour), work exploration, academic skills, understanding of disciplinary subject matter • <u>Reflection and knowledge of the self</u>: career reflection, reflection on qualities, self-profiling, self-awareness, self (understanding personality and interests), strengths (knowing how to use talents and skills), learning through reflection, reflective behaviour • <u>Social</u>: social skills, social competencies, interpersonal skills, leadership skills, teamwork, negotiation skills, networking, networks (identifying who can help you and how), networking (interactive behaviour)	Akkermans et al. (2013); Hooley et al. (2013); Knight and Yorke (2003); Kuijpers and Meijers (2012); Skills Development Scotland (2012); Succi and Canovi (2020); Sultana (2021); Sung, Turner and Kaewchinda (2013); Zinser (2003)
Digital career literacy skills	**Sources**
• Keeping a digital record of personal development and reflecting on progress (for example, digital career portfolios) • Technical skills needed to use computer applications • Maintaining a digital identity and knowing what information to share online in order to enhance employability • The seven Cs of digital career literacy – changing, collecting, critiquing, connecting, communicating, creating, curating	Bennett and Robertson (2015); Goe, Ipsen and Bliss (2018); Hooley (2012); Kaeophanuek, Jaitip and Nilsook (2018); Martin and Grudziecki (2006); Riel, Christian and Hinson (2012); Willis and Wilkie (2009)
Career information literacy skills	**Sources**
• Self-assessment, career searches, career information, job preparation • Functional, interactive and critical skills a student needs to be able to read, understand and make decisions on career-related information • Generic, situated and transformative skills (mapped against self-awareness, opportunity awareness, decision-making and transition learning domains)	Lin-Stephens et al. (2019); Valentine and Kosloski (2021); Zalaquett and Osborn (2007)

2018; Chinyamurindi and Dlaza, 2018, 1). Thus, it might be assumed that all literacies *do* have a digital aspect.

Following this line of reasoning, there is an opportunity to conceptualise career information literacy as a competency for informed career management in the digital age. Framed in such a way, career information literacy encompasses the skills included in the digital career literacy competency cluster. In addition, it contributes to the advancement and popularisation of information skills within career self-management processes and responds to the need for promoting sustainable employability for citizens. The interrelationships and proposed specialisation of existing concepts is further depicted in Figure 6.1. Here, information competencies are highlighted as crucial parts of career self-management. Digital career literacy is nested as an integral component of career information literacy.

Career self-management skills

Information competencies	Self-management competencies
Career information literacy	Planning
	Learning
Digital career literacy	Reflection; self-knowledge
	Social skills; networks

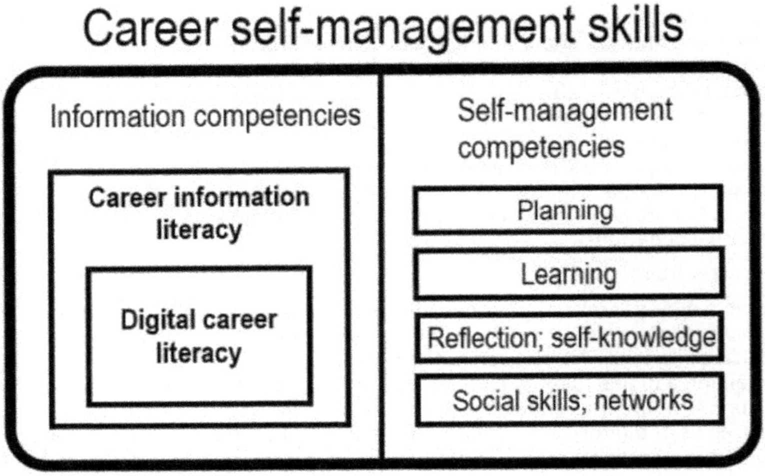

Figure 6.1 *Career information literacy and digital career literacy relative to career self-management skills*

Supporting employability and career: best practices and new directions

Employability information literacy – is skills transferability possible?

Multiple successful employability interventions have been reported in the information literacy literature, with specific reference to the effectiveness of interventions deployed in university libraries (for example, Fiegen, 2011; Mawson and Haworth, 2018; Oakley, 2013;). Yet the general usefulness of subject-specific employability literacy skills beyond the education setting is questionable due to the difficulty of transferring information literacy skills from one context to another. In general, it has been noted that school-to-work, classroom-to-classroom and school-to-university transitions of information literacy skills are difficult to achieve (Lloyd, 2011, 284). Upon entering the workplace, more specifically, recent graduates encounter several challenges. These include vaguely defined workplace tasks, limited or poor feedback and collaborative working arrangements; as a result of these challenges, employer expectations are not ordinarily met at the onset of employment (for example, Hahn and Pedersen, 2020; Head et al., 2013, 4; Lundh, Limberg and Lloyd, 2013).

While little is known about information literacy transitions across the lifespan and, particularly, education-to-work and work-to-work transitions (Markless and Streatfield, 2007), there is ample evidence that the differences between education and work settings are stark and skills transferability between them is likely to be limited. The main issue is that the rather artificial 'practising' of employability information literacy skills in an educational setting cannot replicate the reality of information handling in the workplace. Information literacy performed at work is rarely the product of proficient searching by a single individual to meet a defined information need in the form of textual information held in a particular document, as might be the task for a conventional university assignment. Rather, information needs, sources and practices in the workplace are more diverse and complex and not usually solved through adherence to a linear process of information search and retrieval by one person (Abram, 2013; Bruce, 1999; Crawford and Irving, 2009, 29; Hepworth and Smith, 2008; Kirton and Barham, 2005; Lloyd, 2005, 235; O'Farrill, 2010).

This issue of transferability is further underlined in the findings of empirical work on information literacy outcomes where study participants are both students and practising professionals in their field. Here, they exhibit information literacy outcomes more typical of the workplace setting than of the education setting (D'Angelo, 2012). This is because learners in work settings understand and practise information literacy not only from their perspectives as students, but also as employees and future professionals (Sharun, 2021). Thus, exposure to the workplace is vital in ensuring information literacy skills transferability across different settings. Indeed, according to the environment habit theory of work, work experience and learning are efficient only to the extent that the learning environment replicates the subsequent working environment (Prosser and Quigley, 1949). By extension, workplace training is the most effective method for skills development in the workplace (Oviawe, Uwameiye and Uddin, 2017), including information literacy skills.

There is thus a case for further underscoring the importance of information literacy training in organisations and demonstrating the added value that information literacy skills can bring to the workplace. Two prominent conceptualisations of added value exist in the literature and can be used to support advocacy: *compliant/routine* and *inventive/innovative* information literacy (for example, Collard et al., 2017). In the context of workplace practices, the former type of information literacy safeguards against social, legal, financial and medical risks and contributes towards evidence-based practice (Forster, 2017; Partridge, Edwards and Thorpe, 2010). The latter is invoked in the development of new products, processes and services (D'Angelo, 2012, 639). Information literacy is one of the key informational determinants underpinning workplace learning and knowledge generation (Middleton and Hall, 2021); thus, if innovation is an organisational goal, investment in information literacy training is likely to lead to tangible returns (Cheuk, 2008). If the limits of information literacy training in higher education are indeed recognised and skills are scaffolded through continued training in industry, then the true strategic and sustained potential of information literacy may be unlocked.

Career information literacy – from skills transferability to transition

A different perspective on skills transferability is offered by career information literacy when this is framed as a competency for career transitions in the digital age. This represents a viable alternative to transferring educational information literacy skills to the workplace setting – a challenge that has proven to be arduous. It also provides recourse from focusing solely on school-to-work transitions, which only partially fulfils the promise of developing an employability or career agenda for the information literate life course. In recent years, the notion of *transition* has gained traction within information literacy discourse and shows great promise in supporting ongoing efforts to link graduate employability literacies and adult literacies through a consideration of the role of information literacy in sustainable employability, self-management and career decision-making.

Transition, as a concept in information literacy scholarship, is relatively novel. Yet some granularity is already evident in its articulation. Hicks (2021), for example, indicates that the processes of deploying information literacy skills to navigate changes (such as career transitions) are socially situated and complex. Hicks' work builds on earlier studies that demonstrate the need to become accustomed to the sociocultural determinants of transitional settings during periods of change and to be familiar with the key social and material affordances within those settings (Lloyd et al., 2013, 18–19). In the literature of forced transition and refugees' information practices, transition is understood to be a sociocultural phenomenon, where 'learning as becoming' entails the embodiment of the site-specific systems, practices and cultural values of a given setting (for example, Hicks, 2021; Lloyd et al., 2013, 18–19;

Penuel et al., 2016). Transition, therefore, is an important challenge within everyday settings and needs to be managed effectively through the enactment of specific information literacy practices that mitigate risk, maximise personal success and facilitate inclusion in new communities (Hicks, 2019, 1–5). Managing crises and moving from one mode of being to another requires that mental and behavioural adjustments take place through three main stages: understanding, negotiating and resolving (Ruthven, 2022, 586–90).

When applied to career development, transition may help elucidate the means by which transitional career landscapes are navigated at multiple points across the lifespan. As evidenced in Willson and Given's (2020) paper on the career transitions of doctoral students into early career academics, career transitions are complex endeavours in which impactful decisions need to be made through the utilisation of appropriate information behaviour. The authors of this paper explore the information behaviours of early career academics, establish linkages between affective experiences and specific information behaviours and discuss patterns of information avoidance (Willson and Given, 2020, 4). Information avoidance can be reduced through information literacy training (Karim, Widén and Heinström, 2019), hence there would appear to be a clear benefit in developing career information literacy competencies to facilitate career decision-making during career transitions.

The utilisation of seminal work in career studies can provide further explanation of transitional effects in career development. Adams, Hayes and Hopson's (1976) model of transition, Nicolson's (1990) transition cycle and Williams' transition cycle (1999) are some examples of such work. In each of them, multi-phase transition pathways are presented. Adams, Hayes and Hopson (1976) further supplement their model with a transition typology, in which four types of transitions are discussed: (1) predictable-voluntary; (2) predictable-involuntary; (3) unpredictable-voluntary; and (4) unpredictable-involuntary. In information literacy research, it may be useful to employ similar distinctions between planned transitions (as exhibited during periods of career decision-making) and forced transitions (such as the redundancy transitions discussed by Oakland, MacDonald and Flowers, 2012).

In consideration of the arguments presented in this chapter, the development of supportive structures to enhance citizens' career information literacy skills is an aspirational objective. Much of employability information literacy education is provided by academic librarians due to the focus of this type of literacy on graduate employability. In contrast, career information literacy qualifies multiple transition points and incorporates adult literacies. This suggests that career information literacy needs to be supported through institutions and community structures serving adults regardless of their age and occupation status. Public libraries, career counselling services, job centres, training centres, workplaces, professional associations, labour unions, charities and independent institutions that offer vocational counselling are natural candidates for training delivery and collaboration. Building on the important outreach initiatives of Crawford and Irving (2012) in the public library, novel and more advanced career information literacy programmes may be offered to library users.

The skills and content to be taught as part of career information literacy instruction remain to be established and verified through future research: this chapter serves primarily to introduce this concept and to synthesise the extant associated thematic streams. Overall, it is anticipated that the main goal of such instruction would be to align career education with information literacy education by employing a hybrid approach. By consulting the available literature, as well as Guichard's review of a century of career education (Guichard, 2001), and the latest taxonomy of career information literacy skills (Valentine and Kosloski, 2021), multiple potential approaches can be identified. Individuals could be taught information literacy and digital literacy skills in order to successfully perform career self-management activities such as planning, learning, self-reflection and social engagement. A broader 'career literacy' course could implement career education topics alongside career information literacy instruction. Career education topics may include, but not be limited to: changes in the labour market, including in-demand occupations and job demand projections; local work, education and upskilling opportunities; self-knowledge and personality profiling; financial planning; and many more.

Conclusion

At a time of considerable workplace digitalisation and career precarity, individuals' engagement with work, employability and career development are changing. Two types of work-related information literacy, in particular – employability information literacy and career information literacy – present opportunities for the empowerment of citizens. The former comprises generic and subject-specific skills, while the latter relates to three clusters of competencies: career self-management skills; digital career literacy skills; and career information literacy skills.

However, employability information literacy scholarship, concentrated primarily in the area of graduate employability, fails to address the complexity and longevity of the issues that society faces. Of particular importance in the development of competent, confident and future-ready workers is the notion of sustainable employability, that is, employability that is associated with principles of social justice, decent work and empowerment through personal agency and choice. Indeed, to craft dignified and empowered lives for themselves, individuals need to develop sustainable employability skills for engagement in lifelong career development and self-management. A conceptual roadmap for the development of information literacy competencies in citizens as related to work and for the promotion of personal resilience during career transitions is needed.

In this chapter, such a roadmap is presented through the analysis of extant narratives in employability and career information literacy research. A thematic grouping of career self-management skills, digital career literacy skills and career information literacy skills clusters indicates that there are opportunities to incorporate information literacy within the career self-management skills matrix and to embed digital literacy skills within the career information literacy skills profile.

Opportunities for the advancement of employability and career information literacy research are also highlighted. It is suggested that transition is an overlooked aspect of informed career management in the modern age that merits closer investigation and that the assumed transferability of subject-specific employability information literacy skills from educational settings into the workplace should be addressed through the provision of ongoing workplace training.

Career information literacy has the potential to unify disparate narratives pertaining to information use, career self-management and digitalisation and to pave the way for further research that extends the graduate employability literacy concept beyond higher education. To establish career information literacy as a key competence for personal effectiveness across work and career transitions, however, more research and institutional advocacy is required. Sustainable employability, transition, self-management and career decision-making are key pillars upon which future career information literacy research and advocacy can be predicated.

References

Abdi, E. S. and Bruce, C. (2015) From Workplace to Profession: New Focus for the Information Literacy Discourse. In Kurbanoğlu, S., Boustany, J., Špiranec, S., Grassian, E., Mizrachi, D. and Roy, L. (eds), *European Conference on Information Literacy*, 59–69, Springer.

Abram, S. (2013) Workplace Information Literacy: It's Different. In Hepworth, M. and Walton, G. (eds), *Developing People's Information Capabilities: Fostering Information Literacy in Educational, Workplace and Community Contexts*, I-II, Emerald Group Publishing Limited.

Adams, J., Hayes, J. and Hopson, B. (1976) *Transition: Understanding and Managing Personal Change*, Martin Robertson.

Akkermans, J., Brenninkmeijer, V., Huibers, M. and Blonk, R. W. (2013) Competencies for the Contemporary Career: Development and Preliminary Validation of the Career Competencies Questionnaire, *Journal of Career Development*, **40**, 245–67.

Arur, A. and Sharma, M. (2022) Career Life Skills for 10th Grade Boys in Delhi, India: Mapping Information Literacies for Sustainable Development. In DeJaeghere, J. G. and Murphy-Graham, E. (eds), *Life Skills for Youth: Critical Perspectives*, 169–91, Springer.

Atif, Y. and Chou, C. (2018) Digital Citizenship: Innovations in Education, Practice, and Pedagogy, *Journal of Educational Technology and Society*, **21** (1), 152–4.

Atkins, L. (2013) From Marginal Learning to Marginal Employment? The Real Impact of 'Learning' Employability Skills, *Power and Education*, **5** (1), 28–37.

Barhate, B. and Dirani, K. M. (2021) Career Aspirations of Generation Z: A Systematic Literature Review, *European Journal of Training and Development*, **46** (1/2), 139–57, https://doi.org/10.1108/EJTD-07-2020-0124.

Barkas, L. A. and Armstrong, P. A. (2021) The Price of Knowledge and the Wisdom of Innocence: A Difficult Journey Through the Employability Discourse in Higher Education, *Industry and Higher Education*, **36** (1), 51–62, https://doi.org/10.1177/09504222211016293.

Beer, D. (2017) The Social Power of Algorithms, *Information, Communication and Society*, **20** (1), 1–13.

Bejaković, P. and Mrnjavac, Z. (2020) The Importance of Digital Literacy in the Labour Market, *Emerald Insight*, **42** (4), 921–32, https://doi.org/10.1108/ER-07-2019-0274.

Bennett, D. and Robertson, R. (2015) Preparing Students for Diverse Careers: Developing Career Literacy with Final-Year Writing Students, *Journal of University Teaching and Learning Practice*, **12** (3), 49–65, https://doi.org/10.53761/1.12.3.5.

Bezanson, L., Hopkins, S. and Neault, R. A. (2016) Career Guidance and Counselling in Canada: Still Changing After All These Years, *Canadian Journal of Counselling and Psychotherapy*, **50**, 219–39.

Bimrose, J., Kettunen, J. and Goddard, T. (2015) ICT – The New Frontier? Pushing the Boundaries of Careers Practice, *British Journal of Guidance and Counselling*, **43** (1), 8–23.

Blustein, D. (2019) *The Importance of Work in an Age of Uncertainty: The Eroding Work Experience in America*, Oxford University Press.

Blustein, D. L., Olle, C., Connors-Kellgren, A. and Diamonti, A. J. (2016) Decent Work: A Psychological Perspective, *Frontiers in Psychology*, 7, 407, https://doi.org/10.3389/fpsyg.2016.00407.

Boden, R. and Nedeva, M. (2010) Employing Discourse: Universities and Graduate 'Employability', *Journal of Education Policy*, **25** (1), 37–54, https://doi.org/10.1080/02680930903349489.

Bone, J. (2021) Neoliberal Precarity and Primalization: A Biosocial Perspective on the Age of Insecurity, Injustice, and Unreason, *The British Journal of Sociology*, **72** (4), 1030–45, https://doi.org/10.1111/1468-4446.12884.

Bongard, A. (2019) Automating Talent Acquisition: Smart Recruitment, Predictive Hiring Algorithms, and the Data-Driven Nature of Artificial Intelligence, *Psychosociological Issues in Human Resource Management*, 7 (1), 36–41.

Bridgstock, R. (2019) Graduate Employability 2.0: Learning for Life and Work in a Socially Networked World. In Higgs, J. (ed.), *Education for Employability (Volume 1)*, 97–106, Brill Sense.

Bruce, C. S. (1999) Workplace Experiences of Information Literacy, *International Journal of Information Management*, **19** (1), 33–47, https://doi.org/10.1016/S0268-4012(98)00045-0.

Bufquin, D., Park, J. Y., Back, R. M., de Souza Meira, J. V. and Hight, S. K. (2021) Employee Work Status, Mental Health, Substance Use, and Career Turnover Intentions: An Examination of Restaurant Employees During COVID-19, *International Journal of Hospitality Management*, **93** (1), 102764.

Buheji, M. and Buheji, A. (2020) Planning Competency in the New Normal – Employability Competency in Post-COVID-19 Pandemic, *International Journal of Human Resource Studies*, **10** (2), 237, https://doi.org/10.5296/ijhrs.v10i2.17085.

Bušelić, V. and Banek Zorica, M. (2018) Information Literacy Quest: In Search of Graduate Employability. In Kurbanoğlu, S., Boustany, J., Špiranec, S., Grassian, E., Mizrachi, D. and Roy, L. (eds), *Information Literacy in the Workplace*, 98–108, Springer International Publishing, https://doi.org/10.1007/978-3-319-74334-9_11.

Chan, A. P. C., Chiang, Y. H., Wong, F. K. W., Liang, S. and Abidoye, F. A. (2020) Work–Life Balance for Construction Manual Workers, *Journal of Construction Engineering and Management*, **146** (5), 04020031.

Cheuk, B. (2008) Delivering Business Value Through Information Literacy in the Workplace, *Libri*, **58** (3), 137–43.

Chinyamurindi, W. T. and Dlaza, Z. (2018) Can You Teach an Old Dog New Tricks? An Exploratory Study Into How a Sample of Lecturers Develop Digital Literacies as Part of Their Career Development, *Reading and*

Writing Journal of the Reading Association of South Africa, **9** (1), 1–8.

Christie, F. (2017) The Reporting of University League Table Employability Rankings: A Critical Review, *Journal of Education and Work*, **30** (4), 403–18, https://doi.org/10.1080/13639080.2016.1224821.

Clarke, M. (2012) The (Absent) Politics of Neo-Liberal Education Policy, *Critical Studies in Education*, **53** (3), 297–310, https://doi.org/10.1080/17508487.2012.703139.

Collard, A. S., De Smedt, T., Dufrasne, M., Fastrez, P., Ligurgo, V., Patriarche, G. and Philippette, T. (2017) Digital Media Literacy in the Workplace: A Model Combining Compliance and Inventivity, *Italian Journal of Sociology of Education*, **9** (1), 122–54, https://doi.org/10.14658/pupj-ijse-2017-1-7.

Conley, T. M. and Gil, E. L. (2011) Information Literacy for Undergraduate Business Students: Examining Value, Relevancy, and Implications for the New Century, *Journal of Business and Finance Librarianship*, **16** (3), 213–28, https://doi.org/10.1080/08963568.2011.581562.

Cordell, R. M. (2013) Information Literacy and Digital Literacy: Competing or Complementary?, *Communications in Information Literacy*, **7** (2), 177–83, https://doi.org/10.15760/comminfolit.2013.7.2.150.

Crawford, J. and Irving, C. (2009) Information Literacy in the Workplace: A Qualitative Exploratory Study, *Journal of Librarianship and Information Science*, **41** (1), 29–38.

Crawford, J. and Irving, C. (2012) Information Literacy in Employability Training: The Experience of Inverclyde Libraries, *Journal of Librarianship and Information Science*, **44** (2), 79–89, https://doi.org/10.1177/0961000611436096.

Crawford, J. and Irving, C. (2014) Information Literacy, Policy Issues and Employability, *International Journal of Multidisciplinary Comparative Studies*, **1** (2), 8–25.

D'Angelo, B. (2012) Student Learning and Workplace IL: A Case Study, *Library Trends*, **60**, 637–50.

de Haas, M., Faber, R. and Hamersma, M. (2020) How COVID-19 and the Dutch 'Intelligent Lockdown' Change Activities, Work and Travel Behaviour: Evidence from Longitudinal Data in the Netherlands, *Transportation Research Interdisciplinary Perspectives*, **6**, 100150.

Duffy, B. E. (2020) Algorithmic Precarity in Cultural Work, *Communication and the Public*, **5**, (3–4), 103–7.

Farrar, A., Grays, L., VanderPol, D. and Cox, A. (2007) A Collaborative Voyage to Improve Students' Career Information Literacy. In *35th National LOEX Library Instruction Conference Proceedings*, 9–13, LOEX.

Fiegen, A. M. (2011) Business Information Literacy: A Synthesis for Best Practices, *Journal of Business and Finance Librarianship*, **16**, 267–88, https://doi.org/10.1080/08963568.2011.606095.

Fleuren, B. P., de Grip, A., Jansen, N. W., Kant, I. and Zijlstra, F. R. (2016) Critical Reflections on the Currently Leading Definition of Sustainable Employability, *Scandinavian Journal of Work, Environment and Health*, **42** (6), 557–60, https://doi.org/10.5271/sjweh.3585.

Forster, M. (2017) *Information Literacy in the Workplace*, Facet Publishing.

Gilbert, S. (2017) Information Literacy Skills in the Workplace: Examining Early Career Advertising Professionals, *Journal of Business and Finance Librarianship*, **22** (2), 111–34, https://doi.org/10.1080/08963568.2016.1258938.

Gill, R. (2020) Graduate Employability Skills Through Online Internships and Projects During the Covid-19 Pandemic: An Australian Example, *Journal of Teaching and Learning for Graduate Employability*, **11** (1), 146–58.

Goe, R., Ipsen, C. and Bliss, S. (2018) Pilot Testing a Digital Career Literacy Training for Vocational Rehabilitation Professionals, *Rehabilitation Counseling Bulletin*, **61** (4), 236–43, https://doi.org/10.1177/0034355217724341.

Goldstein, S. (2015) A Graduate Employability Lens for the SCONUL Seven Pillars of Information Literacy; Incorporating a Review of Sources on How Graduate Employability Relates to Information Know-How, https://www.sconul.ac.uk/sites/default/files/documents/Employability%20lens%20and%20report.pdf.

Goldstein, S. (2016) Information Literacy and Graduate Employability. In Kurbanoğlu, S., Boustany, J., Špiranec, S., Grassian, E., Mizrachi, D., Roy, L. and Çakmak, T. (eds), *Information Literacy: Key to an Inclusive Society, 4th European Conference, ECIL 2016, Prague, Czech Republic, 10–13 October, Revised Selected Papers*, 89–98, Springer.

Guichard, J. (2001) A Century of Career Education: Review and Perspectives, *International Journal for Educational and Vocational Guidance*, **1**, 155–76.

Guichard, J. (2009) Self-Constructing, *Journal of Vocational Behavior*, **75** (3), 251–8.

Hagel, P. A. (2015) *What is Good Practice in the Development, Assessment and Evaluation of Digital Literacy for Graduate Employability?*, Deakin University Library.

Hahn, S. E. and Pedersen, J. (2020) Employers Needs Versus Student Skillsets, *Practical Academic Librarianship: The International Journal of the SLA Academic Division*, **10** (1), 38–53.

Head, A. J., Van Hoeck, M., Eschler, J. and Fullerton, S. (2013) What Information Competencies Matter in Today's Workplace?, *Library and Information Research*, **37** (114), 74–104, https://doi.org/10.29173/lirg557.

Helpman, E., Itskhoki, O. and Redding, S. (2010) Inequality and Unemployment in a Global Economy, *Econometrica*, **78** (4), 1239–83.

Hepworth, M. and Smith, M. (2008) Workplace Information Literacy for Administrative Staff in Higher Education, *The Australian Library Journal*, **57** (3), 212–36.

Hepworth, M. and Walton, G. (2013) *Developing People's Information Capabilities: Fostering Information Literacy in Educational, Workplace and Community Contexts*, Emerald Group Publishing.

Hicks, A. (2019) Mitigating Risk: Mediating Transition Through the Enactment of Information Literacy Practices, *Journal of Documentation*, **75** (5), 1190–210.

Hicks, A. (2021) Negotiating Change: Transition as a Central Concept for Information Literacy, *Journal of Information Science*, 0165551520949159.

Higgins, J., Nairn, K. and Sligo, J. (2010) Vocational Imagination and Labour Market Literacy: Young New Zealanders Making Education-Employment Linkages, *Journal of Vocational Education and Training*, **62** (1), 13–25, http://dx.doi.org/10.1080/13636820903491716.

Hirschi, A. (2018) The Fourth Industrial Revolution: Issues and Implications for Career Research and Practice, *The Career Development Quarterly*, **66** (3), 192–204.

Hollister, C. (2005) Bringing Information Literacy to Career Services, *Reference Services Review*, **33** (1), 104–11, https://doi.org/10.1108/00907320510581414.

Hooley, T. (2012) How the Internet Changed Career: Framing the Relationship Between Career Development and Online Technologies, *Journal of the National Institute for Career Education and Counselling*, **29** (1), 3–12.

Hooley, T. (2017) Developing Your Career: Harnessing the Power of the Internet for 'Digital Career Management', *Development and Learning in Organizations: An International Journal*, **31** (1), 9–11, https://doi.org/10.1108/DLO-07-2016-0066.

Hooley, T. and Sultana, R. (2016) Career Guidance for Social Justice, *Journal of the National Institute for Career Education and Counselling*, **36** (1), 2–11, https://doi.org/10.20856/jnicec.3601.

Hooley, T., Watts, A. G., Sultana, R. G. and Neary, S. (2013) The 'Blueprint' Framework for Career Management Skills: A Critical Exploration, *British Journal of Guidance and Counselling*, **41** (2), 117–31.

Horbach, J. and Rammer, C. (2021) Skills Shortage and Innovation, *Industry and Innovation*, **28**, 1–26, https://doi.org/10.1080/13662716.2021.1990021.

Hoskyn, K., Eady, M. J., Capocchiano, H., Lucas, P., Rae, S., Trede, F. and Yuen, L. (2020) GoodWIL Placements: How COVID-19 Shifts the Conversation About Unpaid Placements, *International Journal of Work-Integrated Learning*, **21** (4), 439–50.

Hunter, I. (2018) Digital Literacy in the Workplace: A View from the Legal Sector, *Business Information Review*, **35** (2), 56–9, https://doi.org/10.1177/0266382118772675.

Inskip, C. (2014) *Information Literacy is for Life, Not Just for a Good Degree: A Literature Review* (Information Literacy Project 26), Chartered Institute of Library and Information Professionals (CILIP).

Jacobson, T. E. and Mackey, T. P. (2013) Proposing a Metaliteracy Model to Redefine Information Literacy, *Communications in Information Literacy*, **7** (2), 84–91.

Johnston, N. (2010) Is an Online Learning Module an Effective Way to Develop Information Literacy Skills?, *Australian Academic and Research Libraries*, **41** (3), 207–18.

Kaeophanuek, S., Jaitip, N.-S. and Nilsook, P. (2018) How to Enhance Digital Literacy Skills Among Information Sciences Students, *International Journal of Information and Education Technology*, **8** (4), 292–7, https://doi.org/10.18178/ijiet.2018.8.4.1050.

Karim, M., Widén, G. and Heinström, J. (2019) Influence of Demographics and Information Literacy Self-Efficacy on Information Avoidance Propensity Among Youth. In *Proceedings of CoLIS, the Tenth International Conference on Conceptions of Library and Information Science, Ljubljana, Slovenia, 16–19 June*, https://informationr.net/ir/24-4/colis/colis1909.html.

Kazi, T. B. (2011) Effects of Globalization on Work and Organizations: Exploring Post-Industrialism, Post-Fordism, Work and Management in the Global Era, *Inquiries Journal*, **3** (12), 1693.

Kidd, J. (2008) Exploring the Components of Career Well-Being and the Emotions Associated With Significant Career Experiences, *Journal of Career Development*, **35** (2), 166–86, https://doi.org/10.1177/0894845308325647.

Kingma, S. (2019) New Ways of Working (NWW): Work Space and Cultural Change in Virtualizing Organizations, *Culture and Organization*, **25** (5), 383–406, https://doi.org/10.1080/14759551.2018.1427747.

Kirton, J. and Barham, L. (2005) Information Literacy in the Workplace, *The Australian Library Journal*, **54** (4), 365–76, https://doi.org/10.1080/00049670.2005.10721784.

Klusek, L. and Bornstein, J. (2006) Information Literacy Skills for Business Careers: Matching Skills to the Workplace, *Journal of Business and Finance Librarianship*, **11** (4), 3–21.

Knight, P. T. and Yorke, M. (2003) Employability and Good Learning in Higher Education, *Teaching in Higher Education*, **8** (1), 3–16, https://doi.org/10.1080/1356251032000052294.

Koltay, T. (2011) The Media and the Literacies: Media Literacy, Information Literacy, Digital Literacy, *Media, Culture and Society*, **33** (2), 211–21, https://doi.org/10.1177/0163443710393382.

Kuijpers, M. and Meijers, F. (2012) Learning for Now or Later? Career Competencies Among Students in Higher Vocational Education in the Netherlands, *Studies in Higher Education*, **37** (4), 449–67.

Kwon, J. B. and Lane, C. M. (2016) *Anthropologies of Unemployment: New Perspectives on Work and its Absence*, Cornell University Press.

Lin-Stephens, S., Kubicki, J. M., Jones, F., Whiting, M. J., Uesi, J. and Bulbert, M. W. (2019) Building Student Employability Through Interdisciplinary Collaboration: An Australian Case Study, *College and Undergraduate Libraries*, **26** (3), 234–51.

Lissitsa, S., Chachashvili-Bolotin, S. and Bokek-Cohen, Y. (2017) Digital Skills and Extrinsic Rewards in Late Career, *Technology in Society*, **51**, 46–55, https://doi.org/10.1016/j.techsoc.2017.07.006.

Lloyd, A. (2005) Information Literacy: Different Contexts, Different Concepts, Different Truths?, *Journal of Librarianship and Information Science*, **37** (2), 82–8, https://doi.org/10.1177/0961000605055355.

Lloyd, A. (2011) Trapped Between a Rock and a Hard Place: What Counts as Information Literacy in The Workplace And How is it Conceptualized?, *Library Trends*, **60** (2), 277–96, https://doi.org/10.1353/lib.2011.0046.

Lloyd, A., Kennan, M. A., Thompson, K. M. and Qayyum, A. (2013) Connecting with New Information Landscapes: Information Literacy Practices of Refugees, *Journal of Documentation*, **69** (1), 121–44, https://doi.org/10.1108/00220411311295351.

Longridge, D., Hooley, T. and Staunton, T. (2013) Building Online Employability: A Guide For Academic Departments, University of Derby.

Lundh, A. H., Limberg, L. and Lloyd, A. (2013) Swapping Settings: Researching Information Literacy in Workplace and in Educational Contexts. In *Eighth International Conference on Conceptions of Library and Information Science (CoLIS8), Copenhagen Denmark, 19–22 August*, Vol. 18, No. 3, University of Sheffield: Department of Information Studies.

Lyons, S. T., Schweitzer, L. and Ng, E. S. (2015) How Have Careers Changed? An Investigation of Changing Career Patterns Across Four Generations, *Journal of Managerial Psychology*, **30** (1), 8–21.

Markless, S. and Streatfield, D. (2007) Three Decades of Information Literacy: Redefining the Parameters. In Andretta, S. (ed.) *Change and Challenge: Information Literacy for the Twenty-First Century*, 15–36, Auslib Press.

Martin, A. and Grudziecki, J. (2006) DigEuLit: Concepts and Tools for Digital Literacy Development, *Innovation in Teaching and Learning in Information and Computer Sciences*, **5** (4), 249–67, https://doi.org/10.11120/ital.2006.05040249.

Mawson, M. and Haworth, A. C. (2018) Supporting the Employability Agenda in University Libraries: A Case Study from the University of Sheffield, *Information and Learning Sciences*, **119** (1/2), 101–8, https://doi.org/10.1108/ILS-04-2017-0027.

McCrindle, M. and Fell, A. (2019) *Understanding Generation Z: Recruiting, Training and Leading the Next Generation*, McCrindle Research Pty Ltd, https://generationz.com.au/wp-content/uploads/2019/12/Understanding_Generation_Z_report_McCrindle.pdf.

McDonald, P. K., Brown, K. A. and Bradley, L. M. (2005) Have Traditional Career Paths Given Way to Protean Ones? Evidence from Senior Managers in the Australian Public Sector, *Career Development International*, **10** (2), 109–29.

McGuinness, S., Pouliakas, K. and Redmond, P. (2017) *How Useful is the Concept of Skills Mismatch?*, IZA Discussion Paper, No 10786, Papers from IZA Institute of Labor Economics.

Meijers, F., Kuijpers, M. and Gundy, C. (2013) The Relationship Between Career Competencies, Career Identity, Motivation and Quality Of Choice, *International Journal for Educational and Vocational Guidance*, **13** (1), 47–66.

Meske, C. and Junglas, I. (2020) Investigating the Elicitation of Employees' Support Towards Digital Workplace Transformation, *Behaviour and Information Technology*, **39** (4), 1–17.

Middleton, L. and Hall, H. (2021) Workplace Information Literacy: A Bridge to the Development of Innovative Work Behaviour, *Journal of Documentation*, **77** (6), 1343–63, https://doi.org/10.1108/JD-03-2021-0065.

Milosheva, M., Hall, H., Robertson, P. and Cruickshank, P. (2022) New Information Literacy Horizons: Making the Case for Career Information Literacy. In Kurbanoğlu, S. et al. (eds) Information Literacy in a Post-Truth Era, ECIL 2021, *Communications in Computer and Information Science*, **1533**, 239–52, https://doi.org/10.1007/978-3-030-99885-1_21.

Mishra, K. E., Wilder, K. and Mishra, A. K. (2017) Digital Literacy in the Marketing Curriculum: Are Female College Students Prepared for Digital Jobs?, *Industry and Higher Education*, **31** (3), 204–11, https://doi.org/10.1177/0950422217697838.

Monge, R. and Frisicaro-Pawlowski, E. (2014) Redefining Information Literacy to Prepare Students for the 21st Century Workforce, *Innovative Higher Education*, **39**, 59–73, https://doi.org/10.1007/s10755-013-9260-5.

Newman, S. and Jahdi, K. (2009) Marketisation of Education: Marketing, Rhetoric and Reality, *Journal of Further and Higher Education*, **33** (1), 1–11.

Nicolson, N. (1990) The Transition Cycle: Causes, Outcomes, Processes and Forms. In Fisher, S. and Cooper, C. L. (eds), *On the Move: The Psychology of Change and Transition*, 83–108, John Wiley.

O'Farrill, R. (2010) Information Literacy and Knowledge Management at Work: Conceptions of Effective Information Use at NHS24, *Journal of Documentation*, **66** (5), 706–33, https://doi.org/10.1108/00220411011066808.

Oakland, J., MacDonald, R. A. and Flowers, P. (2012) Re-Defining 'Me': Exploring Career Transition and the Experience of Loss in the Context of Redundancy for Professional Opera Choristers, *Musicae Scientiae*, **16** (2), 135–47, https://doi.org/10.1177/1029864911435729.

Oakley, S. (2013) Information Literacy Meets Employability, *SCONUL Focus*, **58**, 25–6.

Oeij, P. R., Dhondt, S., Rus, D. and Van Hootegem, G. (2019) The Digital Transformation Requires Workplace Innovation: An Introduction, *International Journal of Technology Transfer and Commercialisation*, **16** (3), 199–207.

Oviawe, J., Uwameiye, R. and Uddin, P. (2017) Bridging Skill Gap to Meet Technical, Vocational Education and Training School-Workplace Collaboration in the 21st Century, *International Journal of Vocational Education and Training Research*, **3** (1), 7–14, https://doi.org/10.11648/j.ijvetr.20170301.12.

Paret, M. (2016) Towards a Precarity Agenda, *Global Labour Journal*, **7** (2), 111–22.

Partridge, H., Edwards, S. and Thorpe, C. (2010) Evidence-Based Practice: Information Professionals' Experience of Information Literacy in the Workplace. In Partridge, H., Edwards, S., Clare, T., Lloyd, A. and Talja, S. (eds), *Practising Information Literacy: Bringing Theories of Learning, Practice and Information Literacy Together*, 273–98, Centre for Information Studies, Charles Sturt University.

Patton, W. and McMahon, M. (2001) *Career Development Programs: Preparation for Lifelong Career Decision Making*, ACER.

Pennington, M., Mosley, E. and Sinclair, R. (2013) AGCAS/AGR Graduate Success Project: An Investigation of Graduate Transitions, Social Mobility and the HEAR, AGCAS, http://agcas.org.uk/assets/1519-Graduate-Success-Project-downloads.

Penuel, W. R., DiGiacomo, D. K., Van Horne, K. and Kirshner, B. (2016) A Social Practice Theory of Learning and Becoming Across Contexts and Time, *Frontline Learning Research*, **4** (4), 30–8.

Prosser, C. A. and Quigley, T. H. (1949) *Vocational Education in a Democracy*, American Technical Society.

Riel, J. and Christian, S. (2012) Charting Digital Literacy: A Framework for Information Technology and Digital Skills Education in the Community College, *SSRN Electronic Journal*, March 2012, 2781161, https://doi.org/10.2139/ssrn.2781161.

Riel, J., Christian, S. and Hinson, B. (2012) *Charting Digital Literacy: A Framework for Information Technology and Digital Skills Education in the Community College*, https://ssrn.com/abstract=2781161.

Rodrigues, R. A. and Guest, D. (2010) Have Careers Become Boundaryless?, *Human Relations*, **63** (8), 1157–75.

Ruthven, I. (2022) An Information Behavior Theory of Transitions, *Journal of the Association for Information Science and Technology*, **73** (4), 579–93.

Sampson, J. P., Osborn, D. S., Kettunen, J., Hou, P.-C., Miller, A. K. and Makela, J. P. (2018) The Validity of Social Media-Based Career Information, *The Career Development Quarterly*, **66** (2), 121–34, https://doi.org/10.1002/cdq.12127.

Saunders, L. (2017) Connecting Information Literacy and Social Justice: Why and How, *Comminfolit*, **11** (1), 55–75, https://doi.org/10.15760/comminfolit.2017.11.1.47.

Savickas, M. L. (2013) Career Construction Theory and Practice. In Brown, S. and Lent, R. (eds), *Career Development and Counseling: Putting Theory and Research to Work*, 144–80, John Wiley and Sons, Inc.

Savickas, M. L., Nota, L., Rossier, J., Dauwalder, J.-P., Duarte, M. E., Guichard, J., Soresi, S., Van Esbroeck, R. and Van Vianen, A. E. (2009) Life Designing: A Paradigm for Career Construction in the 21st Century, *Journal of Vocational Behavior*, **75** (3), 239–50.

Secker, J. (2018) The Revised CILIP Definition of Information Literacy, *Journal of Information Literacy*, **12** (1), 156–8.

Sen, A. (1987) *The Standard of Living*, Cambridge University Press.

Sharun, S. (2021) Practicing Information Literacy: Practicum Students Negotiating Information Practice in Workplace Settings, *The Journal of Academic Librarianship*, **47** (1), 102267.

Sheather, J. and Slattery, D. (2021) The Great Resignation – How Do We Support and Retain Staff Already Stretched to Their Limit?, *BMJ*, **375**, 1–2, https://doi.org/10.1136/bmj.n2533.

Skills Development Scotland (2012) *Career Management Skills Framework for Scotland*, https://www.skillsdevelopmentscotland.co.uk/media/40428/career-management-skills-framework.pdf.

Smith, M., Bell, K., Bennett, D. and McAlpine, A. (2018) *Employability in a Global Context: Evolving Policy and Practice in Employability, Work Integrated Learning, and Career Development Learning*, Graduate Careers Australia.

Smith, S. and Edwards, J. A. (2012) Embedding Information Literacy Skills as Employability Attributes, *ALISS Quarterly*, **7** (4), 22–7.

Sofritti, F., Benozzo, A., Carey, N. and Pizzorno, M. C. (2020) Working Precarious Careers Trajectories: Tracing Neoliberal Discourses in Younger Workers' Narratives, *Journal of Youth Studies*, **23** (8), 1054–70, https://doi.org/10.1080/13676261.2019.1654602.

Southwood, I. (2017) Against Precarity, Against Employability. In Armano, E., Bove, A. and Murgia, A. (eds), *Mapping Precariousness, Labour Insecurity and Uncertain Livelihoods*, 70–81, Routledge.

Succi, C. and Canovi, M. (2020) Soft Skills to Enhance Graduate Employability: Comparing Students and Employers' Perceptions, *Studies in Higher Education*, **45** (9), 1834–47, https://doi.org/10.1080/03075079.2019.1585420.

Sultana, R. G. (2014) Pessimism of the Intellect, Optimism of the Will? Troubling the Relationship Between Career Guidance and Social Justice, *International Journal for Educational and Vocational Guidance*, **14**, 5–19.

Sultana, R. G. (2017) Precarity, Austerity and the Social Contract in a Liquid World. In Hooley, T., Sultana, R. G. and Thomsen, R. (eds.), *Career Guidance for Social Justice: Contesting Neoliberalism*, 63–76, Routledge.

Sultana, R. G. (2021) Authentic Education for Meaningful Work: Beyond 'Career Management Skills'. In Robertson, P., Hooley, T. and McCash, P. (eds), *The Oxford Handbook of Career Development*, 1–19, Oxford University Press.

Sung, Y., Turner, S. L. and Kaewchinda, M. (2013) Career Development Skills, Outcomes, and Hope Among College Students, *Journal of Career Development*, **40** (2), 127–45.

Susskind, D. (2020) *A World Without Work: Technology, Automation and How We Should Respond*, Penguin UK.

Todolí-Signes, A. (2017) The 'Gig Economy': Employee, Self-Employed or the Need for a Special Employment Regulation?, *Transfer: European Review of Labour and Research*, **23** (2), 193–205.

Toven-Lindsey, B. A. (2017) *Digital Literacy and Career Capital: How College Experiences are Preparing Students for the Transition to Work*, PhD dissertation, UCLA, https://escholarship.org/content/qt3234k0v6/qt3234k0v6.pdf.

Towlson, K. and Rush, N. (2013) Carving the Information Literacy Niche within Graduate Employability, *New Review of Academic Librarianship*, **19** (3), 300–15, https://doi.org/10.1080/13614533.2013.825212.

Tsekeris, C. (2018) Industry 4.0 and the Digitalisation of Society: Curse or Cure?, *Homo Virtualis*, **1** (1), 4–12.

Valenduc, G. and Vendramin, P. (2017) Digitalisation, Between Disruption and Evolution, *Transfer: European Review of Labour and Research*, **23** (2), 121–34.

Valentine, K. S. and Kosloski, M. F. (2021) Developing the Key Constructs of Career Literacy: A Delphi Study, *Journal of Research in Technical Careers*, **5**, 1, https://doi.org/10.9741/2578-2118.1095.

van der Klink, J. J., Bültmann, U., Burdorf, A., Schaufeli, W. B., Zijlstra, F. R., Abma, F. I., Brouwer, S. and van der Wilt, G. J. (2016) Sustainable Employability – Definition, Conceptualization, and Implications: A Perspective Based on the Capability Approach, *Scandinavian Journal of Work, Environment and Health*, **42** (1), 71–9, https://doi.org/10.5271/sjweh.3531.

Vrana, R. (2016) Digital Literacy as a Boost Factor in Employability of Students. In *Information Literacy: Key to an Inclusive Society: 4th European Conference Communications in Computer and Information Science, Prague, Czech Republic, 10–13.10.2016, Revised Selected Papers*, 169–78, https://doi.org/10.1007/978-3-319-52162-6_17.

Waters, N., Kasuto, E. and McNaughton, F. (2012) Partnership Between Engineering Libraries: Identifying Information Literacy Skills for a Successful Transition from Student to Professional, *Science and Technology Libraries*, **31** (1), 124–32, https://doi.org/10.1080/0194262X.2012.648104.

Webber, S. and Johnston, B. (2014) Transforming Information Literacy for Higher Education in the 21st Century: A Lifelong Learning Approach. In Hepworth, M. and Walton, G. (eds), *Developing People's Information Capabilities: Fostering Information Literacy In Educational, Workplace and Community Contexts*, 15–30, Emerald.

Wiernik, B. M. and Kostal, J. W. (2019) Protean and Boundaryless Career Orientations: A Critical Review and Meta-Analysis, *Journal of Counseling Psychology*, **66** (3), 280–307.

Williams, D. D. (1999) Human Responses to Change, *Futures*, **31**, 609–16.

Williams, D., Cooper, K. and Wavell, C. (2014) *Information Literacy in the Workplace – An Annotated Bibliography*, Institute for Management, Governance and Society (IMaGeS), in association with InformAll.

Willis, L. and Wilkie, L. (2009) Digital Career Portfolios: Expanding Institutional Opportunities, *Journal of Employment Counseling*, **46** (2), 73–81, https://doi.org/10.1002/j.2161-1920.2009.tb00069.x.

Willson, R. and Given, L. M. (2020) 'I'm in Sheer Survival Mode': Information Behaviour and Affective Experiences of Early Career Academics, *Library & Information Science Research*, **42**, 101014, https://doi.org/10.1016/j.lisr.2020.101014.

Woods, E. and Murphy, E. (2013) Get the Digital Edge: A Digital Literacy and Employability Skills Day for Students, *Journal of Information Literacy*, **7** (2), 156–7, https://doi.org/10.11645/7.2.1856.

Wu, M. S. (2019) Information Literacy, Creativity and Work Performance, *Information Development*, **35** (5), 676–87.

Yam, J. and Skorburg, J. A. (2021) From Human Resources to Human Rights: Impact Assessments for Hiring Algorithms, *Ethics and Information Technology*, **23** (3), 1–13.

Zalaquett, C. P. and Osborn, D. S. (2007) Fostering Counseling Students' Career Information Literacy Through a Comprehensive Career Web Site, *Counselor Education and Supervision*, **46** (3), 162–71, https://doi.org/10.1002/j.1556-6978.2007.tb00022.x.

Zhang, X., Majid, S. and Foo, S. (2010) Environmental Scanning: An Application of Information Literacy Skills at the Workplace, *Journal of Information Science*, **36** (6), 719–32.

Zinser, R. (2003) Developing Career and Employability Skills: A US Case Study, *Education + Training*, **45** (7), 402–10.

7

The Importance of Information Literacy for Work Satisfaction in a World-Wide-Workplace Context

Angela Djupsjöbacka, Jannica Heinström and Eva Österbacka

Introduction

The aim of this chapter is to investigate one central component of workplace information literacy, namely information sharing at the workplace and its impact on work satisfaction.

Workplace information sharing has been defined as the activities of sharing day-to-day work-related information (Savolainen, 2017). In this chapter, we will consider information and knowledge sharing as synonyms, applying the term used in the literature we cite. Both the concepts of information and knowledge sharing essentially describe the activity of sharing (Pilerot, 2012; Savolainen, 2017).

In essence, white-collar work is about creating knowledge. Knowledge sharing among employees is, in turn, key for individual and organisational performance, innovation and efficiency (Ahmad and Karim, 2019). Ferguson and Lloyd (2007) argue that information literacy and knowledge management share many similarities in organisational contexts; both are applied to maximise the use of knowledge in organisations and foster knowledge sharing. Knowledge sharing is, therefore, a key component of information literacy (Leith and Yerbury, 2015).

In previous research, workplace information literacy has largely been investigated in the context of work performance and innovation (for example, Ahmad, Widén and Huvila, 2020). Less is known about the impact of workplace information literacy on socio-emotional aspects of work, such as work satisfaction. Worker wellbeing and work satisfaction are, however, just as important factors of working life as productivity. One key factor in work satisfaction is self-determination (Brunelle and Fortin, 2021). In this chapter, information sharing is investigated as a part of self-determination in the workplace, which in turn results in work satisfaction. This shows that aspects of workplace information literacy, such as information sharing, do not only influence work performance, but also psycho-social factors such as work satisfaction. In Chapter 2, Mård and Hallin refer to Lloyd's (2010) concept of information sharing as a key component of information literacy as a sociomaterial practice. In this chapter, information sharing is investigated as an individual practice related to work satisfaction. These chapters work in tandem, demonstrating that information sharing is part of the sociomaterial practice at work (see Chapter 2) and, at the same time, a factor influencing the individual employee's experiences and activity at work.

In this chapter, information sharing is investigated using data from the *Programme for the International Assessment of Adult Competencies (PIAAC)*. This is a large-scale quantitative dataset, which contains a rich set of worker characteristics, working conditions and employee use of information. This also includes several measures of employee communication as well as problem-solving skills using different sources of information (written, graphical, numerical and technological). PIAAC is therefore highly suited for studying information sharing as well as information literacy generally. This dataset has been used extensively for research in the social sciences, but not by information scientists per se. This may sound surprising, considering that PIAAC contains variables of interest to information scientists. We believe that this is due to a lack of tradition within information science for exploiting pre-collected datasets such as PIAAC and similar large-scale surveys. Information scientists have considerable experience in gathering their own qualitative and quantitative data but have rarely analysed pre-collected survey data in their research. The aim of this study is to respond to this research gap. Research using data collected by large-scale surveys has the potential to give important new insights in the field.

Previous research has mostly explored workplace information literacy (WIL) qualitatively by emphasising how factors in the specific workplace context shape and determine which practices can be regarded as elements of workplace information literacy in that particular workplace context (Lloyd, 2017). When quantitative studies have been conducted, they have for the most part been within a local context, such as a particular workplace (Widén et al., 2021). Studies of WIL across several workplaces and countries have, however, to the authors' knowledge, largely been neglected. Large-scale quantitative studies of WIL are, however, important to further our understanding of factors influencing WIL and the impact of WIL on workplace processes and employees. It has been argued that when studying WIL quantitatively, it is beneficial to focus on one particular aspect of WIL (Widén et al., 2021). In this chapter, we will demonstrate how one aspect of WIL, namely information sharing, can be measured using a large-scale dataset. We investigate these connections further by using self-determination theory, together with other external and individual characteristics to explain work satisfaction in a global context.

In the next section, we describe the self-determination theory and how the theory has been related to information sharing and work satisfaction in previous research. We continue by describing the PIAAC dataset, our method and results, and conclude by discussing our results.

Self-determination theory, information sharing and work satisfaction

Social contexts can catalyse individual development, performance and work satisfaction, around which the self-determination theory is formalised. These positive processes among individuals are fostered by three psychological needs: (1) the need for competence; (2) relatedness; and (3) autonomy. In a work environment, competence refers to workers' capability to accomplish their tasks and achieve their objectives. Relatedness refers to the feeling of belonging and connectedness with others. Autonomy relates to the workers' experience of being able to choose what they are doing and having authority over work processes (Ryan and Deci, 2000; Deci and Ryan, 2014; Meyer, 2014).

The self-determination theoretical framework is based on the idea that motivation facilitates individual functioning. Intrinsic motivation is the highest degree of motivation emanating from the self, which determines interest, enjoyment and satisfaction. Amotivation leads to lack of drive and lower performance, while individuals can reach self-control or awareness also through extrinsic motivation (Ryan and Deci, 2000). Previous research has identified intrinsic motivation and work engagement as factors that increase information sharing (Cabrera, Collins and Salgado, 2006; Kim and Park, 2017; Matzler et al., 2011; van den Hooff and de Leeuw van Weenen, 2004). People who are intrinsically motivated for their work are driven to share more information with their colleagues and are also motivated to reach out for and receive more information.

Previous studies exploring knowledge or information sharing using self-determination theory have explored components of self-determination as factors influencing information sharing. Studies using self-determination theory have found that intrinsic (Suwanti, 2019) and autonomous motivation increase both knowledge sharing intent and behaviour (Stenius et al., 2017; Wu, Wang and Hsieh, 2021). Self-determination theory has not only been used in the context of the employees' own motivation to share knowledge with their colleagues, but also in regards to the perception of colleagues' willingness to share. One study found that autonomy particularly influences the perception of colleagues' willingness to share (Coun, Peters and Blomme, 2019). Interestingly, relatedness, as a central element of self-determination theory, was less influential on knowledge sharing (Coun, Peters and Blomme, 2019). Based on previous studies emphasising close collegial relationships and trust as key factors behind knowledge sharing (Bălău and Utz, 2017; Hau et al., 2013), relatedness could have been expected to be important. Competence as part of self-determination was not influential on knowledge sharing, leaving autonomy as the most influential factor (Coun, Peters and Blomme, 2019). Autonomy is, however, an essential element in today's virtual work environment where knowledge is shared across platforms. In this context, independence and self-determination may increase the value employees give to knowledge sharing (Coun, Peters and Blomme, 2019). Self-determination could, therefore, be particularly important for knowledge sharing in today's digital work environment.

The connection between work satisfaction and knowledge sharing is well-established in previous research. Rafique and Mahmood (2018) report on 28 studies showing the connection between these two factors. The relationship between work satisfaction and knowledge sharing has been explored both from the direction of work satisfaction influencing knowledge sharing and from the direction of knowledge sharing influencing work satisfaction. Most studies have examined this relationship by using work satisfaction as the independent variable, investigating how work satisfaction influences knowledge sharing (for example, Kucharska and Bedford, 2019; Rehman et al., 2014; Suliman and Al-Hosani, 2014). These studies show that employees who are motivated and enjoy their work also tend to share more knowledge with their colleagues (Kucharska and Bedford, 2019; Rehman et al., 2014; Suliman and Al-Hosani, 2014). This finding is comparable to research showing that other measures of wellbeing and stress resilience, such as subjective wellbeing (Bhatti et al., 2020; Chumg, Cooke and Hung, 2015; Wang, Yang and Xue, 2017) and sense of coherence (Heinström et al., 2020), increase information sharing. A contented and stress-free employee is hence more likely to share information than a discontented and over-worked colleague. However, work satisfaction doesn't only influence knowledge sharing. Studies have demonstrated the relationship working in the opposite direction where knowledge sharing increases work satisfaction (for example, Kianto, Vanhala and Heilmann 2016; Saeed, 2016). Here, knowledge sharing is the independent variable and work satisfaction the outcome. An explanation for this is that knowledge sharing is often part of a generally positive work environment where employees are encouraged to share ideas and skills (Rafique and Mahmood, 2018). Such environments, which include active knowledge sharing among colleagues, consequently increase employees' satisfaction at work (Rafique and Mahmood, 2018). A positive workplace atmosphere and collegial support foster knowledge sharing, which in turn results in work satisfaction (Kianto, Vanhala and Heilmann, 2016).

In summary, self-determination theory can be used to explain how work environments can support workers to become healthy, highly creative, effective and productive, and furthermore how workplaces can reduce stress, burnout and turnover (for an overview, see Gagné, 2014). In other words, the degree of satisfaction of the three psychological needs (competence, relatedness and autonomy) has a positive impact on work satisfaction. Information sharing is not necessarily a consequence of, but rather a factor behind self-determination, which in turn is related to work satisfaction.

Below, we describe how a large-scale dataset can be used to investigate information sharing. The aim is to demonstrate that WIL factors may be investigated using large samples. We explain which data was used and the empirical model that we developed. We further explain how the three self-determination needs are measured and how we operationalise information sharing.

Data and variables

We used survey data from the first and second rounds of PIAAC, which targeted adults (16–65 years) from 31 countries in total (Austria, Belgium, Canada, Chile, Cyprus, Czech Republic, Denmark, Estonia, Finland, France, Germany, Greece, Ireland, Israel, Italy, Japan, Korea, Lithuania, Netherlands, New Zealand, Norway, Poland, Russia, Singapore, Slovak Republic, Slovenia, Spain, Sweden, Turkey, the UK and the US). The dataset was collected by OECD in 2011–2012 (first round) and in 2014–2015 (second round), mainly in order to assess adult cognitive performances as measured by literacy, numeracy and technological problem-solving skills. (Since we started this project, a third round has been published.) However, the dataset also contains a rich set of worker and company characteristics. For our purposes, these are the variables of main interest. (See www.oecd.org/skills/piaac/BQ_MASTER. HTM for a complete list of the PIAAC questions and possible responses.)

The dataset gives us the ability to measure the three psychological needs (competence, relatedness and autonomy) as well as a range of external and individual characteristics. In previous research on the relationship between self-determination and knowledge sharing, the measures of self-determination needs have varied substantially (see, for example, van den Broeck et al., 2010; Stenius et al., 2017; Coun, Peters and Blomme, 2019; Suwanti, 2019; Wu, Wang and Hsieh, 2021). Data availability partly determines how the theoretical concepts can be measured. We measure *relatedness* using two variables: *information sharing* and *co-operation*. Information sharing is an index composed of five questions measuring direct information sharing among co-workers, but also factors such as instructing and giving presentations, as well as learning from others. All questions are answered on 5-point scales:

1 F_Q02a: How often does your job involve sharing work-related information with co-workers?
2 F_Q02b: How often does your job involve instructing, training or teaching people, individually or in groups?
3 F_Q02c: How often does your job involve making speeches or giving presentations in front of five or more people?
4 F_Q02e: How often does your job involve advising people?
5 D_Q13a: In your own job, how often do you learn new work-related things from co-workers or supervisors?

The measure covers both aspects of sending and receiving information.

Co-operation is measured as 'time spent co-operating or collaborating with co-workers'. The possible responses are: None of the time; Up to a quarter of the time; Up to half of the time; More than half of the time; or All the time. In the analysis, we treat this as a quantitative variable.

Autonomy is an index composed of six questions, which together capture the degree of flexibility in how and when you perform your work tasks. All questions are answered on 5-point scales:

1 D_Q11a: To what extent can you choose or change the sequence of your tasks?
2 D_Q11b: To what extent can you choose or change how you do your job?
3 D_Q11c: To what extent can you choose or change the speed or rate at which you work?
4 D_Q11d: To what extent can you choose or change your working hours?
5 F_Q03a: How often does your job usually involve planning your own activities?
6 F_Q03: How often does your job usually involve organising your own time?

For both indices (information sharing and autonomy), the responses are summed together with weights determined by principal component analysis. (Cronbach's Alfa is 0.69 and 0.81 for information sharing and autonomy, respectively, suggesting that both measures reach recommended levels for basic/preliminary research (Peterson, 1994)).

The last need, *competence*, is measured both as formal and subjective competence using a set of dummy variables. *Formal competence* is measured by comparing an individual's educational degree to the one formally required for the job. *Subjective competence* is measured by combining two variables (F_Q07a and F_Q07b). The latter question – Do you feel that you need further training in order to cope well with your present duties? – is answered by 'yes' or 'no'. For individuals answering 'no', we measure further with F_Q07a: Do you feel that you have the skills to cope with more demanding duties than those you are required to perform in your current job? (also answered by 'yes' or 'no').

The outcome variable – *work satisfaction* – is measured using the question: All things considered, how satisfied are you with your current job? The response is measured on a 5-point scale, ranging from 'Extremely dissatisfied' to 'Extremely satisfied', with the typical respondent being 'Satisfied'.

In total, the first and second rounds of PIAAC cover roughly 200,000 individuals. For our purposes, some restrictions on this sample are needed. Firstly, we exclude individuals who are currently not working. Among the working population, we include employees as well as self-employed workers. We exclude individuals with missing values on key variables including work satisfaction, information sharing, co-operation, autonomy and gender. We allow for missing values on all other variables and code for these accordingly. For qualitative (factor) variables, we use a dummy for the missing group. For continuous variables, we use a dummy for the 'non-missing group' and the variable of interest (for example, earnings) becomes an interaction term (earnings x non-missing). For some variables, missing values are quite common. This is especially true for monthly earnings and 'type of contract'. This leaves us with a sample covering roughly 130,000 individuals, of whom 55% are men having an average work experience of 18.2 years and 12.9 years of schooling.

Method

The aim is to measure the effects of relatedness, which are measured by information sharing and co-operation, autonomy and competence on work satisfaction. We do this using a set of linear regressions, where we also control a large set of external characteristics, which includes company characteristics, job position and type, as well as working hours and earnings. Furthermore, we also control a set of individual characteristics, such as education, experience and skills. As a general skill measure, we use numeracy (the ability to use, apply, interpret and communicate mathematical information and ideas, www.oecd.org/skills/piaac/piaacdesign) and exploit the first plausible value. The testing is based on item response theory and multiple imputations. Hence, instead of a single measure on numeracy, we have access to ten draws or 'plausible values' from each individual distribution on numeracy. One possibility is to exploit all plausible values in a step-wise estimation procedure. Here, we follow the strategy chosen by some other authors (such as Hanushek et al., 2015) and exploit the first plausible value instead. In all regressions, we use within-country variation only, that is, all regressions include country fixed effects. In the estimations, observations are weighted to account for the country-specific survey designs; on a cross-country level, all countries are weighted equally. Standard errors are estimated using jackknife replicate sampling weights.

Now, since the outcome variable – work satisfaction – is ordinal, one would usually apply ordinal logit or probit techniques. However, these estimators are computationally heavy for large datasets with complex survey designs. The standard errors are estimated using jackknife replicate sampling weights, which here means that a model needs to be re-estimated 80 times (with different weights each time). Considering the size of the dataset and the number of parameters to be estimated, computational time becomes an issue with probit and logit. As this is the case here, we applied adjusted-POLS instead. Adjusted-POLS estimates the latent variable model underlying ordered probit using OLS, with the exception that the variance of the latent variable – as opposed to the error – is constrained to one (Djupsjöbacka, 2020). This is done in two steps. First, we quantify the ordinal scale to fit a standard normal distribution; that is, we calculate your expected value on the latent variable given your ordinal score. For example, if 10% of individuals are 'extremely dissatisfied' with their jobs, they receive a score at -1.755 since $E[Z|Z \leq F^{-1}(0.1)] \approx -1.755$, where Z is a standard normal variable and $F^{-1}(0.1)$ is the inverse of its cumulative distribution function (here, evaluated at the tenth percentile). Secondly, we divide this 'new' quantified variable by its variance. (In both steps, when calculating the expected score and its variance, we adjust for the sampling weights.) This becomes our outcome variable in the regressions, which are then estimated by weighted least squares. Assuming that the latent version of work satisfaction is normally distributed, adjusted-POLS produces consistent estimates for the parameters in the latent variable model (Djupsjöbacka, 2020).

It is worth noting that the estimates cannot be given a causal interpretation. The data is observational in nature, meaning that any estimated effects are likely to also pick up on unobservable heterogeneity. For this data, one of the main concerns is that 'rating norms' may induce artificial correlation between the outcome and the independent variables of main interest. It makes intuitive sense that individuals make use of 'reference points' or 'default options' when answering subjective questions regarding satisfaction, relatedness or autonomy, and that this 'reference point' may vary systematically between individuals and cause artificial correlation across questions. For example, over half of the individuals in our sample answered that they are 'satisfied' with their jobs (which is the second-best option below 'extremely satisfied'). Although speculative, it seems likely that this rather pointy distribution is also a result of many individuals using 'satisfied' as their default option. However, this may not be the case for everyone. For example, being 'extremely satisfied' is the most common answer for individuals from Norway, Sweden and Denmark, with nearly half of respondents giving this answer; for Japanese and South Korean workers, only around 10% perceive themselves as 'extremely satisfied'. Naturally, this considerable difference may reflect a 'real' gap in worker satisfaction, but it is also likely that cultural differences in rating norms contribute.

How large a problem is this? If 'rating norms' are constant within countries, such norms will be picked up by the country dummies entering the model. To the degree 'rating norms' also vary between individuals from the same country, however, estimates are likely to be biased. The size of this bias cannot be determined empirically, but we can make some theoretical inferences. Assume that we have access to the latent variable distributions for two (subjectively scaled) variables denoted by L:

$$L_{ji} = \alpha_i + e_{ji}$$

where j is an index for variable j ($j = 1, 2$) and i is an index for individual i ($i = 1, 2, ..., n$). α_i denotes the reference point for individual i and e_{ji} is the 'real part' of the latent variable. Here, we assume that α_i is independent of e_{ji}. For the sake of simplicity, we also assume that $Var(L_{1i}) = Var(L_{2i})$, which isn't restrictive – it's only a matter of scaling.

In a simple regression – regressing L_2 on L_1 – the bias is proportional to the variance of α as compared to the variance of L (a detailed derivation can be retrieved from the authors upon request):

$$(\hat{\beta}) = \frac{Cov(\alpha_i + e_{1i}, \alpha_i + e_{2i})}{Var(L_{ji})} = \frac{Var(\alpha_i) + Cov(e_{1i}, e_{2i})}{Var(L_{ji})} = \frac{\sigma_a^2 + \beta \sigma_e^2}{\sigma_L^2}$$

$$bias = (\hat{\beta}) - \beta = \frac{\sigma_a^2 + \beta \sigma_e^2}{\sigma_L^2} - \beta = \frac{\sigma_a^2}{\sigma_L^2}(1 - \beta)$$

For example, if $Cov(e_{1i}, e_{2i})=0$ so that $\beta=0$, and if $Var(\alpha_i)$ is making up 20% of the variance in L, then $plim(\hat{\beta}) = 0.2$, hence producing a bias at 0.2 units. As β increases towards 1, this bias decreases towards 0. (Note that is a correlation coefficient as the variances for both variables have been equalised.) Also, the bias may decrease as several variables are included as controls, since you could partially control for the influence of α that way. For example, if the variation could be fully explained by other control variables entering the model (such as gender, schooling or work experience) then that would eliminate the bias in estimating β, that is, the conditional effect of one latent variable on the outcome.

Hence, the existence of 'rating norms' is likely to bias estimates upwards. On the other hand, measurement errors in relatedness, autonomy or competency are likely to bias the estimates towards zero. It is not clear if these problems are significant or negligible. However, the estimates for the effects of relatedness, autonomy and competency are insensitive to including a large set of control variables, which does increase the credence in these estimates.

Results

The data is largely consistent with self-determination theory. When comparing two observably identical individuals – A and B – where A has a job measuring one standard deviation higher on information sharing, co-operation and autonomy than B, then work satisfaction is predicted to be roughly 30% of a standard deviation higher for A. This can be translated into an 8.5-percentile point move up the latent variable distribution on work satisfaction, or a 10 percentage point increase in the probability of being 'extremely satisfied' when fitting a linear probability model to the data. Competence is also of some importance: work satisfaction is predicted to be 0.09 standard deviations higher for those who have the skills to cope, as compared to those lacking in skills (holding all other factors constant). Of equal importance is to not be bored with simple tasks; individuals who feel that they could handle more demanding tasks are no better off than those who feel that they don't possess the skills to cope. These estimates are presented in Table 7.1 opposite. The first specification (1) only includes the self-determination factors of main interest and country fixed effects. The second specification (2) includes the full set of controls, including external and individual characteristics.

Table 7.1 Effects of self-determination factors, external and individual characteristics on work satisfaction, weighted adjusted-POLS

	(1) Coefficient	Se	(2) Coefficient	Se
Self-determination factors				
Information sharing (z)	0.10***	(0.0044)	0.098***	(0.0048)
Co-operation (z)	0.027***	(0.0044)	0.047***	(0.0046)
Autonomy (z)	0.15***	(0.0044)	0.15***	(0.0045)
Qualified on paper (ref. yes):				
Underqualified	-0.17***	(0.0095)	-0.13***	(0.010)
Overqualified	0.076***	(0.012)	0.056***	(0.013)
Have the skills to cope? (ref. no):				
Yes	0.11***	(0.012)	0.088***	(0.012)
x would handle more demand. Tasks	-0.13***	(0.011)	0.098***	(0.011)
Company characteristics				
Sector (ref. private):				
Public			0.044***	(0.013)
Non-profit			0.046*-	(0.023)
Size (ref. very small: 1–10 people):				
Small (11–50 people)			-0.063***	(0.0094)
Medium (51–250 people)			-0.091***	(0.0099)
Large (251–1000 people)			-0.089***	(0.014)
Very large (>1000 people)			-0.036**	(0.015)
Performance (ref. stable):				
Growing			0.043***	(0.0095)
Declining			-0.26***	(0.010)
Industry, $F_{21,59}$ (p-value)			13.78***	(0.000)
Position and job type				
Position (ref. subordinate):				
Manager			-0.023**	(0.0096)
Self-employee			-0.028	(0.021)
x with employees			-0.0022	(0.025)
Skill-level (ref. elementary):				
Semi-skilled blue-collar			0.053***	(0.016)
Semi-skilled white-collar			0.065***	(0.016)
Skilled			0.10***	(0.018)
Physically demanding? (ref. no):				
Somewhat			-0.044***	(0.0092)
Very			-0.089***	(0.010)
Type of contract (ref. indefinite):				
Temporary/Fixed-term			-0.0029	(0.013)
No contract/other			-0.050***	(0.016)
Not stated (don't know)			-0.15***	(0.038)
Working hours and earnings				
Hours per week (ref. 1–10):				
11–20			-0.030	(0.025)
21–30			-0.079***	(0.023)
31–40			-0.064***	(0.024)
41–50			-0.063**	(0.025)
51–60			-0.089***	(0.029)
61–80			-0.14***	(0.037)
81–125			-0.30***	(0.067)
Ln(monthly earnings, PPP$)			0.038***	(0.0057)

Table 7.1 Continued

	(1) Coefficient	Se	(2) Coefficient	Se
Education, experience and skills				
Schooling (years)			-0.0046**	(0.0021)
Numeracy (z)			-0.042***	(0.0047)
Educational area, $F_{10, 70}$ (p-value)			4.39***	(0.000)
Work experience (years)			-0.0066***	(0.0012)
Work experience ^{2}			0.00018***	(0.000027)
Other individual characteristics				
Female			0.019**	(0.0078)
Living with partner			0.026***	(0.0085)
Have children			0.051***	(0.010)
Immigrant			-0.054***	(0.014)
Country, $F_{30, 50}$ (p-value)	196.65	(0.000)	128.35	(0.000)
Observations	131,295		131,295	
R^2	0.117		0.139	

Notes: All observations are weighted to account for the country-specific survey designs; on a cross-country level all countries are weighted equally. Standard errors (in parentheses) are estimated using jackknife replicate sampling weights. (z) denotes that this variable is measured on a standardised scale. 'Missing categories' are left out from the Table. For the factor *Type of contract*, we do, however, include 'not stated (don't know)' in the Table considering the size of this group and the effect size. Some variables are specific to employees (not asked of self-employed workers): *Qualified on paper*, *Performance* and *Type of contract*. Industries are based on ICIC (A, B, ..., U; 21 categories in total with G='Wholesale and retail trade; repair of motor vehicles and motorcycles' being the most common). *Educational area* is based on ISCED and measured in 10 categories (the 9 main categories + 1 for those with only primary or lower secondary schooling, i.e. no specific area). *** $p<0.01$, ** $p<0.05$, * $p<0.1$***

Among the external characteristics, some effects are worth mentioning. Although most effects are rather modest, we do observe that individuals working at declining companies feel distinctly less satisfied with their jobs as compared to those at stable or growing companies. For example, if individual B (from the example above) is working at a growing company – and A at a declining one – that would fully compensate B for his otherwise comparatively poor satisfaction of self-determination needs.

Table 7.1 also reveals that earnings have a surprisingly small effect on work satisfaction. For example, a 50% wage cut is predicted to decrease work satisfaction by merely 0.026 standard deviations – an ignorable effect (Ln(2)*0.038 = 0.026). Self-reported earnings are, however, likely fraught with measurement errors (as well as widespread attrition) and the size of the earnings-effect is best interpreted with caution.

One might also think that the negative effects of schooling and numeracy are surprising. Note, however, that these are conditional effects, that is, conditional on several job characteristics that are endogenous to schooling and numeracy. For example, higher education might allow you to hold a 'better' job than you would have held otherwise, hence increasing your work satisfaction. This pathway would not be captured by the schooling-effect.

It is reasonable to suspect that the effects of information sharing, co-operation, autonomy or competence may differ between social groups. For example, highly educated individuals who are prone to working in intellectually or technically challenging environments, might value autonomy more than workers with routine tasks. Usually, one would associate these high-skilled jobs with a higher requirement on worker creativity and problem-solving, which could be hampered by rigid schedules or strict management. Similar arguments can be made concerning information sharing and competence. We find that the effects of co-operation, autonomy and subjective competence are, indeed, somewhat larger for highly educated individuals, but find no evidence of a difference in the effect of information sharing. For example, workers with tertiary degrees, a one standard deviation increase in autonomy is predicted to increase work satisfaction by 0.20 standard deviations (based on specification (2)). For those without a tertiary degree, this effect is 0.13. Also, we find no evidence of any meaningful heterogeneity in effects based on gender; dropping the self-employed also does not affect the other estimates in any noteworthy way. These estimates are not presented in Table 7.1 but results are available from the authors upon request.

One may ask which is more important in explaining work satisfaction – self-determination (as captured by information sharing, co-operation, autonomy and competence) – or external characteristics (as captured by job position and type, earnings and working hours, as well as other company characteristics). In order to separate the predictive power of different attributes, we perform a Shapley-based R^2-decomposition using specification (2) (Israeli, 2007; see also Nikolova and Cnossen, 2020, who use this approach in a similar setting). This decomposition is based on the concept of the Shapley value known from game theory, where a Shapley value is the marginal contribution of a player in a co-operative game. Consider first that one player at a time enters the game. Each player demands a fair compensation for entering, that is, a compensation equal to the value added by that player. The Shapley value is then the average compensation to a player when considering all possible permutations describing how a set of N players may enter the game. In this case, the players are the variables (or groups of variables) entering the regression model and the payoff is given by R^2. The sum of all such Shapley values equals R^2 for the full model, which is the basis for the decomposition.

This decomposition suggests that self-determination is an important contributor, accounting for 30% of the explained variance in work satisfaction. External characteristics are also of importance, accounting for 23% of the explained variance, while individual characteristics contribute less. For this data, the country of residence is the most important in a statistical sense, which may not be that surprising considering the wide set of countries included. See Figure 7.1 for an illustration of the R^2-decomposition.

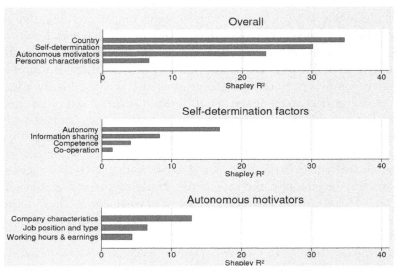

Figure 7.1 *Shapley decomposition of R^2 based on specification (2)*

Among the self-determination factors, autonomy contributes the most to the explained variance in work satisfaction, namely 17%. In other words, being able to decide how you approach a certain work task, or flexibility with regards to working schedules and task sequencing, are all factors that may be of importance in explaining work satisfaction. Information sharing is also a significant contributor, accounting for roughly 8% of the explained variance in work satisfaction, while competence and co-operation contribute less in a statistical sense. In other words, this analysis suggests that a work environment where employees have the opportunity to learn from each other and openly share knowledge and insights may inspire better performances and job satisfaction overall.

Among the external characteristics, company characteristics contribute the most, namely 13%. It is worth noting that this category includes a rather wide set of variables, however (i.e., sector, size, performance and industry;

see Table 7.1). Working hours and earnings, on the other hand, are relatively unimportant, accounting for 4% of the explained variance. One possible interpretation is that individuals mostly ignore financial aspects of their work situation when judging their overall level of satisfaction. This is also the conclusion of Nikolova and Cnossen (2020).

Discussion and conclusion

This chapter demonstrates that information sharing can be investigated using large-scale samples. Information sharing was found to be associated with work satisfaction, which confirms previous results using smaller company-specific samples (Kianto, Vanhala and Heilmann, 2016; Saeed, 2016).

We've shown that self-determination is an important factor behind work satisfaction, accounting for about 30% of the explained variance of satisfaction at work. Self-determination was more important for work satisfaction than external characteristics were, such as company characteristics, job position, working hours and salary, or individual characteristics. Among the self-determination dimensions, autonomy had the strongest impact on work satisfaction, followed by information sharing, competence and co-operation.

Information sharing was measured as part of relatedness. The findings showed that information sharing had a stronger impact on work satisfaction than the other measure of relatedness, co-operation. Information sharing is often conducted as an independent activity, albeit involving colleagues, rather than sharing work tasks, such as in the case of co-operation. As information sharing is often an independent activity, the stronger impact of information sharing on work satisfaction, as compared to co-operation, could therefore be explained by the importance of autonomy for work satisfaction. Today's workplace is increasingly moving towards autonomy and the independence of employees. In this context, WIL also gains importance as facilitating independent work and work satisfaction. On the other hand, co-operation was measured only by one variable, whereas a scale measured information sharing. This means that there could be a measurement bias towards information sharing, as this was a stronger measure.

Viewing information sharing as part of self-determination underlines the complexity of encouraging and developing WIL at the workplace. Self-determination, and hence information sharing, is not a learnt or acquired skill but rather something that springs from favourable conditions that motivate and allow for autonomy in the workplace. This also underlines that WIL should be regarded holistically as encompassing not only skills but also mindset and motivation. Although management may encourage and facilitate information sharing by providing tools and platforms for it, actual information sharing depends on the employees' willingness and motivation to share.

In this chapter, a measure of information sharing was derived from a pre-collected large-scale dataset. The findings underline the cross-contextual impact of information sharing on work satisfaction. Information sharing impacted work satisfaction across a multitude of workplaces, including both white-collar and blue-collar professions. Studies that investigate WIL within a specific context are valuable to show how specific contexts form how WIL is defined within that specific workplace. Investigating WIL across contexts, on the other hand, shows a more abstract yet powerful impact of WIL features. This in turn provides robust evidence for the importance of WIL across workplaces and across countries. Further research should investigate other dimensions of WIL using large-scale data to increase our understanding of its role in workplaces.

References

Ahmad, F. and Karim, M. (2019) Impacts of Knowledge Sharing: A Review and Directions for Future Research, *Journal of Workplace Learning*, **31** (3), 207–30.

Ahmad, F., Widén, G. and Huvila, I. (2020) The Impact of Workplace Information Literacy on Organizational Innovation: An Empirical Study, *International Journal of Information Management*, **51**, 102041.

Bălău, N. and Utz, S. (2017) Information Sharing as Strategic Behaviour: The Role of Information Display, Social Motivation and Time Pressure, *Behaviour and Information Technology*, **36** (6), 589–605.

Bhatti, M. H., Akram, U., Bhatti, M. H., Rasool, H. and Su, X. (2020) Unraveling the Effects of Ethical Leadership on Knowledge Sharing: The Mediating Roles of Subjective Well-Being and Social Media in the Hotel Industry, *Sustainability*, **12** (20), 8333.

Brunelle, E. and Fortin, J. A. (2021) Distance Makes the Heart Grow Fonder: An Examination of Teleworkers' and Office Workers' Job Satisfaction through the Lens of Self-determination Theory, *SAGE Open*, **11** (1), 2158244020985516.

Cabrera, A., Collins, W. C. and Salgado, J. F. (2006) Determinants of Individual Engagement in Knowledge Sharing, *The International Journal of Human Resource Management*, **17** (2), 245–64.

Chumg, H-F., Cooke, L., Fry, J. and Hung, I-H. (2015) Factors Affecting Knowledge Sharing in the Virtual Organisation: Employees' Sense of Well-Being as a Mediating Effect, *Computers in Human Behavior*, **44**, 70–80.

Coun, M. M., Peters, P. C. and Blomme, R. R. (2019) 'Let's Share!' The Mediating Role of Employees' Self-Determination in the Relationship between Transformational and Shared Leadership and Perceived Knowledge Sharing among Peers, *European Management Journal*, **37** (4), 481–91.

Deci, E. L. and Ryan, R. M. (2014) The Importance of Universal Psychological Needs for Understanding Motivation in the Workplace. In Gagné, M. (ed.), *The Oxford Handbook of Work Engagement, Motivation, and Self-Determination Theory*, 13–32, Oxford University Press.

Djupsjöbacka, A. (2020) *Human Capital: Formation, Maintenance and Transmission*, Åbo Akademi University Press.

Ferguson, S. and Lloyd, A. (2007) Information Literacy and the Leveraging of Corporate Knowledge. In Ferguson, S. (ed.), *Libraries in the Twenty-First Century: Mapping Future Directions in Information Services*, 221–39, Centre for Information Studies.

Gagné, M. (ed.) (2014) *The Oxford Handbook of Work Engagement, Motivation, and Self-Determination Theory*, Oxford University Press.

Hanushek, E. A., Schwerdt, G., Wiederhold, S. and Woessmann, L. (2015) Returns to Skills around the World: Evidence from PIAAC, *European Economic Review*, **73**, 103–30.

Hau, Y. S., Kim, B., Lee, H. and Kim, Y. G. (2013) The Effects of Individual Motivations and Social Capital on Employees' Tacit and Explicit Knowledge Sharing Intentions, *International Journal of Information Management*, **33** (2), 356–66.

Heinström, J., Ahmad, F., Huvila, I. and Ek, S. (2020) Sense of Coherence as Influencing Information Sharing at the Workplace, *Aslib Journal of Information Management*, **73** (2), 201–20.

Israeli, O. (2007) A Shapley-Based Decomposition of the R-Square of a Linear Regression, *The Journal of Economic Inequality*, **5**, 199–212.

Kianto, A., Vanhala, M. and Heilmann, P. (2016) The Impact of Knowledge Management on Job Satisfaction, *Journal of Knowledge Management*, **20** (4), 621–36.

Kim, W. and Park, J. (2017) Examining Structural Relationships Between Work Engagement, Organizational Procedural Justice, Knowledge Sharing, and Innovative Work Behavior for Sustainable Organizations, *Sustainability*, **9** (2), 205.

Kucharska, W. and Bedford, D. A. (2019) Knowledge Sharing and Organizational Culture Dimensions: Does Job Satisfaction Matter?, *Electronic Journal of Knowledge Management*, **17**, 1–18.

Leith, D. and Yerbury, H. (2015) Organizational Knowledge Sharing, Information Literacy and Sustainability: Two Case Studies from Local Government. In Kurbanoğlu, S., Boustany, J., Špiranec, S., Grassian, E., Mizrachi, D. and Roy, L. (eds), *Information Literacy: Moving Toward*

Sustainability, ECIL 2015, *Communications in Computer and Information Science*, **552**, 13–21, Springer.

Lloyd, A. (2010) Framing Information Literacy as Information Practice: Site Ontology and Practice Theory, *Journal of Documentation*, **66** (2), 245–58, https://doi.org/10.1108/00220411011023643.

Lloyd, A. (2017) Learning Within for Beyond: Exploring a Workplace Information Literacy Design. In Forster, M. (ed.), *Information Literacy in the Workplace*, 97–112, Facet Publishing.

Matzler, K., Renzl, B., Mooradian, T., von Krogh, G. and Mueller, J. (2011) Personality Traits, Affective Commitment, Documentation of Knowledge, and Knowledge Sharing, *The International Journal of Human Resource Management*, **22** (2), 296–310.

Meyer, J. P. (2014) Employee Commitment, Motivation, and Engagement: Exploring the Links. In Gagné, M. (ed.), *The Oxford Handbook of Work Engagement, Motivation, and Self-Determination Theory*, 33–49, Oxford University Press.

Nikolova, M. and Cnossen, F. (2020) What Makes Work Meaningful and Why Economists Should Care About It, *Labour Economics*, **65**, 101847.

Peterson, R. A. (1994) A Meta-Analysis of Cronbach's Coefficient Alpha, *Journal of Consumer Research*, **21** (2), 381–91.

Pilerot, O. (2012) LIS Research on Information Sharing Activities – People, Places, or Information, *Journal of Documentation*, **68** (4), 559–81.

Rafique, G. M. and Mahmood, K. (2018) Relationship Between Knowledge Sharing and Job Satisfaction: A Systematic Review, *Information and Learning Sciences*, **119** (5–6), 295–312.

Rehman, M., Mahmood, A. K., Salleh, R. and Amin, A. (2014) Job Satisfaction and Knowledge Sharing Among Computer and Information Science Faculty Members: A Case of Malaysian Universities, *Research Journal of Applied Sciences, Engineering and Technology*, **7** (4), 839–48.

Ryan, R. M. and Deci, E. L. (2000) Self-Determination Theory and the Facilitation of Intrinsic Motivation, Social Development, and Well-Being, *American Psychologist*, **55** (1), 68–78.

Saeed, M. S. (2016) The Impact of Job Satisfaction and Knowledge Sharing on Employee Performance, *Journal of Resources Development and Management*, **21**, 16–23.

Savolainen, R. (2017) Information Sharing and Knowledge Sharing as Communicative Activities, *Information Research*, **22** (3), http://InformationR.net/ir/22-3/paper767.html.

Stenius, M., Haukkala, A., Hankonen, N. and Ravaja, N. (2017) What Motivates Experts to Share? A Prospective Test of the Model of Knowledge Sharing Motivation, *Human Resource Management*, **56** (6), 871–85.

Suliman, A. and Al-Hosani, A. A. (2014) Job Satisfaction and Knowledge Sharing: The Case of the UAE, *Business Management and Economics*, **2** (2), 24–33.

Suwanti, S. (2019) Intrinsic Motivation, Knowledge Sharing, and Employee Creativity: a Self-Determination Perspective, *International Journal of Scientific & Technology Research*, 8 (7), 623–8.

van den Broeck, A., Vansteenkiste, M., Witte, H., Soenens, B. and Lens, W. (2010) Capturing Autonomy, Competence, and Relatedness at Work: Construction and Initial Validation of the Work-Related Basic Need Satisfaction Scale, *Journal of Occupational and Organizational Psychology*, 83 (4), 981–1002.

van den Hooff, B. and de Leeuw van Weenen, F. (2004) Committed to Share: Commitment and CMC Use as Antecedents of Knowledge Sharing, *Knowledge and Process Management*, **11** (1), 13–24.

Wang, J., Yang, J. and Xue, Y. (2017) Subjective Well-Being, Knowledge Sharing and Individual Innovation Behavior: The Moderating Role of Absorptive Capacity, *Leadership & Organization Development Journal*, **38** (8), 1110–27.

Widén, G., Ahmad, F., Nikou, S., Ryan, B. and Cruickshank, P. (2021) Workplace Information Literacy: Measures and Methodological Challenges, *Journal of Information Literacy*, **15** (2), 26–44.

Wu, S.-Y., Wang, W.-T. and Hsieh, Y.-H. (2021) Exploring Knowledge Sharing Behavior in Healthcare Organizations: An Integrated Perspective of the Empowerment Theory and Self-Determination Theory, *Kybernetes*, **51** (8), 2529–53.

8
Entrepreneurs' Digital Information Sources Selection: A Perspective on the Impact of Information Literacy and Generational Differences

Thao Orrensalo, Malin Brännback and Shahrokh Nikou

Introduction

The emergence of digitalisation has transformed the ways entrepreneurs seek and acquire information from available digital information sources. The vast amount of digital information sources offers unprecedented opportunities to entrepreneurs and small- and medium-sized enterprises (SMEs) to enhance their business performance. However, acknowledging the benefits that digital information sources provide, especially in terms of quality and accessibility, entrepreneurs should develop their literacy skills, such as information literacy (IL hereinafter). In an information-based society, IL is defined as the necessary skills and competencies to find, handle and use information and individuals are required to acquire such skills. Some authors argue that IL is the most important literacy in our contemporary society as it enables us to achieve both personal and professional goals, as well as supporting economic development (Virkus, 2011). Besides IL, social norms, 'the influence of peers' (Brännback et al., 2018) and types of tasks may also affect entrepreneurs' perception of digital information sources and, in turn, their digital information sources selection (Nikou et al., 2020). Moreover, the continuous expansion of digitalisation has been associated with a substantial reduction of entry barriers for entrepreneurs, in particular, access to critical business information (Kristiansen, Furuholt and Wahid, 2003).

For example, digitalisation enables and improves entrepreneurs' access to information through digital information sources, such as social media and web-based platforms (Guan et al., 2017; Jansen, van de Wijngaert and Pieterson, 2010; Orrensalo and Nikou, 2021a). The use of digital information sources (Ivanytska et al., 2021), reduces the cost of infrastructure, time constraints and human labour (Dinet, 2014). Information acquired from digital sources allows entrepreneurs to reach relevant, accurate and timely information for their business needs (Chatterjee, Dutta Gupta and Upadhyay, 2020), which leads to an increase in entrepreneurs' understanding of the market environments that support their activities, decision-making process and the business growth and outcome (Sahut, Iandoli and Teulon, 2021). Although literature has shown the benefits of digital information sources for entrepreneurial activities to compete in high pressure and dynamic environments (Sahut, Iandoli and Teulon, 2021), current research does not present a comprehensive conceptual model that examines the entrepreneurs' digital information sources selection. The selection of digital information sources may not happen in isolation but requires the identification of factors influencing such behaviour (for example, Zaremohzzabieh et al., 2016). In addition, IL and other factors – like characteristics of information sources and type of tasks – have shown their relevance and significance in examining entrepreneurs' digital information source selection in the context of digitalisation (for example, Bolek et al., 2018; Mothe and Nguyen-Thi, 2013; Nikou et al., 2020).

We argue that entrepreneurs' digital information source selection is a critical business issue, since in the digital era, where competition is intense, entrepreneurs' competencies on how to locate appropriate channels to conduct business activities is critical to their growth and success. Simić, Slavković and Ognjanović (2020) claim that in the age of information explosion, we need to assess workplaces' readiness in their journey towards digital transformation, particularly in terms of information management. Therefore, considering the importance of literacy skills, the objective of this chapter is to explore the impact of factors that influence entrepreneurs' digital information sources selection, with the focus on the gender and generational differences.

The research question guiding this chapter is: *'What factors influence entrepreneurs' digital information sources selection and is there any difference between the age and gender when selecting digital information sources?'*

To answer the research question, a research conceptual model demonstrating the determinants of entrepreneurs' digital information sources selection has been developed. In the proposed model, IL, social norms and the type of tasks have been conceptualised to influence characteristics of information sources (the accessibility and quality of an information source) and consequently influencing entrepreneurs' digital information sources selection. The analysis goes further as it assesses the significance of these factors from generational and gender perspectives. To examine and assess the proposed model, a survey questionnaire has been developed and the final dataset is composed of 145 Finnish entrepreneurs. The data analysis was performed through Structural Equation Modelling (SEM).

This chapter aims to make the following contributions: firstly, to better understand the factors influencing entrepreneurs' digital information sources selection; and, second, to provide in-depth analysis and rich theoretical insights towards understanding entrepreneurs' digital information source selection.

The next section describes the theoretical background of entrepreneurs' digital information sources selection and develops the hypotheses. We then describe the sample and empirical methods. Finally, we present the results and discuss the main findings, theoretical contributions and managerial implications and make suggestions for future research.

Literature review

Entrepreneurs' digital sources selection

Due to the development of digital technologies, the distribution and availability of information have increased significantly within the last decade. This has further complicated the dynamics of entrepreneurs' information sources selection behaviours (Sahut, Iandoli and Teulon, 2021). Moreover, Bronstein (2010) highlighted that the advancement of technologies, access to a full spectrum of contemporary information technology and the explosion of digital information positively influence information users in source preferences. Recent studies, for example, Mack, Marie-Pierre and Redican (2017) and Yuldinawati, van Deursen and van Dijk (2018), also pointed to the complexity and uniqueness of the intention to use digital information sources in an entrepreneurship context. Understanding the impact of digitalisation on the selection of digital information sources, along with the role of different factors, is critical because it represents the primary stage for entrepreneurs to reach the required information efficiently and effectively to fulfil their information needs and complete their tasks (Roetzel, 2019). However, researchers like Motoyama, Goetz and Han (2018) and Mothe and Nguyen-Thi (2013) have expressed their concern regarding a scarcity of empirical contributions in the literature focusing on the factors that influence entrepreneurs' digital information sources selection.

Bringing attention to this gap in the literature, recent studies (for example, van Laar et al., 2017) emphasised the importance of entrepreneurs' information skills such as IL in an information-based society. The authors pointed out that IL positively impacts both the exploration (information processing capability) and exploitation (information acquisition, evaluation and synthesis capabilities for a better understanding of the distribution and utilisation of available resources) of information. In addition to IL, studies have also identified several factors, such as characteristics of information sources, social norms and the type of tasks, that can impact entrepreneurs' digital information sources selection (Nikou et al., 2020). Susanto and Aljoza (2015) pointed out that characteristics of information sources include their accessibility and quality and that information seekers (entrepreneurs) form their perception of digital information sources based on the usefulness, ease, social cost and risk associated with the use of digital sources. In addition, Xie and Joo (2010) argued that the type of task has a significant influence on the source selection. For example, an urgent task may require immediate access to information, while other tasks may not be urgent and can wait. Social norms additionally influence entrepreneurs' behaviours as they represent a homogenous group. Calvo-Porral and Pesqueira-Sanchez (2020) argued that people in different age groups can vary in the way they select digital information sources. In other words, young entrepreneurs who are familiar with digital devices and technology might be more confident in selecting digital information sources, whereas the older generation of entrepreneurs, who are still adopting digital technology and trying to adapt to digitalisation, might find it more difficult (Pathak, Xavier-Oliveira and Laplume, 2013). In addition, the gender perspective may interfere with the differences in the digital information source selection process (Jansen, van de Wijngaert and Pieterson, 2010). This proposes a pattern of gender and generational differences in individuals' perception of digital information sources selection and the use of such sources.

In the digital age, access to information is critical for business survival and growth (Orrensalo and Nikou, 2021b). The use of information is an essential part of business success, controlling business operations and achieving business goals. Conroy and Weiler (2019) stated that high-quality information supports managerial decisions and improves organisational performance. Entrepreneurs need to continuously learn and update information to assure their competitiveness. For example, Najat (2017) emphasised the necessity of customers' information to strengthen business models, products and services and to meet customers' requirements and expectations. In addition, Sagarik et al. (2018) pointed out that regulatory information, such as tax, business registration and business policy, is essential to the entrepreneurial process, especially for newly established businesses. A constant update of such information helps promote entrepreneurial business success. Information is important for entrepreneurs' needs at all stages of the entrepreneurial lifecycle.

Entrepreneurs seek and acquire information from various sources, employing different mediums (for example, digital tools and applications) to solve their information needs (Jansen, van de Wijngaert and Pieterson, 2010). In this regard, information source selection is a significant part of information seeking behaviour (Case, 2012). Purposeful information seeking begins when a seeker selects information sources by applying multiple criteria to gain value and prioritise different information sources (Bronstein, 2010). Due to the growth of digital information sources in entrepreneurship, researchers have become increasingly interested in this topic (Ardakani and Avorgani, 2021; Orrensalo and Nikou, 2021a). Such understanding contributes to the development of IL education and the provision of information services, which increases the efficiency of entrepreneurs' information behaviour.

The information source selection process is a complex and important step in the business operation, especially for entrepreneurs when considering the limited resources, risks associated with source choices and the business environment (Dinet, 2014). Limited resources, especially human resources, force entrepreneurs to deal with the information need on their own (Eze et al., 2018). Therefore, it is crucial that they direct themselves to the appropriate sources that will provide sufficient information to solve their business problem. By doing so, the process of identifying trends, visualising bottlenecks and obtaining insights for business decisions will be effective and efficient. Entrepreneurs can then focus on the most pressing issues and better align their organisations to the turbulent and ambiguous environmental conditions (Sahut, Iandoli and Teulon, 2021; Zaremohzzabieh et al., 2016).

According to the findings of multiple studies, digital information sources have profoundly impacted how entrepreneurs discover answers to their business demands and acquire information. For example, Jansen, van de Wijngaert and Pieterson (2010) discuss how people prefer online information sources because of the financial and time-saving advantages compared to traditional sources, such as phone calls, libraries and printed materials. Entrepreneurs select a digital information source based on its ability to enhance the productivity of information access (Sahut, Iandoli and Teulon, 2021), the efficiency of entrepreneurial action and new venture creation (Jaska and Werenowska, 2018), and the entrepreneurs' professional growth (Hafeez et al., 2019; Zamani and Mohammadi, 2018). Studies also show a positive relationship between the preference for digital information sources and the ease of conducting business, as well as the expansion of this trend from urban to rural areas with the growth of the availability and accessibility of digital information and technology (Guan et al., 2017; Sagarik et al., 2018).

However, entrepreneurs will not utilise all available information sources. This is because of restrictions on time and processing capacity or lack of literacy skills. They will instead use what they perceive to be the most accessible information, while minimising the cost. Entrepreneurs' selection of information sources can be influenced by various factors and this chapter will examine these with a focus on the differences between genders and generations.

Theoretical background and hypotheses development

According to Savolainen (1995, 267), the act of selecting and using an information source varies depending on different criteria, such as the valuation or attitude towards the problem, social capital, material capital, cultural and cognitive capital, and the current state of life. Other studies also identified several factors associated with the users' information source selection. Xie and Joo (2010) indicate that multiple factors co-interfere with the users' choice of information sources. In the following, we will show and discuss some of these factors.

Information literacy

There is a significant and growing body of research (for example, Orrensalo and Nikou, 2021a; Zhang, Majid and Foo, 2010) that has addressed entrepreneurs' IL skills when selecting digital information sources. The concept of IL originally refers to the ability to think and reason logically to solve complex, open-ended problems, a skillset that contributes directly to the ability to conduct searches actively and successfully (Malafi, Liu and Goldstein, 2017). It further expands towards the skills needed to use digital materials and tools to solve an information need in the digital age (Rayna and Striukova, 2021). Ng (2012) added that in the digital information environment, IL also covers critical thinking and the capability to efficiently search, identify and evaluate digital information sources. It enables information seekers to evaluate and make a knowledgeable assessment about an information source's accessibility and quality (Kim and Sin, 2011).

Information is currently exposed to digital sources that are generated and distributed more quickly and easily than ever before. The number of available digital information sources is triggering the uncertainty and confusion of entrepreneurs when dealing with the quality of information sources, as well as their capacity to process risks like information overload, information avoidance and fake news (Karia, Bathula and Gaur, 2020; Roetzel, 2019). This complex situation requires entrepreneurs to raise their awareness in identifying and selecting what source is suitable and ensure their efficiency in accessing and using information (Sariwulan et al., 2020). Information literacy has a positive influence on other important entrepreneurs' activities: opportunity recognition; exploratory innovation (information processing capability and market awareness); and exploitation innovation (information acquisition, evaluation and synthesis capabilities for a better understanding of the distribution and utilisation of available resources, as well as the potential areas of improvement) (Ahmad, Widén and Huvila, 2020; Erdogan et al., 2019). Bolek et al. (2018) connect IL with the lifelong learning process of entrepreneurs, which is important for them to remain on the cutting edge in a dynamic and competitive digital environment. Researchers like Eze et al. (2018) and Dulle, Gichohi and Onyancha (2017) also noted that a major barrier to the efficient utilisation of information resources, especially digital resources, is the relatively low level of IL skills. Insufficient IL skills can lead to entrepreneurs' poor evaluation of the affordability, reliability and accessibility of information sources (Eze et al., 2018). All in all, this implies that IL skills can and will influence entrepreneurs' perception of the characteristics of information sources and consequently the selection of digital information sources, hence:

H1: *Information literacy significantly influences how entrepreneurs perceive the characteristics of information sources.*

Social norms

Researchers like Xie and Joo (2010) consider social norms as an effective factor that motivates or demotivates the information seekers' behaviours in selecting and using an information source. According to Lapinski and Rimal (2005), social norms refer to the informal rules that are accepted and used as guidance for the perception and behaviour of members in a group. The concept of social norms has been widely employed in social sciences, especially when examining technology adoption generally and digital information source selection particularly (for example, Naeem, 2020; Nikou, Mezei and Brännback, 2018; Nguyen and Luu, 2020). To elucidate this, an individual's attitude and choice to utilise e-government services are heavily impacted by the expectations and suggestions of others around them, such as their family members, friends and colleagues (Belanche Gracia, Casaló Ariño and Flavián Blanco, 2012). In an entrepreneurial context, Nguyen and Luu (2020) illustrate that entrepreneurs use technology under the influence of their stakeholders, like partners, customers and suppliers. This statement is similar to the finding from other researchers, like Raymond, Julien and Ramangalahy (2001), that social surroundings have a relation to the expectations or opinions of entrepreneurs' perceptions of digital information sources in terms of their usefulness and ease of use, hence:

H2: *Social norms significantly influence entrepreneurs' perceptions of the characteristics of information sources.*

Type of tasks

The other factor that influences information source selection behaviour is the type of tasks. It represents different dimensions of a task including its complexity, its stage, its nature and its subject (Li et al., 2019). For instance, the type of tasks can be classified according to complexity, such as automatic information processing tasks, normal (routinised) information processing tasks, normal decision tasks and known-genuine decision tasks (Byström, 2002). The complex work tasks might require a different approach to information sources (Byström and Järvelin, 1995). The type of task can also be categorised based on the themes of information required, such as customer information, administrative information, partnership information, and so on. Many researchers have shown that based on the type of tasks, an individual will perceive the characteristics of information sources differently, thus influencing their information source selection, their decision-making process and completing the tasks (Raymond, Julien and Ramangalahy, 2001; Söderlund and Lundin, 2017; Woudstra and van den Hooff, 2008). To illustrate, existing literature has revealed entrepreneurs' preference for using their social capital to seek for sensitive, timely, relevant and critical information, which they might not get easy access to from other sources (Soetanto, 2017); hence:

H3: *The type of tasks significantly influences entrepreneurs' perceptions of the characteristics of information sources.*

Characteristics of information sources

When it comes to the perception of information sources, researchers like Agarwal, Xu and Poo (2011), Woudstra, van den Hooff and Schouten (2016) and Xie and Joo (2010) focus on the two main elements of the source: accessibility and quality. The accessibility of the information source represents the effort and time required to access the source (for example, availability, convenience and comprehensiveness), the psychological perspectives of the user (for example, ease-of-use, familiarity and understandability) and the monetary cost. The quality of information sources covers relevance, reliability, credibility, trustworthiness and authoritativeness (Zhang, 2013). Stohl, Stohl and Leonardi (2016) argue that the quality of an information source depends heavily on who produces and provides the information. Together, these characteristics of the information source become the primary determination for entrepreneurs when selecting and using a particular source. This impact of these characteristics on the source selection refers to the cost–benefit principle. This principle suggests that information seekers tend to select and use information sources that require the least cost and effort (accessibility characteristic) to access but still provide more benefits (quality characteristic) (Case, 2012; Woudstra, van den Hooff and Schouten, 2016).

For entrepreneurs, due to the high pressure and limited resources of their working environment, the efficiency of an information source reflected through its characteristics is valuable. Haase and Franco (2011) highlight entrepreneurs' preferences for a digital information source when handling business decisions due to accessibility and relevance and how it helps them overcome the traditional barriers caused by resource constraints. Supporting this argument, Dinet (2014) further argues that entrepreneurs' use of digital information sources for technology advancement significantly reduces the amount of manual work and time spent on retrieving the information. Other researchers, like Guan et al. (2017), mention unfamiliarity with digital tools and platforms. Truong, Teruaki and Yosuke (2016) refer to the cost of digital information sources hindering entrepreneurs in rural areas, hence:

H4: *Entrepreneurs' perceptions of the characteristics of information sources influence digital information sources selection.*

As mentioned, the aim of this chapter is to explore the impact of factors, including IL, the type of tasks and social norms, on the characteristics of information sources, as well as how the characteristics of information sources influence digital information sources selection among entrepreneurs. Previous studies have presented a potential direct relationship between entrepreneurs' literacy skills and entrepreneurs' perceptions of characteristics of information sources (Eze et al., 2018). Moreover, they also illustrate how the type of tasks and social norms affect these perceptions, thus motivating entrepreneurs to use digital information sources. Figure 8.1 on the next page proposes the research model to capture the relationships depicted. We will evaluate the model through empirical research and use gender and age as moderating variables (Jansen, van de Wijngaert and Pieterson, 2010; Nikou, Brännback and Widén, 2019).

Methodology
Study design and sampling
This chapter adopts a quantitative approach to data collection and hypotheses testing. This approach is increasingly popular in social science for predicting behavioural intention, in a similar vein to in the field of entrepreneurship research (see, for example, Ayeh, Au and Law, 2013; Chao, 2019; Nikou, Brännback and Widén, 2019). A survey instrument was developed for the data collection based on established measures of constructs

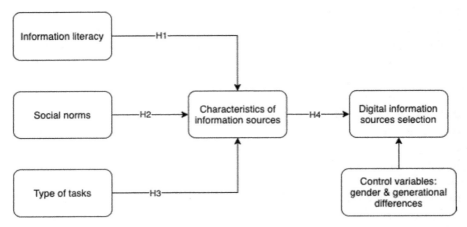

Figure 8.1 *Proposed conceptual model*

from different information behaviour literature on social norms (Belanche Gracia, Casaló Ariño and Flavián Blanco, 2012); IL (Kurbanoğlu, Akkoyunlu and Umay, 2006); characteristics of information sources, such as accessibility and quality (Xie and Joo, 2010); the type of tasks (Bronstein, 2010); and entrepreneurs' digital information sources selection (Ayeh, Au and Law, 2013). If necessary, the measures were slightly modified to make them applicable to the context of the study. Participants answered survey questions using seven-point scales, with anchors ranging from strongly disagree (1) to strongly agree (7). Each scale presents a pair of bipolar adjectives describing the attitudes of the respondents on the influence of social norms (3 items), characteristics of information sources (5 items), the type of tasks (4 items), IL (6 items) and digital information sources selection (6 items).

The research was conducted in Finland. The survey questionnaire was available through the web, using the Webropol. Furthermore, we sent an invitation to potential participants via LinkedIn private messages, as well as via e-mails to different groups of entrepreneurial organisations, including Upgraded Finland, Tribe Tampere, Boost Turku, the Hub, VietES, Nuoret Yrittäjät, Young Entrepreneurs of Finland and Startup Finland. We also approached entrepreneurs and invited them to join our survey through different entrepreneurial events organised by Kiuas, Boost Turku and NewCo Helsinki. The survey was voluntarily filled by entrepreneurs online. The questionnaire consists of questions on the participants' demographic background, their frequency of use of digital tools and information sources and their self-reported proficiency. The study developed the survey questions based on related literature and finalised the questions through two pilot tests.

Sample characteristics

A total of 145 entrepreneurs in Finland participated in the study; 27% of them were female and 73% were male entrepreneurs. Sixty-nine participants were born after 1980 and 76 were born before 1980. Limited liability companies make up the majority (79%) of the type of entrepreneurial ventures included. Most of the participants were originally from Finland and approximately 19% were immigrant entrepreneurs. Regarding academic background, 72% of the participants had higher education degrees (bachelor's or master's), around 11% attended college but had not graduated, and 7% had a high school diploma or equivalent. Most of them use digital devices, especially mobile phones, laptops and the internet, almost all the time. For digital information sources, search engines (Google, Bing, Yahoo) seem to be the most popular sources. 84.4% of the respondents reported using search engines several times a day, followed by almost 70% using social media (Facebook, Instagram, Twitter, LinkedIn, YouTube). Remarkably, e-government websites and e-libraries were the least used sources. The results also showed that most of the respondents considered themselves proficient with their internet skills, with six items including searching information through search engines (mean = 6.5), downloading/sending a file (mean = 6.3), opening an attachment (mean = 6.4), sharing and asking for information on social media (mean = 6.1), and navigating information on a website (mean = 6.4). The questions were rated, with 1 being not proficient at all, to 7 being very proficient. In addition, respondents' competencies with using digital information sources were measured. The results showed that search engines had the highest mean value (mean = 6.4), followed by social media (mean = 6.0), organisational/institutional websites (mean = 5.9), e-newspapers (mean = 5.1), e-government websites and forums (mean = 4.9), forums (mean = 4.8) and e-libraries (mean = 4.2).

Study analysis

For data analysis, the research applied Structural Equation Modelling (SEM) using SmartPLS 3.0. In the context of social science research, this method is appropriate due to its ability to determine the construct validity of the proposed model's variables (Gefen, Straub and Boudreau, 2000). SEM is a statistical technique that allows researchers to simultaneously test and estimate the hypothesised relationships given in the conceptual model by depicting the pattern of relationships between multiple dependent and independent variables (Tarka, 2018). This approach is also known as *path analysis* and *covariance structure analysis*. It is suitable for constructing concepts and theories and elucidating a systematic follow-up for further research questions without using a variety of statistical methods (Gefen,

Straub and Boudreau, 2000; Tabachnick and Fidell, 2013). Moreover, this approach allows studying the measurement errors of the observed variables as an integral part of the model, thus ensuring more rigorous analysis (Ringle, Sarstedt and Straub, 2012).

Results

Measurement model

Confirmatory factor analysis (CFA) was employed to assess the measurement model and test the reliability and validity of the latent variables. We used three criteria to examine the reliability and validity of the conceptualised research model: Cronbach's alpha (α); composite reliability (CR); and average variance extracted (AVE) (Hair et al., 2019). We measured Cronbach's alpha for the internal consistency of latent constructs. The ideal value should be higher than 0.70 (Hair et al., 2019) and all our Cronbach's alpha values meet this standard. The result of CR is used for measuring the internal consistency reliability and is recommended to be above 0.70. Our CR values range from 0.886 to 0.906. Finally, AVE reflects the convergence among a set of items in a latent construct. Our AVE scores vary from 0.612 to 0.729, which are higher than the recommended threshold level of 0.50. The analysis results are shown in Table 8.1 opposite.

We used the square root of AVE for each latent variable to establish discriminant validity and all the values were higher than other correlation values among the latent variables, thus confirming discriminant validity (see Table 8.2).

Structural model

We examined the path coefficients by using SmartPLS 3.0 to test the hypotheses and the significance of relationships between constructs in the model. The results showed that entrepreneurs' digital information sources selection was explained by a variance of 53%, which indicates that the prediction explained more than half of the variation. In addition to this result, the characteristics of information sources were also explained by a variance of 54%. Furthermore, hypotheses were tested to ascertain the significance of the relationship. H1 evaluates whether IL has a significant impact on entrepreneurs' perceptions of characteristics of information sources. The result confirmed this hypothesis ($\beta = 0.250$, $t = 2.897$, $p < 0.01$). The SEM analysis results show that the path between social norms to entrepreneurs' digital information sources selection is not significant, thus rejecting H2. However, the SEM results showed that the path between the type of tasks and entrepreneurs' perceptions towards characteristics of information sources was significant ($\beta = 0.511$, $t = 6.070$, $p < 0.001$), thus confirming H3. The SEM

Table 8.1 Construct reliability and validity

Constructs	Items	Factors loading	α	CR	AVE
Information literacy	IL1	0.782	0.873	0.904	0.612
	IL2	0.868			
	IL3	0.803			
	IL4	0.761			
	IL5	0.754			
	IL6	0.719			
Characteristics of information sources	SC1	0.767	0.867	0.905	0.656
	SC2	0.857			
	SC3	0.883			
	SC4	0.787			
	SC5	0.747			
Social norms	SN1	0.889	0.811	0.889	0.729
	SN2	0.892			
	SN3	0.774			
Type of tasks	TOT1	0.867	0.828	0.886	0.663
	TOT2	0.712			
	TOT3	0.903			
	TOT4	0.758			
Digital information sources selection	DISS1	0.824	0.875	0.906	0.616
	DISS2	0.755			
	DISS3	0.738			
	DISS4	0.807			
	DISS5	0.781			
	DISS6	0.801			

Note α: Cronbach's alpha, CR: composite reliability, AVE: average variance extracted

Table 8.2 Discriminant validity

Constructs	IL	DISS	CS	SN	TOT
Information literacy (IL)	.782				
Digital information sources selection (DISS)	.543	.785			
Characteristics of information sources (CS)	.576	.731	.810		
Social norms (SN)	.471	.558	.468	.854	
Type of tasks (TOT)	.553	.779	.696	.503	.814

result also showed a positive association between characteristics of information sources and entrepreneurs' digital information sources selection, thus supporting H4 ($\beta = 0.731$, $t = 14.520$, $p < 0.001$). Hypotheses testing results are summarised in Figure 8.2. Moreover, in the further analysis, we found an indirect significant impact between IL and entrepreneurs' digital information sources selection through the mediation of characteristics of information sources ($\beta = 0.183$, $t = 3.007$, $p < 0.01$). The SEM analysis also revealed that characteristics of information sources mediate the path relationship between the type of tasks and entrepreneurs' digital information sources selection (β = 0.374, t = 4.782, p < 0.001). However, no mediation effect of characteristics of information sources was found between social norms and entrepreneurs' digital information sources selection.

Multigroup analysis

The assessment of the moderating effect of gender and generation on the path relationships revealed interesting results. We found that the path between IL and the characteristics of information sources was significant for male entrepreneurs (β = 0.183, t = 3.007, p = 0.01), but not significant for female entrepreneurs. Furthermore, considering the generation as a moderator, an intriguing contrast in the path between IL and entrepreneurs' digital information sources selection was also found. For entrepreneurs born before 1980, IL significantly impacted their perceptions towards characteristics of information sources (β = 0.326, t = 3.374, p = 0.001), while IL was not significant for those born after 1980. In addition, we also found a significant path between social norms and characteristics of information sources for the group of entrepreneurs who were born before 1980 (β = 0.326, t = 3.374, p = 0.05). Interestingly, the path between social norms and characteristics of information sources was only significant for this group. No further difference was found in other path relationships.

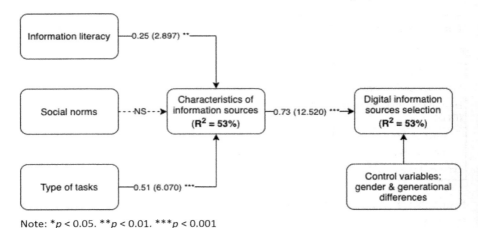

Note: *p < 0.05. **p < 0.01. ***p < 0.001.

Figure 8.2 *Structural model results*

Through the mediation test, we also found that for female entrepreneurs, there were not any significant indirect paths between IL, the type of tasks or social norms and entrepreneurs' digital information sources selection through the perception of characteristics of information sources. However, the result was slightly different in the male group where both IL ($\beta = 0.202$, $t = 3.001$, $p = 0.01$) and the type of tasks ($\beta = 0.388$, $t = 4.200$, $p = 0.001$) had indirect effects on entrepreneurs' digital information sources selection. For the moderating effect of generational difference, there was only one significant indirect path between the type of tasks and entrepreneurs' digital information sources selection and that was found for the group of entrepreneurs who were born after 1980 ($\beta = 0.363$, $t = 3.613$, $p = 0.001$). On the other hand, for entrepreneurs born before 1980, the SEM results confirmed that characteristics of information sources mediates the path relationship between IL ($\beta = 0.259$, $t = 3.640$, $p = 0.001$), the type of tasks ($\beta = 0.324$, $t = 3.140$, $p = 0.01$), social norms ($\beta = 0.187$, $t = 2.411$, $p = 0.05$) and entrepreneurs' digital information sources selection.

Discussion

This study examined the effects of different factors influencing entrepreneurs' digital information sources selection. We developed an integrated conceptual model comprising five constructs: IL, social norms, the type of tasks, characteristics of information sources and entrepreneurs' digital information sources selection (the outcome variable). In line with previous studies, IL and the type of tasks significantly impact entrepreneurs' perceptions of characteristics of information sources (Eze et al., 2018; Söderlund and Lundin, 2017) and consequently their digital information sources selection (Guan et al., 2017; Haase and Franco, 2011). This result indicates that characteristics of information sources have a decisive mediating effect on the relationships between IL, the type of tasks and entrepreneurs' digital information sources selection. In today's world of digital technologies and information, entrepreneurs need to possess sufficient IL skills to evaluate and make judgements about the quality and availability of sources, such as accuracy, adequacy, relevance and trustworthiness, in order to select the most appropriate information sources to efficiently solve their problems (Sariwulan et al., 2020). However, unlike previous research (for example, Nguyen and Luu, 2020), this study found that not only do social norms not have a significant impact on entrepreneurs' perceptions of characteristics of information sources but also do not have any impact on digital information sources selection through the mediation of characteristics of information sources.

Furthermore, we also observed the moderating role of gender and found generational differences in the path between IL and entrepreneurs' digital information sources selection. We found that this path was significant for male entrepreneurs. This may suggest that male entrepreneurs with IL skills are more likely to be more confident in their digital information sources selection. This finding supports the strand of research indicating that female entrepreneurs are often less willing and confident to adopt information and communication technologies than men due to their lower perception of critical skills, that is, IL (Mack, Marie-Pierre and Redican, 2017).

This chapter also revealed that the effect of social norms is only positive for the group of entrepreneurs who were born before 1980. This group of entrepreneurs might be new to exposing themselves to digital information sources, thus their perceptions of digital characteristics of information sources and their digital information sources selection depends more on their soundings (social norms), such as their peers' opinions or market demands (Raymond, Julien and Ramangalahy, 2001). For younger entrepreneurs who were born after 1980, the type of tasks is the only factor that influences entrepreneurs' digital information sources selection. This group of individuals is more familiar and equipped with essential IL skills and understands better the benefits of digital information sources. This quality makes them more confident and efficient in utilising digital information sources compared to the older group of entrepreneurs who migrate to the digital agenda (Kusuma et al., 2020).

Conclusion

The results show that IL and the type of tasks significantly influence entrepreneurs' perceptions towards characteristics of information sources. In turn, characteristics of information sources mediate the relationship between these two factors and entrepreneurs' perceptions towards characteristics of information sources. This supports the earlier findings of Centobelli, Cerchione and Esposito (2017) about similar factors influencing entrepreneurs' digital sources selection. The results confirm the moderating role of gender and generational differences in observing the impact of different factors on entrepreneurs' digital information sources selection. The results contribute to and enrich literature on entrepreneurship and information behaviour research in the digital age and provide practical implications and suggestions for future research agendas. The findings help practitioners and policymakers whose role is to develop policies and strategies that increase digital information access for entrepreneurs, thereby contributing to economic growth.

In light of the lack of research on entrepreneurs' information-seeking behaviours in the digital age, the findings contribute to the literature on information behaviour studies and entrepreneurship in terms of digital information sources selection. We validated the proposed models and examined the impact of factors such as IL, social norms, the type of tasks and characteristics of information sources on entrepreneurs' digital information sources selection. In addition, the findings reveal that the extent to which these factors influence entrepreneurs' digital information sources selection could vary across different genders and generations. Such assessment of sociodemographic variables provides new insights and knowledge on our current understanding of entrepreneurs' information behaviour. We further suggest that female entrepreneurs and the older generation of entrepreneurs should be empowered with a higher level of IL through specific IL training and programmes. Thus, we recommend that entrepreneurial education programmes focus on IL as a motivational factor for entrepreneurs to adopt digital information sources, while including gender and generation sensitivity in designing and implementing such programmes. This approach will reduce the digital inequality between male and female entrepreneurs, as well as the younger and older entrepreneurs. In addition, it reinforces entrepreneurs' self-confidence and efficacy beliefs in digital information sources.

Policymakers and other stakeholders need to facilitate and encourage entrepreneurs to learn and improve their IL skills over time, alongside continuously developing digital information technologies. Therefore, it is vital to integrate IL education and training for entrepreneurs at all stages of life and the entrepreneurial career. This implies that policymakers come up with policies that shape and raise the awareness of the value and importance of digital information sources for entrepreneurs in society and especially in entrepreneurial circles, for example, entrepreneurial ecosystems.

Finally, the results of this chapter reveal a positive effect of social norms on the older entrepreneurs' digital information sources selection, but not for their younger counterparts. A plausible reason might be the fact that the younger generation of entrepreneurs is highly confident in its ability to locate appropriate digital information sources and is able to better use technology to access information.

Like many other studies, this research is also subject to a few limitations. By discussing them here, we present some possible directions for future research. First, most of the data collected was from three entrepreneurial centres in Finland: Helsinki, Turku and Tampere. These cities are the most dynamic regions of entrepreneurship in Finland. The use of advanced technologies is pervasive and extensive markets, young entrepreneurs and active entrepreneurial organisations are located in these areas. Therefore, we suggest that future research should examine the situation in other regions of the country, such as the rural areas or where entrepreneurs belong to a more aging population. Furthermore, we only investigated the effect of cultural values in one country/culture; therefore, we suggest conducting a multi-country study to have more generalisable results. Future studies may examine entrepreneurs from, for example, Nordic countries and investigate whether our proposed conceptual framework is applicable in a different context or not. The data was collected based on being self-reported, thus there might be a bias in the perceptions, emotions and knowledge of the participants. Further research can use the qualitative method to increase the breadth and depth of insights of entrepreneurs' digital information sources selection. Finally, future research could replicate this study at the firm level to assess whether IL could be a source of competitive advantage.

References

Agarwal, N. K., Xu, Y. and Poo, D. C. C. (2011) A Context-Based Investigation into Source Use by Information Seekers, *Journal of the American Society for Information Science and Technology*, **62** (6), 1087–104.

Ahmad, F., Widén, G. and Huvila, I. (2020) The Impact of Workplace Information Literacy on Organizational Innovation: An Empirical Study, *International Journal of Information Management*, **51**, 102041.

Ardakani, M. F. and Avorgani, R. K. (2021) Decision Making of Entrepreneurs in Small and Medium-Sized Enterprises (SMEs), *International Journal of Academic Research in Business and Social Sciences*, **11** (3), 1412–24.

Ayeh, J. K., Au, N. and Law, R. (2013) Predicting the Intention to Use Consumer-Generated Media for Travel Planning, *Tourism Management*, **35**, 132–43.

Belanche Gracia, D., Casaló Ariño L. V. and Flavián Blanco, C. (2012) Understanding the Influence of Social Information Sources on E-Government Adoption, *Information Research*, **17** (3), paper 531.

Bolek, V., Kokles, M., Romanova, A. and Zelina, M. (2018) Information Literacy of Managers: Models and Factors, *Journal of Business Economics and Management*, **19** (5), 722–41.

Brännback, M., Nikou, S., Carsrud, A. L. and Hechavarria, D. (2018) Context, Cognition and Female Entrepreneurial Intentions: It is All About Perceived Behavioural Control. In Greene, P. G. and Brush, C. G. (eds), *A Research Agenda for Women and Entrepreneurship*, 169–86, Edward Elgar Publishing.

Bronstein, J. (2010) Selecting and Using Information Sources: Source Preferences and Information Pathways of Israeli Library and Information Science Students, *Information Research*, **15** (4), 2–15.

Byström, K. (2002) Information and Information Sources in Tasks of Varying Complexity, *Journal of the American Society for Information Science and Technology*, **51** (14), 581–91.

Byström, K. and Järvelin, K. (1995) Task Complexity Affects Information-Seeking and Use, *Information Processing & Management*, **31** (2), 191–213.

Calvo-Porral, C. and Pesqueira-Sanchez, R. (2020) Generational Differences in Technology Behaviour: Comparing Millennials and Generation X, *Kybernetes*, **49** (11), 2755–72.

Case, O. D. (2012) *Looking for Information: A Survey of Research on Information Seeking, Needs and Behaviour*, 3rd edn, Emerald Group Publishing.

Centobelli, P., Cerchione, R. and Esposito, E. (2017) Knowledge Management in Start-ups: Systematic Literature Review and Future Research Agenda, *Sustainability*, **9** (3), 361.

Chao, C. (2019) Factors Determining the Behavioural Intention to Use Mobile Learning: An Application and Extension of the UTAUT Model, *Frontiers in Psychology*, **10**, 1652.

Chatterjee, S., Dutta Gupta, S. and Upadhyay, P. (2020) Technology Adoption and Entrepreneurial Orientation for Rural Women: Evidence from India, *Technological Forecasting & Social Change*, **160**, 120236.

Conroy, T. and Weiler, S. (2019) Local and Social: Entrepreneurs, Information Network Effects, and Economic Growth, *The Annals of Regional Science*, **62** (3), 681–713.

Dinet, J. (2014) *Information Retrieval in Digital Environments*, John Wiley & Sons, Inc.

Dulle, F., Gichohi, P. and Onyancha, O. (2017) Capacity Building Modules for Public Libraries to Support Small-Scale Business Enterprises in Meru County, Kenya, *South African Journal of Library and Information Science*, **83** (1), 49–58.

Erdogan, D. G., Güngören, Ö. C., Hamutoğlu, N. B., Uyanık, G. K. and Tolaman, T. D. (2019) The Relationship Between Lifelong Learning Trends, Digital Literacy Levels and Usage of Web 2.0 Tools with Social Entrepreneurship Characteristics, *Croatian Journal of Education*, **21** (1), 45–76.

Eze, S. C., Olatunji, S., Chinedu-Eze, V. C. and Bello, A. O. (2018) Key Success Factors Influencing SME Managers' Information Behaviour on Emerging ICT (eICT) Adoption Decision-Making in UK SMEs, *The Bottom Line*, **31** (3/4), 250–75.

Gefen, D., Straub, D. and Boudreau, M. (2000) Structural Equation Modelling and Regression: Guidelines for Research Practice, *Communications of the Association for Information Systems*, **4** (1), 1–77.

Guan, L., Zhao, H., Xu, P., Xie, L. and Zhang, W. (2017) Problems and Suggestions of Rural Information Service Platform Construction in China, *Proceedings of the 2017 2nd International Conference on Automation, Mechanical and Electrical Engineering*, **87**, 259–62, Atlantic Press.

Haase, H. and Franco, M. (2011) Information Sources for Environmental Scanning: Do Industry and Firm Size Matter?, *Management Decision*, **49** (10), 1642–57.

Hafeez, K., Alghatas, F. M., Foroudi, P., Nguyen, B. and Gupta, S. (2019) Knowledge Sharing by Entrepreneurs in a Virtual Community of Practice (VCoP) *Information Technology & People (West Linn, Or.)*, **32** (2), 405–29.

Hair, J. F., Risher, J. J., Sarstedt, M. and Ringle, C. M. (2019) When to Use and How to Report the Results of PLS-SEM, *European Business Review*, **31** (1), 2–24.

Ivanytska, N., Tymoshchuk, N., Dovhan, L., Osaulchyk, O. and Havryliuk, N. (2021) Effectiveness of Digital Resources in the Learning Management System Within Online Education of Future Entrepreneurs, *Journal of Entrepreneurship Education*, **24** (4), 1–8.

Jansen, J., van de Wijngaert, L. and Pieterson, W. (2010) Channel Choice and Source Choice of Entrepreneurs in a Public Organizational Context: The Dutch Case. In *International Conference on Electronic Government*, 144–55, Springer.

Jaska, E. and Werenowska, A. (2018) The Availability and Use of Media Information Sources in Rural Areas, *Rural Development and Entrepreneurship Production and Co-operation in Agriculture*, **47**, 115–22.

Karia, M., Bathula, H. and Gaur, S. S. (2020) Information Overload and the Entrepreneurs' Behaviour: Mediating Role of Entrepreneurial Self-Efficacy, *Journal of New Business Ventures*, **1** (1–2), 48–68.

Kim, K. and Sin, S. J. (2011) Selecting Quality Sources: Bridging the Gap Between the Perception and Use of Information Sources, *Journal of Information Science*, **37** (2), 178–88.

Kristiansen, S., Furuholt, B. and Wahid, F. (2003) Internet Cafe Entrepreneurs: Pioneers in Information Dissemination in Indonesia, *The International Journal of Entrepreneurship and Innovation*, **4** (4), 251–63.

Kurbanoglu S. S., Akkoyunlu B. and Umay A. (2006) Developing the Information Literacy Self-Efficacy Scale, *Journal of Documentation*, **62** (6), 730–43.

Kusuma, H., Muafi, M., Aji, H. M. and Pamungkas, S. (2020) Information and Communication Technology Adoption in Small- and Medium-Sized Enterprises: Demographic Characteristics, *The Journal of Asian Finance, Economics, and Business*, **7** (10), 969–80.

Lapinski, M. and Rimal, R. (2005) An Explication of Social Norms, *Communication Theory*, **15** (2), 127–47.

Li, Y., Li, Y., Pan, Y. and Han, H. (2019) Work-Task Types, Stages, and Information-Seeking Behaviour of Strategic Planners, *Journal of Documentation*, **75** (1), 2–23.

Mack, E. A., Marie-Pierre, L. and Redican, K. (2017) Entrepreneurs' Use of Internet and Social Media Applications, *Telecommunications Policy*, **41** (2), 120–39.

Malafi, E., Liu, G. and Goldstein, S. (2017) Business and Workplace Information Literacy: Three Perspectives, *Reference and User Services Quarterly*, **57** (2), 79–85.

Mothe, C. and Nguyen-Thi, T. U. (2013) Sources of Information for Organisational Innovation: A Sector Comparative Approach, *International Journal of Technology Management*, **63** (1–2), 125–44.

Motoyama, Y., Goetz, S. and Han, Y. (2018) Where Do Entrepreneurs Get Information? An Analysis of Twitter-following Patterns, *Journal of Small Business & Entrepreneurship*, **30** (3), 253–74.

Naeem, M. (2020) Developing the Antecedents of Social Influence for Internet Banking Adoption Through Social Networking Platforms: Evidence from Conventional and Islamic Banks, *Asia Pacific Journal of Marketing and Logistics*, **33** (1), 185–204.

Najat, B. (2017) Importance of Customer Knowledge in Business Organizations, *International Journal of Academic Research in Business and Social Sciences*, **7** (11), 175–87.

Ng, W. (2012) Can We Teach Digital Natives Digital Literacy?, *Computers & Education*, **59** (3), 1065–78.

Nguyen, X. T. and Luu, Q. K. (2020) Factors Affecting Adoption of Industry 4.0 by Small- and Medium-Sized Enterprises: A Case in Ho Chi Minh City, Vietnam, *The Journal of Asian Finance, Economics and Business*, **7** (6), 255–64.

Nikou, S., Brännback, M. and Widén, G. (2019) The Impact of Digitalization on Literacy: Digital Immigrants vs Digital Natives. In *Proceedings of the 27th European Conference on Information Systems (ECIS)*, Stockholm & Uppsala, Sweden, 8–14 June, https://aisel.aisnet.org/ecis2019_rp/39.

Nikou, S., Brännback, M., Orrensalo, T. P. and Widén, G. (2020) Social Media and Entrepreneurship: Exploring the Role of Digital Source Selection and Information Literacy. In Schjoedt, L., Brännback, M. and Carsrud, A. L. (eds), *Understanding Social Media and Entrepreneurship*, Springer, 29–46.

Nikou, S., Mezei, J. and Brännback, M. (2018) Digital Natives' Intention to Interact with Social Media: Value Systems and Gender, *Telematics and Informatics*, **35** (2), 421–35.

Orrensalo, T. and Nikou S. (2020) Review of the Nexus Between Trust and Respect in Entrepreneurs' Information-Seeking Behaviour. In Bandi, R. K., Ranjini, C. R., Klein, S., Madon, S. and Monteiro, E. (eds), *The Future of Digital Work: The Challenge of Inequality*, IFIPJWC 2020, IFIP Advances in Information and Communication Technology, vol. 601, 23–37, Springer.

Orrensalo, T. and Nikou, S. (2021a) Digital Source Adoption and Information-Seeking Behaviours of Entrepreneurs: A Systematic Literature Review. In *Proceedings of the 23rd ITS Biennial Conference*, Online Conference, Gothenburg 2021, www.econstor.eu/bitstream/10419/238044/1/Orrensalo-Nikou.pdf.

Orrensalo, T. and Nikou, S. (2021b) Entrepreneurs' Information Retrieval: The Role of Affective Aspects through the Media Richness Theory, *IEEE International Conference on Technology and Entrepreneurship (ICTE)*, 1–6, IEEE, https://doi.org/10.1109/ICTE51655.2021.9584789.

Pathak, S., Xavier-Oliveira, E. and Laplume, A. O. (2013) Influence of Intellectual Property, Foreign Investment, and Technological Adoption on Technology Entrepreneurship, *Journal of Business Research*, **66** (10), 2090–101.

Raymond, L., Julien, P. A. and Ramangalahy, C. (2001) Technological Scanning by Small Canadian Manufacturers, *Journal of Small Business Management*, **39** (2), 123–38.

Rayna, T. and Striukova, L. (2021) Fostering Skills for the 21st Century: The Role of Fab Labs and Makerspaces, *Technological Forecasting & Social Change*, **164**, 120391.

Ringle, C. M., Sarstedt, M. and Straub, D. W. (2012) Editor's Comments: A Critical Look at the Use of PLS-SEM in 'MIS Quarterly', *MIS Quarterly*, **36** (1), iii–xiv.

Roetzel, P. G. (2019) Information Overload in the Information Age: A Review of the Literature from Business Administration, Business Psychology, and Related Disciplines with a Bibliometric Approach and Framework Development, *Business Research*, **12** (2), 479–522.

Sagarik, D., Chansukree, P., Cho, W. and Berman, E. (2018) E-government 4.0 in Thailand: The Role of Central Agencies, *Information Polity: The International Journal of Government & Democracy in the Information Age*, **23** (3), 343–53.

Sahut, J. M., Iandoli, L. and Teulon, F. (2021) The Age of Digital Entrepreneurship, *Small Business Economics*, **56**, 1159–69.

Sariwulan, T., Suparno, S., Disman, D., Ahman, E. and Suwatno, S. (2020) Entrepreneurial Performance: The Role of Literacy and Skills, *The Journal of Asian Finance, Economics, and Business*, **7** (11), 269–80.

Savolainen, R. (1995) Everyday Life Information Seeking: Approaching Information Seeking in the Context of 'Way of Life', *Library and Information Science Research*, **17**, 259–94.

Simić, M., Slavković, M. and Ognjanović, J. (2020) Information Literacy Competencies in Digital Age: Evidence from Small- and Medium-Sized Enterprises. In *Proceedings of the 6th International Scientific Conference on*

Contemporary Issues in Economics, Business and Management (EBM 2020), Faculty of Economics in Kragujevac, Republic of Serbia, 9–10 October, www.researchgate.net/publication/350499090_INFORMATION_ LITERACY_COMPETENCIES_IN_DIGITAL_AGE_EVIDENCE_FROM _SMALL-_AND_MEDIUM-SIZED_ENTERPRISES.

Söderlund, C. and Lundin, J. (2017) What is an Information Source? Information Design Based on Information Source Selection Behavior, *Communication Design Quarterly Review*, **4** (3), 12–19.

Soetanto, D. (2017) Networks and Entrepreneurial Learning: Coping with Difficulties, *International Journal of Entrepreneurial Behaviour & Research*, **23** (3), 547–65.

Stohl, C., Stohl, M. and Leonardi, P. M. (2016) Digital age| Managing Opacity: Information Visibility and the Paradox of Transparency in the Digital Age, *International Journal of Communication*, **10**, 123–37.

Susanto, T. and Aljoza, M. (2015) Individual Acceptance of e-Government Services in a Developing Country: Dimensions of Perceived Usefulness and Perceived Ease of Use and the Importance of Trust and Social Influence, *Procedia Computer Science*, **72**, 622–9.

Tabachnick, B. and Fidell, L. (2013) *Using Multivariate Statistics*, 6th edn, Pearson.

Tarka, P. (2018) An Overview of Structural Equation Modelling: Its Beginnings, Historical Development, Usefulness and Controversies in the Social Sciences, *Quality and Quantity*, **52** (1), 313–54.

Truong, T. L., Teruaki, N. and Yosuke, C. (2016) Factors Affecting Farmers' Uses of Information Sources in Vietnam, *Agricultural Information Research*, **25** (3), 96–104.

Van Laar, E., Van Deursen, A. J., Van Dijk, J. A. and De Haan, J. (2017) The Relation Between 21st century skills and digital skills: A systematic literature review. *Computers in Human Behaviour*, **72**, 577–88.

Virkus, S. (2011) Information Literacy as an Important Competency for the 21st Century: Conceptual Approaches, *Journal of the Bangladesh Association of Young Researchers*, **1** (2), 15–29.

Woudstra, L. and van den Hooff, B. (2008) Inside the Source Selection Process: Selection Criteria for Human Information Sources, *Information Processing & Management*, **44** (3), 1267–78.

Woudstra, L., van den Hooff, B. and Schouten, A. (2016) The Quality Versus Accessibility Debate Revisited: A Contingency Perspective on Human Information Source Selection, *Journal of the Association for Information Science and Technology*, **67** (9), 2060–71.

Xie, I. and Joo, S. (2010) Selection of Information Sources: Accessibility of and Familiarity with Sources, and Types of Tasks, *Proceedings of the American Society for Information Science and Technology*, **46** (1), 1–18.

Yuldinawati, L., van Deursen, A. J. and van Dijk, J. A. (2018) Exploring the Internet Access of Indonesian SME Entrepreneurs, *International Journal of Business*, **23** (3), 235–47.

Zamani, N. and Mohammadi, M. (2018) Entrepreneurial Learning as Experienced by Agricultural Graduate Entrepreneurs, *Higher Education*, **76** (2), 301–16.

Zaremohzzabieh, Z., Samah, B. A., Muhammad, M., Omar, S. Z., Bolong, J., Hassan, S. B. H. and Mohamed Shaffril, H. A. (2016) Information and Communications Technology Acceptance by Youth Entrepreneurs in Rural Malaysian Communities: The Mediating Effects of Attitude and Entrepreneurial Intention, *Information Technology for Development*, **22** (4), 606–29.

Zhang, X., Majid, S. and Foo, S. (2010) The Role of Information Literacy in Environmental Scanning as a Strategic Information System – A Study of Singapore SMEs. In *International Symposium on Information Management in a Changing World*, 95–109, Springer.

Zhang, Y. (2013) The Effects of Preference for Information on Consumers' Online Health Information Search Behaviour, *Journal of Medical Internet Research*, **15** (11), 234.

9

Conclusion: Workplace Information Literacy as the Literacy of the Digital Workplace

Isto Huvila, Gunilla Widén,
Farhan Ahmad and José Teixeira

The starting point of this book has been a growing realisation of the impact of digitalisation and digital information on the transformation of the contemporary workplace. Today's workplace is very different from how a place of work has been conceptualised previously. Information and informational skills, competencies and capabilities have a similarly radically different role in how people work and how work and workplaces are organised. All this makes workplace information literacy a crucial condition for their successful digitalisation.

Underlining the impact of digital information and informational competencies might sound like stating the obvious, especially when the massive impact on information literacies established itself as a cliché more than a decade ago (Francke, Sundin and Limberg, 2011). However, it has become all the more apparent that information literacies are a fleeting target that evolve alongside digitalisation and its contexts. Among literacies, workplace information literacy (WIL) and workplace as a site of literacies has so far received comparatively less attention than other information literacies in education and library contexts. This is an issue that this book aimed to address by introducing and discussing perspectives and approaches to how information literacy can function as a key concept in not only understanding but also making a difference in the workplaces of today and tomorrow.

In the preceding chapters, we have made excursions to different aspects of WIL and its role in the contemporary and future workplace. Some of these explorations have pointed to theoretical and conceptual issues, methodological considerations on how to investigate WIL, processual and transitional perspectives on what it takes to be information literate in different contexts, and what the outcomes and implications are in the workplace.

From a conceptual and theoretical perspective, the extensive literature review conducted by Teixeira and Karim (Chapter 1) points to the diversity of perspectives on the information literacy concept. The diversity can be seen both as an opportunity and a complication. It is a strength as long as it helps to address different aspects of being (information) literate in increasingly digitalising (information) work. However, it can become a burden if WIL research and practice loses sight of the essence of the concept: skills, competencies and mastery of the complex informational landscape of the contemporary workplaces. A prominent risk is also if the various WILs are too violently torn apart from each other by overemphasising their differences. In this respect (and as briefly touched upon in Chapter 1), the tendency to introduce new literacy concepts can be useful in helping to pinpoint new aspects and dimensions of being literate in the contemporary digital workplace, from artificial intelligence (Ng et al., 2021) to data (Koltay, 2015), and, for example, data infrastructure literacy (Gray, Gerlitz and Bounegru, 2018). At the same time, however, too much fragmentation easily obscures the fact that the different literacy concepts have much in common and relate to each other. Rather than demarcating different literacy concepts from each other in the contemporary workplace context, it would be much more important to focus on the complementarities and links between individual concepts in the broader landscape of WIL. Instead of putting too much weight to the individual elements of the informational landscape in the workplace by introducing a plethora of increasingly specific literacy concepts, mastering it as a whole could be fruitfully approached from a more holistic literacy perspective (see Limberg, Sundin and Talja, 2012) by framing WIL as the totality of the literacies of workplace information.

A close reading of the chapters reveals the benefits and opportunities offered by an integrative perspective. A conceptual argument for considering WIL as a constellation of literacies is the linkage of the individual concepts, diverse information-related skills, competencies and mastery through and in their broad and complex sociomaterial underpinnings. The sociomateriality of literacies and the intermingling of their social, material and technological underpinnings has been one of the key emphases in earlier information literacy literature (Sundin, 2015; Pilerot, 2016; Budd and Lloyd, 2014). It has remained less obvious in technology-related informational literacies that often come with fairly specific emphasis on individual technologies and conceptualisations of the technology landscape. Mård and Hallin elaborate on this in Chapter 2 in the context of post-digital digital literacy by drawing on the sociomaterialist perspectives of Orlikowski (2010) and others to expand on Lloyd's (2010) sociocultural perspective on information literacy.

The two methodology-oriented chapters in this book highlight the need for and the opportunities offered by previously little-used methods for addressing some of the earlier acknowledged problems in studying WIL practices caused by their contextuality and variety (Williamson, 2007; Forster, 2017). Even if many of the challenges of investigating and measuring information literacy both in workplace and other contexts stem from the general diversity and mutability of information literacy practices, it is apparent that the digitalisation of workplaces makes discerning information practices and catching up with indicators of information literacies both increasingly difficult and just plain different. This requires new approaches and methods to find and capture it in the contemporary workplace. Rather than resorting to post hoc and self-reported qualitative or quantitative only designs (with their respective strengths and weakness) or laborious mixed-methods studies, new methods – like the fuzzy-set Qualitative Comparative Analysis (fsQCA) discussed in Chapter 3, the use of digital trace data (Chapter 4) and the OECD PIAAC (Survey of Adult Skills) dataset (Chapter 7) – provide complementary opportunities to capture more of the totality of WILs and their underpinnings. There are obviously many other options available that have been tried out to different degrees. Modern technologies allow us to record and retrieve real-time data, which offers endless opportunities for digging deeper into human information behaviour. For example, event logs can show exactly what individuals, teams, machines and organisations have been doing and in which order over a period of time. Such data can be extremely useful in gaining an in-depth understanding of not only what was done but how successful and literally 'literate' these doings have been. Further, rather than providing mere snapshots, the technologies allow continuous collecting of such data, which makes them particularly useful for longitudinal research. At the same time, these possibilities are only examples of what opportunities there might be to embrace new means and approaches to further our understanding of information literacies. In the future – while acknowledging the need for ethical reflection and not doing whatever is possible without considering its consequences – there is undoubtedly room for a further broadening of the palette of both methods and types of empirical material that can help to shed light on WIL practices.

Similar to studies of information literacy in general, a closer look at WIL as it is unfolding in practice in Chapters 5 and 6 points to its diversity and the multiplicity of its facets in sociomaterial space and time. As the decades of information science research on human information behaviour and practices show, there are few limits to what informational things, material and immaterial processes, matters and ideas can be informative (Case and Given, 2016; Khosrowjerdi, Sundqvist and Byström, 2020). The studies show how people seek, find, encounter and appropriate information in manifold different ways (Case and Given, 2016; Huvila, 2022). This means that being information literate in different types of workplace contexts requires different types of literacies – as Lammi and Hallin demonstrate in Chapter 5 with their investigation of information sharing in a secretive organisation. Milosheva describes in parallel in Chapter 6 how career transitions require specific informational competencies and literacies that traverse and bridge workplace-specific skills and mastery of the transition itself. Both chapters point to situations that often evade the attention of both researchers and practitioners in the study and management of daily work.

Finally, the last two chapters take a deep dive into a much debated aspect of information literacy – its impact – adding another lens to the diversity and totality of the experiences and impact of WIL. In Chapter 8, Orrensalo, Brännback and Nikou demonstrate how information source use and WIL are critical business issues. Similarly, as Chapter 7 shows, being and becoming informed in a digital workplace affects not only information sharing and flows but also has an impact on workers' wellbeing and satisfaction in the workplace. This aligns with earlier research and expands perspectives on how literacies have been demonstrated to have an influence on information sharing (Pálsdóttir, 2021) and how information sharing has been demonstrated to relate to individuals' sense of coherence (Heinström et al., 2020), perceptions of organisational changes (Ahmad, Widén and Huvila, 2020) and social capital (Widén, Ahmad and Huvila, 2021). It highlights that WIL is a key factor both to study and to put into practice to improve work satisfaction and the success of work, working and workplaces.

It is difficult to pinpoint only a handful of conclusions that stand out from these remarks. That said, we think there are three critical takeaways that warrant specific attention.

First, we argue that future research needs to take a more inclusive stance towards the concept of information literacy in the workplace context and beyond. The failure to make a real effort to explore the complementarities and bridge the differences between different (information) literacies is a real problem. In this book, we have adopted an inclusive stance where the different conceptualisations of information literacy – as sociomaterial practice, a set of transitive competencies and collective information behaviour – are brought together in different chapters. We do not consider these conceptualisations as mutually exclusive and are inclined to suggest that others should not make such a demarcation either, at least not a priori. Instead, we see the conceptualisations as highlighting different facets of information literacy, some of which are more pertinent in certain contexts of enquiry and perhaps less so in others. Similarly, the different takes on information literacy help to highlight complementary aspects of mastering information rather than right or wrong ones. Considering the existing, and even more so the potential complementarities, we suggest that future research should also be geared towards a comparable inclusive stance instead of the demarcation of concepts and losing itself in theoretical intricacies. Bringing the diverse understandings of information literacy together to inform each other comes with both theoretical and practical benefits for understanding the enabling role of information literacy in today's technologically driven workplaces.

Second, there is an obvious need to continue exploring information literacy in the context of emerging technologies. Currently, such key technologies include artificial intelligence, big data analytics, process mining and cloud computing. Whether fortunate or not, many of the emerging technologies and how they are deployed share a fundamental characteristic: in one way or another, they directly influence information sharing and the management status quo in workplaces. For example, self-service business intelligence (Alpar and Schulz, 2016), an emerging contemporary approach to big data analytics, requires that common employees are capable of employing advanced technical and analytical big data techniques to process information for their job related decision-making. Instead of relying on dedicated expertise, this is projected to happen with minimal support from informational technology and data analysis professionals. It changes the nature of work by altering not only how and how efficiently work is done but also its underpinning information work – what is relevant information in the new technology landscape and how the information should be interacted with – hence turning the introduction of emerging technologies into an information literacy issue. In this sense, the dearth of research on the role of information literacy in the context of emerging technologies becomes a problem that needs to be solved not only by efforts to enquire into the implications and particularities of specific technologies but to develop a sensitivity to the changing technology landscape as an organic aspect of all information literacy research.

Finally, we posit that WIL has the potential to bring conceptual order to the understanding of the diversity and messiness of the skills and competencies required and emerging in the equally heterogeneous and complex digital workplace. In this book, WIL doesn't unfold as just one crucial literacy of the information age among the many others. We suggest that it has the potential to *bring together* the totality of the literacies of workplace information. WIL is technology-agnostic and a specific competence of mastering information (rather than particular technologies in the contemporary and future post-digital workplaces where digital has become a norm and a non-issue).

Information literacy has emphasised different aspects in different time periods, depending on what the key challenges are in relation to mastering information. However, the key issue is that while technologies change, information persists – in one form or another, explicit and implicit – and the literacies needed to master it will retain their significance into the future.

References

Ahmad, F., Widén, G. and Huvila, I. (2020) The Impact of Workplace Information Literacy on Organizational Innovation: An Empirical Study, *International Journal of Information Management*, **51**, 102041, https://doi.org/10.1016/j.ijinfomgt.2019.102041.

Alpar, P. and Schulz, M. (2016) Self-Service Business Intelligence, *Business & Information Systems Engineering*, **58** (2), 151–5, https://doi.org/10.1007/s12599-016-0424-6.

Budd, J. M. and Lloyd, A. (2014) Theoretical Foundations for Information Literacy: A Plan for Action, *Proceedings of the American Society for Information Science and Technology*, **51** (1), 1–5, https://doi.org/10.1002/meet.2014.14505101001.

Case, D. O. and Given, L. M. (2016) *Looking for Information*, Emerald.

Forster, M. (2017) Information Literacy and the Workplace: New Concepts, New Perspectives?. In Forster, M. (ed.), *Information Literacy in the Workplace*, 1–9, Facet Publishing.

Francke, H., Sundin, O. and Limberg, L. (2011) Debating Credibility: The Shaping of Information Literacies in Upper Secondary School, *Journal of Documentation*, **67** (4), 675–94.

Gray, J., Gerlitz, C. and Bounegru, L. (2018) Data Infrastructure Literacy, *Big Data & Society*, **5** (2), https://doi.org/10.1177/2053951718786316.

Heinström, J., Ahmad, F., Huvila, I. and Ek, S. (2020) Sense of Coherence as Influencing Information Sharing at the Workplace, *Aslib Journal of Information Management*, **73** (2), 201–20, https://doi.org/10.1108/ajim-03-2020-0077.

Huvila, I. (2022) Making and Taking Information, *JASIST*, **73** (4), 528–41, https://doi.org/10.1002/asi.24599.

Khosrowjerdi, M., Sundqvist, A. and Byström, K. (2020) Cultural Patterns of Information Source Use: A Global Study of 47 Countries, *JASIST*, **71** (6), 711–24, https://doi.org/10.1002/asi.24292.

Koltay, T. (2015) Data Literacy: In Search of a Name and Identity, *Journal of Documentation*, **71** (2), 401–15, https://doi.org/10.1108/JD-02-2014-0026.

Limberg, L., Sundin, O. and Talja, S. (2012) Three Theoretical Perspectives on Information Literacy, *Human IT*, **11** (2), 93–130.

Lloyd, A. (2010) Framing Information Literacy as Information Practice: Site Ontology and Practice Theory, *Journal of Documentation*, **66** (2), 245–58, https://doi.og/10.1108/00220411011023643.

Ng, D. T. K., Leung, J. K. L., Chu, K. W. S. and Qiao, M. S. (2021) AI Literacy: Definition, Teaching, Evaluation and Ethical Issues, *Proceedings of the Association for Information Science and Technology*, **58** (1), 504–9, https://doi.org/10.1002/pra2.487.

Orlikowski, W. J. (2010) The Sociomateriality of Organisational Life: Considering Technology in Management Research, *Cambridge Journal of Economics*, **34** (1), 125–41, https://doi.org/10.1093/cje/bep058.

Pálsdóttir, Á. (2021) Data Literacy and Management of Research Data – A Prerequisite for the Sharing of Research Data, *Aslib Journal of Information Management*, **73** (2), 322–41, https://doi.org/10.1108/AJIM-04-2020-0110.

Pilerot, O. (2016) Connections Between Research and Practice in the Information Literacy Narrative: A Mapping of the Literature and Some Propositions, *Journal of Librarianship and Information Science*, **48** (4), 313–21, https://doi.org/10.1177/0961000614559140.

Sundin, O. (2015) Invisible Search: Information Literacy in the Swedish Curriculum for Compulsory Schools, *Nordic Journal of Digital Literacy*, **9** (4), 193–209.

Widén, G., Ahmad, F. and Huvila, I. (2021) Connecting Information Literacy and Social Capital to Better Utilise Knowledge Resources in the Workplace, *Journal of Information Science*, https://doi.org/10.1177/01655515211060531.

Williamson, K. (2007) The Broad Methodological Contexts of Information Literacy Research – Monash University. In Lipu, S., Williamson, K. and Lloyd, A. (eds), *Exploring Methods in Information Literacy Research*, 1–12, Centre for Information Studies, https://research.monash.edu/en/publications/the-broad-methodological-contexts-of-information-literacy-researc.

Index

abilities enabled by information literacy 1–2
age influence, entrepreneurs' digital sources selection 124, 134–7
attitudes to work 71–2

career information literacy 74, 78–82
  see also employability
  career competencies 79–82
  career information literacy skills 79–82
  career self-management skills 79–82
  digital career literacy skills 79–82
  from skills transferability to transition 84–6, 87
career options 78
company characteristics, work satisfaction 110–16
competence
  digital literacy 16–18
  work satisfaction 107
competencies, information literacy 71–87
  attitudes to work 71–3
  career competencies 79–82
  job precarity 71
  Programme for the International Assessment of Adult Competencies (PIAAC) 102
compliant/routine information literacy 84
country of residence, work satisfaction 110–14

digital literacy 15–25
  as a competence in a particular site 16–18
  consequences of sociomaterial approach 24–5
  defining 16–17
  emergent emphasis 25
  Google searches 22–3
  influence work 19–20
  information coupling 23–4
  information sharing 22–3
  information work 20–2
  online meetings 21–2, 23–4
  reCAPTCHA 24
  as a sociomaterial practice 15–25
  subjectivities of materialities 25
digital sources selection, entrepreneurs' *see* entrepreneurs' digital sources selection
digital trace data 45–56
  characteristics 46
  defining 46
  information and communication 48–9, 51
  information behaviour 49–52
  information retrieval 51–2
  information seeking 47–50, 52–3, 54–6
  information sharing 47–50, 51–6
  literature review 46–52
  operationalisation of the study of information cycles 49–52
  ownership 47
diversity of perspectives, information literacy 145–6

education, experience and skills, work satisfaction 110–16
Education Resources Information Center (ERIC) database 3, 4
emerging technologies, workplace information literacy (WIL) 149
employability
see also career information literacy
best practices and new directions 82–6
compliant/routine information literacy 84
inventive/innovative information literacy 84
supporting employability and career 82–6
sustainable employability 76–8
transferability 74, 82–6
employability information literacy 73, 74–6
entrepreneurs' digital sources selection 121–38
age influence 124, 134–7
benefits of digital information 121–2, 124
characteristics of information sources: influencing factor 128–9
conclusion 136–8
confirmatory factor analysis (CFA) 132
covariance structure analysis 131–2
discussion 135–6
factors influencing choice of information sources 126–9
gender influence 124, 134–5
information literacy: influencing factor 126–7
literature review 123–6

measurement model 132, 133
methodology 129–32
multigroup analysis 134–5
path analysis 131–2
results 132–5
sample characteristics 131
social norms: influencing factor 127
Structural Equation Modelling (SEM) 131–2
structural model 132–4
study analysis 131–2
study design and sampling 129–30
theoretical background and hypotheses development 126–9
types of tasks: influencing factor 128
ERIC see Education Resources Information Center database

formal competence, work satisfaction 107
FORTE (Swedish Research Council for Health, Working Life and Welfare) 60
fragmentation, workplace information literacy (WIL) 146
fragmented knowing, high-security settings/organisations 60, 62–3, 66
fsQCA see fuzzy-set Qualitative Comparative Analysis
future research 9–10
fuzzy-set Qualitative Comparative Analysis (fsQCA) 29–30, 34–40
calibration 36
procedures 36–7
sufficiency analysis 36–7

workplace information literacy 34–7

gender influence, entrepreneurs' digital sources selection 124, 134–7
generic employability literacy skills 75, 76
Google Drive 8
Google Scholar search engine 3–4, 6
Google searches 22–4

high-security settings/organisations
 analysis 62
 data collection 61–2
 fragmented knowing 60, 62–3
 hinting 60, 63–4
 interpersonal trust 65–6
 limited information 59–67
 organisational trust 65–6
 sensitive information 59–67
 trust 64–6
hinting, high-security settings/organisations 60, 63–4, 66–7

inclusive stance, workplace information literacy (WIL) 148, 149–50
individual characteristics, work satisfaction 110–16
information literacy
 see also workplace information literacy
 abilities enabled 1–2
 concept 59
 context 17
 defining 1, 121
 diversity of perspectives 145–6
 literature review 3–5
 meanings 5–7, 10
 mixed-method research 31–2
 qualitative research 31–2
 quantitative research 31–2
 research methodologies 30–2
 research surge 2
 as sociocultural practice 16, 17–18
information sharing
 digital literacy 22–3
 digital trace data 47–50, 51–6
 work satisfaction 103–7, 110–11, 113–16
integrative perspective, workplace information literacy (WIL) 146
interpersonal trust 65–6
inventive/innovative information literacy 84

job precarity 71, 76

Library, Information Science & Technology Abstracts (LISTA) 3, 4
Library and Information Science Abstracts (LISA) 3, 4
limited information 59–67
 see also high-security settings/organisations; sensitive information
LISA *see* Library and Information Science Abstracts
LISTA *see* Library, Information Science & Technology Abstracts
literature review, entrepreneurs' digital sources selection 123–6
literature review, information literacy 3–5
 analysis and communication 4–5
 future research 9–10
 methodological lessons 7–9

search and storage 3–4
software tools 8
sources 3–4
methodological choices of information literacy in the workplace 29–40
future work 39–40
fuzzy-set Qualitative Comparative Analysis (fsQCA) 29–30, 34–40
limitations 39–40
research methodologies in information literacy 30–2
mixed-method research, information literacy 31–2
Moodle 8

online meetings 21–2, 23–4
operationalisation of the study of information cycles 49–52
organisational trust 65–6

PIAAC (Programme for the International Assessment of Adult Competencies) 102, 105–8
position and job type, work satisfaction 110–16
'professional information literacy' 73
Programme for the International Assessment of Adult Competencies (PIAAC) 102, 105–8

qualitative research
information literacy 31–2
workplace information literacy 33
quantitative research
information literacy 31–2
workplace information literacy 33

reCAPTCHA 24
RefWorks (bibliographic database) 8
regression-based analysis, workplace information literacy 35–6
research methodologies in information literacy 30–2
research surge, information literacy 2

satisfaction, work *see* work satisfaction
SCONUL *see* Society of College, National and University Libraries
self-determination factors, work satisfaction 103–5, 110–16
SEM *see* structural equation modelling
sensitive information 59–67
see also high-security settings/organisations
'Seven Pillars of IL' model, SCONUL 75
sharing information *see* information sharing
skills
see also competencies, information literacy
career information literacy skills 79–82
career self-management skills 79–82
digital career literacy skills 79–82
generic employability literacy skills 75, 76
skills transferability 74, 82–6, 87
transition 84–6, 87

INDEX

Society of College, National and University Libraries (SCONUL), 'Seven Pillars of IL' model 75
sources selection, entrepreneurs' *see* entrepreneurs' digital sources selection
structural equation modelling (SEM), workplace information literacy 36
subjective competence, work satisfaction 107
subject-specific employability literacy 75–6
sustainable employability 76–8
Swedish Research Council for Health, Working Life and Welfare (FORTE) 60

technologies, emerging, workplace information literacy (WIL) 149
top 20 journal publications 9
transferability, skills 74, 82–6, 87
transition, skills transferability 84–6, 87
trust, high-security settings/ organisations 64–6

WIL *see* workplace information literacy
working hours and earnings, work satisfaction 110–16
workplace information literacy (WIL) 33–7, 73, 145–50
  assessment 34–7
  emerging technologies 149
  fragmentation 146
  fuzzy-set Qualitative Comparative Analysis 34–7
  inclusive stance 148, 149–50
  integrative perspective 146
  methodological challenges of workplace information literacy assessment 34–7
  qualitative research 33
  quantitative research 33
  regression-based analysis 35–6
  structural equation modelling (SEM) 36
  work satisfaction 102–3
work satisfaction 101–16
  company characteristics 110–16
  competence 107
  country of residence 110–14
  data and variables 105–7
  education, experience and skills 110–16
  formal competence 107
  individual characteristics 110–16
  information sharing 103–7, 110–11, 113–16
  knowledge creation 101
  method of determining work satisfaction 107–10
  position and job type 110–16
  Programme for the International Assessment of Adult Competencies (PIAAC) 102
  results 110–15
  self-determination factors 103–5, 110–16
  subjective competence 107
  working hours and earnings 110–16
  workplace information literacy 102–3